WHO RUNS FOR
CONGRESS?

WHO RUNS FOR CONGRESS?
Ambition, Context, and Candidate Emergence

Edited by
Thomas A. Kazee

Congressional Quarterly Inc.
Washington, D.C.

Library of Congress Cataloging-in-Publication Data

Who runs for Congress? : ambition, context, and candidate emergence /
    edited by Thomas A. Kazee.
        p.   cm.
Includes bibliographical references (p.   ) and index.
ISBN 0-87187-985-9 (hard) -- ISBN 0-87187-984-0 (pbk.)
1. United States.   Congress.   House--Election districts.   2. United States.
Congress.   House--Elections, 1992.   I. Kazee, Thomas A., 1952-   .
JK1341.W47   1994
328.73' 07347 -- dc20   94-18139
                                                                        CIP

For Estelle Kazee

Contents

Contributors

Douglas D. Abel is a partner in Paragon Research & Communication Associates in Houston, Texas. He received his Master's degree from the University of Houston and has presented academic papers at numerous conferences in the South and Southwest. His primary area of interest is in electoral politics and political communication.

David T. Canon is associate professor of political science at the University of Wisconsin-Madison. He received his Ph.D. from the University of Minnesota in 1987. He is the author of *Actors, Athletes, and Astronauts: Political Amateurs in the United States Congress* (1990). He is currently working on a book titled *Race, Redistricting, and Representation in the U.S. House.*

Gary W. Copeland joined the Carl Albert Center at the University of Oklahoma in 1980 and became an associate professor of political science and the associate director of the Center in 1986. He received his Ph.D. from the University of Iowa in 1979. His research has been published in several journals, including the *Journal of Politics* and *Legislative Studies Quarterly*. He coedited *Congressional Budgeting* (1984) and *Parliaments in the Modern World: Changing Institutions* (1994).

John Haskell teaches in the Political Science Department at Drake University. His writing has appeared in *Western Political Quarterly*. His research interests include southern state politics, superdelegates, and reform in presidential nomination campaigns.

Paul S. Herrnson is associate professor of government and politics at the University of Maryland at College Park. He received his Ph.D. from the University of Wisconsin-Madison in 1986. He is the author of *Campaigning for Congress: Candidates, Parties, and PACs* (CQ Press, 1994) and *Party Campaigning in the 1980s* (1988). He is also coeditor of *Risky Business? PAC Decisionmaking and Strategy in Congressional Elections* (1994) and has written numerous articles on political parties, campaign finance, and congressional elections.

Allen D. Hertzke is assistant director, Carl Albert Congressional Research Center, and associate professor, Department of Political Science,

University of Oklahoma. He received his Ph.D. from the University of Wisconsin-Madison in 1986. He is the author of *Echoes of Discontent: Jesse Jackson, Pat Robertson, and the Resurgence of Populism* (CQ Press, 1993) and *Representing God in Washington: The Role of Religious Lobbies in the American Polity* (1988), and coeditor of *The Atomistic Congress: An Interpretation of Political Change* (1993).

Thomas A. Kazee is professor of political science and chair of the Department of Political Science at Davidson College. He received his Ph.D. from Ohio State University and served as an American Political Science Association Congressional Fellow (1987-1988). He is the author of various articles on the emergence of congressional candidates, public opinion, and state elections.

Anne C. Layzell is a legislative assistant in the Wisconsin state legislature and a research specialist at the University of Wisconsin System. She is completing her doctoral studies at Loyola University of Chicago. She has coauthored papers on political parties and elections; her current research focuses on the use of collaborative programs in higher education.

Bruce I. Oppenheimer is professor of political science at Vanderbilt University. He received his Ph.D. from the University of Wisconsin. He has been a Brookings Fellow (1970-1971) and a Congressional Fellow (1974-1975). In addition to writing numerous articles, he is the author of *Oil and the Congressional Process* (1974), coauthor of *Congress Reconsidered* (CQ Press, 1993), and primary author of *A History of the Committee on Rules* (1983). He served as coeditor of *Legislative Studies Quarterly* (1988-1992).

L. Marvin Overby is an assistant professor of political science at the University of Mississippi. He earned his Ph.D from the University of Oklahoma where he was a fellow at the Carl Albert Congressional Research and Studies Center. His articles on the Congress and southern politics have appeared in journals such as the *American Political Science Review, Political Research Quarterly, Polity, Legislative Studies Quarterly*, and *Congress and the Presidency*.

Susan L. Roberts is associate professor of political science at Davidson College. She received her Ph.D. from the University of Notre Dame and has written about the legislative veto, Congress, and constitutional interpretation. Her current research is on women's PACs.

Matthew M. Schousen is an instructor in the Department of Government at Franklin & Marshall College. His areas of teaching interest include Congress, the presidency, and research methods. His research interests include voting behavior, congressional institutions, minorities in politics, and political ambition. He has published an article in *Legislative Studies Quarterly* on split-ticket voting.

Patrick J. Sellers is a member of the Political Science Department at Indiana University. He also is a Ph.D. candidate in political science at Duke University. He has worked as an assistant to former U.S. representative James McClure Clark and on a number of political campaigns. His research interests include congressional elections, legislative decision-making, the politics of race and redistricting, and voting behavior.

Peverill Squire is professor and chair of the Department of Political Science at the University of Iowa. His articles on congressional elections, and other aspects of American politics have appeared in *American Political Science Review, Journal of Politics, Public Opinion Quarterly, Legislative Studies Quarterly,* and other scholarly journals.

Kerry Sutten is a regional economist with the Northeast-Midwest Institute in Washington, D.C. He also served as legislative assistant to Rep. David Nagle (D-Iowa). He is a Ph.D. candidate at the University of Iowa.

Robert M. Tennant is a Ph.D. candidate in government and politics at the University of Maryland where he is completing a dissertation on congressional financing and committee voting. He is coauthor of *A Congressional Simulation.* His research interests include political action committees, health care interest group politics, and political parties.

Preface

S everal dozen scholars of Congress and congressional elections met on the campus of Colby College in July 1986 to consider a question central to democracy. Why do some people run for office while others do not? Those of us at the meeting enjoyed the Maine summer and the companionship of our colleagues, but we agreed on little except the critical need for a systematic study of congressional candidate recruitment.

Eight years later we still know relatively little about the decisions that potential candidates make. We know that incumbents usually win, and we have reason to believe that one of the key reasons they win is the weaknesses of their opponents. What we do not know is *why* so few experienced, attractive challengers emerge to run for House seats.

As has been my habit at professional meetings, several years ago at a conference I lamented our disciplinary ignorance of the factors affecting candidate recruitment. "Won't *someone*," I asked, "take up where the Colby group left off and organize a multi-district study of candidate emergence?" I had the good sense—or perhaps it was simply bad timing—to direct this question to an audience that included Bruce Oppenheimer. Bruce collared me after the session and called my bluff: He suggested that perhaps I should answer my own challenge. "And if you get the ball rolling," he said, "I'll do a district." It seemed like an offer I could not refuse.

Four years later the ball has rolled quite a distance. Along the way, sixteen political scientists from eleven colleges and universities nationwide joined the team. We descended on nine congressional districts—making contacts, observing, always asking questions—to explore the decision-making process of a district's prospective congressional candidates. Our districts include two children of reapportionment, the 1st District of North Carolina and the 29th District of Texas, both created to increase the likelihood of minority representation in the House. The election of an Anglo candidate in Texas's 29th proves once again the law of unanticipated consequences—as well as the profound importance of the candidate emergence process. We include as well districts with incumbents at various stages of their careers, from first-term incumbent James Moran in Virginia's 8th District to twenty-term incumbent Sidney Yates in Illinois's 9th District.

We base our study on the premise that the best way to understand politics in America is to talk to the people—the politicians and political activists—who are at its heart. The texture of a congressional district and the complexity of its people cannot be appreciated adequately without spending time in the district, without seeing local politics through the lens of an activist who someday might run for a House seat. Recognizing the limits of single case studies, however, we widened our gaze to nine districts while maintaining a common approach to each.

Perhaps our most important conclusion is that diminished competition for House seats is traceable to an emergence process that tells all but the most optimistic prospects that the incumbent cannot be beaten. America does not suffer for lack of ambition; we discover in almost every district a pool of ambitious potential candidates looking for an opportunity to run for Congress. What is lacking is the opportunity that any strategic politician must have: a reasonable chance to win. How we create such opportunities is the task of public policy makers. That may be the rub, for it is in the interest of policy makers—of incumbents—to ensure that the "latent competition" present in most districts does not become actual competition.

A study of this kind, requiring as it does a tremendous investment of time in each district, could not have been completed without the energy and enthusiasm of my collaborators. Their unfailing commitment to the Candidate Emergence Project puts me in their great debt. I am especially grateful to the Carl Albert Congressional Research and Studies Center at the University of Oklahoma and to the Faculty Research Committee of Davidson College for providing funds for a conference in February 1992 at which this plot was fully hatched. Thanks also to Linda Fowler, whose work on candidate recruitment and whose advice on this book have been invaluable.

Finally, I would be remiss if I did not say a special word of thanks to my family. Sharon, who is the best teacher I know, and Nicole and Geoff, as busy as active seventh and tenth graders can be, were always there when I needed them. My ambition is to return the favor.

1

The Emergence of
Congressional Candidates

Thomas A. Kazee

*Who sent us the political leaders we have? There is a simple answer
to that question. They sent themselves* (Ehrenhalt 1991, 19).

The four years preceding the 1992 election were not kind to the U.S.
Congress. In 1989 and 1990 Congress was buffeted by the winds of
scandal, highlighted by allegations that the "Keating Five"—a group of U.S.
senators including Alan Cranston (D-Calif.) and John Glenn (D-Ohio)—had
used their influence to help financier Charles Keating in return for more than
$1 million in campaign contributions. In the House of Representatives,
Speaker Jim Wright (D-Texas) was accused of numerous ethical violations,
charges that eventually led to his resignation. Moreover, radio talk shows
crackled with indignation over a proposed pay raise for members of Congress—a proposal that was first defeated and then adopted after the initial
publicity subsided. The savings and loan crisis surfaced during this period, with
Democrats and Republicans hurling charge and countercharge over who was
responsible for a regulatory disaster that eventually would cost taxpayers hundreds of billions of dollars. The federal budget deficit continued to mushroom,
as it did throughout the previous two decades, and Congress and President
George Bush could not agree on a course of action to address the problem.
Finally, after five months of protracted negotiations, the so-called budget sum-
mit produced a deficit-reduction deal—announced a week before the 1990
midterm elections—that raised taxes while trimming federal services.

With that as prologue, it is not surprising that the results of the 1990
midterm elections signaled voter unrest. Although only 15 of 406 House
incumbents lost their seats, the share of the vote won by the average incumbent dropped by more than 4 percent, affecting incumbents of both
parties. More than one hundred incumbents saw their reelection percentages drop to the lowest points since they were first elected (Cook 1991,
483), and about fifty House incumbents lost at least 10 percentage points
from their showing at the polls in 1988. Measures to limit the terms of U.S.
House and Senate members passed in Colorado, and voters in California
passed a similar measure for state legislators.

It is possible that the anti-incumbent tenor of the 1990 election would
have been more pronounced if a stronger group of congressional challeng-

ers had emerged to run against House and Senate incumbents. Writing in April 1990, Gary Jacobson described House aspirants as the "most unpromising group of challengers in any postwar election" (cited in Hershey 1993, 162). Most challengers raised little money and only about 10 percent—a figure less than half the level a decade earlier—previously had held elective office. Jacobson concludes, "In 1990 voters had a good reason . . . to reject incumbents, but acceptable replacements and money for their campaigns were in exceedingly scarce supply" (Hershey 1993, 161).

The months following the midterm election brought even more dramatic shifts in the ground on which incumbents stood. One force propelling these shifts all could have forseen: the decennial redistricting process mandated by the U.S. Constitution. Demographic changes in the 1980s had produced major population shifts, creating, for example, seven new House districts in California and eliminating five districts in New York. Even in most states that neither gained nor lost seats, population movements required a redrawing of district boundaries by state legislators. Redistricting invariably produces increased House turnover because some incumbents lose their districts, some are forced into districts with other incumbents, and some must run in districts made more competitive by the addition or subtraction of territory.

For many incumbents, however, redistricting was the least of their problems. In October 1991 the Senate confirmation of Supreme Court nominee Clarence Thomas was jolted by allegations of sexual harassment leveled against Thomas by university law professor Anita Hill, a former associate. Televised hearings of the Senate Judiciary Committee broadcast nationally, replete with explicit accusations, aggressive efforts to discredit Hill, and charges of duplicity by Senate staffers, seemed symptomatic of a Congress more concerned about scoring partisan and ideological points than dealing with pressing national problems. Those watching at home may have disagreed about whether to believe nominee Thomas or accuser Hill, but most agreed that the Senate had botched its handling of the situation. Many women, in particular, perceived the all-male Judiciary Committee as emblematic of a Congress insensitive to the needs of half of the population. A few months later, the House banking scandal broke; eventually it was publicized that 325 members of Congress (267 of whom were currently serving in the House) had overdrawn their accounts at the House bank. The banking scandal hit home precisely because it was an issue—unlike arcane policy areas such as the federal budget or trade policy—to which voters could easily and immediately relate.

Public perception of Congress reached a low point in February 1992. Only 16 percent of Americans in a national survey said they approved of the way Congress was handling its job, down from 49 percent a year earlier (Hershey 1993, 164). Confidence in the country's economic performance, a factor linked to voter confidence in governmental performance, also had eroded dramatically: only 17 percent of respondents in a February 1992 survey rated the economy as "good" or "very good" (Jacobson 1993, 162). The country might not be going to hell in a hand basket, but something was amiss and Congress (and the president) appeared to be doing little about it.

The most tangible manifestation of public dissatisfaction with Congress was the growing national flirtation with term limits for members of the House and Senate. By November 1992 measures to limit congressional terms appeared on ballots in fourteen states (subsequently passing in every state). As John Tierney notes, "[t]hrough their growing support for term limitation, a scornful public was sending an increasingly clear message that it was no longer in the mood to suffer fools gladly—especially on Capitol Hill, where there seemed such a high concentration of them" (1993, 29).

Carpe Diem: The 1992 Election and Emergence Decisions

Men and women considering a House race in 1991 and 1992 thus had reason to believe factors that typically conspire to frustrate their ambitions, such as incumbent advantages in fund-raising, media coverage, and party support, were offset by a new and more favorable array of forces. The 1990 midterm elections, an economy in recession, recurring allegations of congressional misconduct, redistricting—all were much discussed developments during the period in which most prospective candidates were deciding whether to run. If timing is everything, 1992 might have appeared to be the year to move. As *Congressional Quarterly Weekly Report* declared on its cover of the February 29, 1992, issue: "New Districts, Angry Mood Stir Competition for Congress."

Perhaps stimulated by this more favorable political climate, a larger and more experienced batch of challengers ran for Congress in 1992. More candidates ran for major party House nominations than in any election in the preceding decade: almost 3,000 congressional nominees filed with the Federal Election Commission (FEC) in 1992, compared with 1,792 in 1990 and 1,873 in 1988 (Jacobson 1993, 167). More districts saw two-party competition, as the number of uncontested House seats fell from the previous decade's average of seventy-one to thirty-four in 1992. The proportion of experienced challengers increased as well; candidates with previous elective-office experience comprised 22.1 percent of all challengers in 1992, compared to 10.4 percent two years earlier—indeed, 1992 saw the largest number of experienced challengers since 1982 (Jacobson 1993, 167).

This enriched pool of challengers may help to explain an increase in the number of closely contested elections, increases in the number of incumbent retirements, and a higher incidence of incumbent primary and general election defeats. Marginal incumbents—that is, those winning with less than 60 percent of the two-party vote—increased to 33.4 percent from 23.5 percent in 1990; as recently as 1988 only 12.7 percent of incumbents won with less than 60 percent of the vote. Nineteen House incumbents were defeated in primary elections in 1992, compared to a *total* of seven in the preceding four congressional elections. Sixty-six House members retired, a number totaling more than the two previous elections combined and eighteen more than in any year since 1946. Retirements, primary defeats, and general election losses produced a House turnover of 110 seats, the highest number in the postwar period. The demographics of the House were affected greatly, as women increased their representation from twenty-eight to forty-seven members, Hispanics increased their numbers from eleven to seventeen members, and African Americans increased their numbers from twenty-five to thirty-eight members (Jacobson 1993, 153).

Notwithstanding the more competitive 1992 environment, however, incumbents continued to attract overwhelming support in most congressional districts. Only twenty-four House incumbents lost in the general election, a 93 percent success rate for those who sought reelection. In a year in which nearly 20 percent of all presidential ballots were cast for outsider Ross Perot, the share of the vote won by the average House incumbent was 63.6 percent, down less than half a point from 1990 (Jacobson 1993, 167). The turnover of House seats, though high by the standards of recent elections, fell well short of the 150-mark predicted by some analysts.

Indeed, perhaps the key question for the 1992 election is why most incumbents were able to fare so well despite the apparently pervasive anti-politician tone of the campaign and dramatically declining confidence in Congress as an institution. In short, why did an electorate that appeared ready to chop at the core of American politics instead pick away at the margins?

It is the premise of this book that the decisions of potential candidates—decisions made well before the first campaign speech is given or the first advertising dollar is spent—shape the universe of winners in congressional elections. The authors of this collection of essays went into a variety of congressional districts during the 1991-1992 election cycle to find out about those decisions, to understand more fully why some people ran for Congress and why others opted to stay on the sidelines. Our interviews revealed that most prospective candidates carefully weighed the political, financial, and personal factors present in each district. Perhaps most important, information critical to candidacy decisions was filtered through the sometimes distorting prism of political ambition. How important was winning a seat in Congress? What price was an aspiring legislator willing to pay? Ultimately, in 1992 most attractive potential candidates decided to wait for a more opportune moment, or to eschew congressional candidacy for more rewarding public service or private sector careers. These decisions helped to ensure, in the short term, that most incumbents were returned to office, and to determine, in the long term, the character of representation and the direction of policy making in the United States.

Candidate Emergence and American Politics

Competition for legislative seats, democratic theory tells us, makes certain that those elected will be held accountable for their actions; if the performances of our representatives are unsatisfactory, we will "throw the rascals out" and replace them with individuals of greater competence—or at least greater sensitivity to the wishes of those who elected them. Such competition depends on an adequate supply of candidates, which, in turn, ultimately depends on ambition; men and women must, for whatever reasons, have the desire to get elected. Joseph Schlesinger (1966, 2) summarizes this argument:

> A political system unable to kindle ambitions for office is as much in danger of breaking down as one unable to restrain ambitions. Representative government, above all, depends on a supply of men so driven; the desire for election and, more important, for reelection becomes the electorate's restraint upon its public officials.

Linda Fowler (1993, 19) echoes this claim in her study of candidacy and American politics: "Candidates are indispensable links between citizens and their government. . . . [I]t is hard to imagine a regime that is both legitimate and dynamic that does not have a healthy supply of candidates." [1]

We have long assumed that ambition for public office in America is widespread, that the number of people seeking elective positions is adequate to ensure both a steady supply of able public servants and a level of electoral competition sufficient to hold officeholders accountable for their actions. Recently, however, the number of potentially strong candidates willing to challenge incumbents for congressional seats has declined—as has the competitiveness of U.S. House elections. Using election data from 1982 to 1988, Linda Fowler and L. Sandy Maisel (1991, 1) report that ". . . a record number of House races went entirely uncontested, while electoral outcomes grew steadily more one-sided in those districts where both parties fielded an opponent." In a report prepared for the Joyce Foundation entitled "The Vanishing American Candidate," Lawrence Hansen (1991, 20) laments the decline in the number and quality of candidates willing to run for public office, concluding that "too much competition is being wrung out of the system."

It seems clear, then, that candidate emergence is a key to understanding competition in American elections, but it may be less obvious that emergence is central to American politics in other important respects. Synthesizing and assessing the substantial but disparate literature on candidate recruitment and congressional elections, Fowler (1993, 11) contends that ". . . recruitment indisputably matters—not just to legislative politics, but to a range of concerns within the field of American politics," including divided government, partisan realignments, congressional policy making, and representation.[2]

Fowler notes that divided government, an issue much discussed in recent years (Mayhew 1991; Jacobson 1990), may be the product of an emergence process that consistently produces stronger Democratic House and Senate candidates than Republican candidates (Fowler 1993, 109-110).[3] In *The United States of Ambition*, Alan Ehrenhalt explains this phenomenon by arguing that philosophical differences between Democrats and Republicans lead to differing career decisions. Democrats have a natural (that is, ideologically reinforced) affinity for elective office; Republicans are less likely to be drawn to candidacy because they see government as a source of much that ails America:

> For all the shortcomings of the national Democratic party over the last two decades, this much must be said for its candidates: They wanted to be the government. And so, throughout the 1970s and 1980s, the Democratic party strengthened itself as the vehicle for people who grew up interested in government and politics and wanted to make a career of them. And the Republican party was forced to compete as the vehicle of those who felt that government was a dirty business and that they were demeaning themselves to take part in it (1991, 222).

More generally, partisan shifts in Congress may be triggered by candidate emergence, if Gary Jacobson and Samuel Kernell's (1983) theory of "strategic politicians" is correct. A weak economy or an unpopular president may encourage a stronger set of challengers to run in the out-party, producing a congressional seat change in favor of that party. This, too, may contribute to divided government.

Citing recent work by several researchers (Canon 1990b; Campbell 1990; and Brady 1988), Fowler notes that partisan realignments may be traceable to changes in the frequency and quality of candidates willing to contest for elective office. The absence of an often-predicted Republican realignment in recent decades, for example, may be a result of the GOP's inability to recruit strong candidates to take advantage of a shift in voters' willingness to support Republicans, a willingness seen most clearly in Republican control of the White House for much of the past four decades and more recently in a gradual closing of the party identification gap between Democrats and Republicans. Fowler concludes that "the intermediaries [candidates] who provide the linkage between the mass public and the government have obstructed the normal process of reconstituting a new political order" (1993, 36). A realignment cannot take place without standard-bearers, and the Republicans simply have been unable to place enough candidates in the field to press their advantage.

Policy making and the representation of diverse interests also are affected by candidate emergence, Fowler contends. The election of a larger number of women or African Americans, for example, is likely to affect the policy orientation of the Congress as a whole. She cites several studies that show that female legislators are more liberal than males (Poole and Ziegler

1985; Welch 1985), and have (at the state level, at least) been "more likely to introduce and pass bills dealing with issues relating to children, families and women's well-being" (Fowler 1993, 125). African American legislators, for their part, have been a consistently liberal presence in the Congress, and have used the Congressional Black Caucus as a vehicle for promoting a variety of procedural and policy changes (Cunningham 1993).[4]

Candidate Emergence from a Theoretical Perspective

If candidate emergence is a key to understanding American politics, we need to know more about the factors that push some people toward candidacy but that discourage others. David Canon, Matthew Schousen, and Patrick Sellers (1992, 1) summarize an extensive literature on candidate emergence—usually referred to in the literature as candidate "recruitment"[5]—as consisting of three theoretical approaches: sociological, psychological, and rational (or ambition theory).[6]

The sociological approach, perhaps best exemplified in the American context by the work of Donald Matthews (1954), is based on the premise that eligibility for public office is dependent primarily on considerations such as occupation, economic status, and social standing. Though sociological theory reminds us that eligibility for public office may be determined by factors over which individuals have little control, it cannot explain why "only some members of a social category, group, or occupation with recruitment-relevant characteristics seek a political career while others do not" (Czudnowski 1975, 209).

Leadership studies took on a more individual focus when students of political recruitment, reflecting an evolving emphasis within political science as a whole, began to shift their focus away from institutions and social groups and toward the attitudes, predispositions, and behaviors of political activists. Harold Lasswell (1930; 1948), for example, speculated about the existence of a "political personality," that is, a "motivational syndrome characteristic of politicians only" (Czudnowski 1975, 210). More recent works (Payne 1984; Browning 1968; Barber 1965) have identified personality traits associated with different patterns of recruitment and behavior in office.

Ambition theory represented the next step in the evolution of recruitment studies. Building on the seminal work of Schlesinger (1966), ambition theorists argue that potential candidates behave rationally, that is, they assess the costs and benefits of alternative courses of action and choose the course that they perceive to be most consistent with their political ambitions.[7] Thus, while psychological and social differences are important, the decision to run results primarily from a matching of individual ambition and the context of opportunities available to the potential candidate. Schlesinger used aggregate data to describe this "structure of opportunities," noting that in many states identifiable career ladders delimited the options available to ambitious would-be politicians.

Ambition theory assumes that all politicians are ambitious; as Schlesinger puts it, "ambition lies at the heart of politics" (1966, 5). Incumbent officeholders, for example, would always run for a higher office if they could obtain those positions without cost (Rohde 1979; Black 1972). The theory further assumes that politicians are rational decision makers, and "do not hanker after offices they cannot hope to attain, and they minimize their uncertainty and maximize their chances of success by following clear-cut and predictable patterns of advancement" (Fowler 1993, 8).

In the past twenty years or so this "rational actor" approach has become dominant in the literature on candidate emergence. Research drawing on the assumptions made by ambition theorists has formalized a theory of costs/benefits assessment (Black 1972), tested hypotheses concerning career advancement from the House to the Senate (Rohde 1979), and evaluated the impact of various local factors on the likelihood that an individual will run for Congress (Bianco 1984). And, as noted previously, Jacobson and Kernell (1983) have built an entire theory around the assumption that potential congressional candidates behave strategically—that is, they are most likely to run for Congress when national conditions are most propitious for their party. This research stream has dovetailed nicely with the candidate-centered paradigm of American congressional elections. As Canon, Schousen, and Sellers have argued, in an environment dominated by candidates it is sensible analytically to "make assumptions about the rational calculations of the individual political entrepreneur. If, indeed, the candidate bears the 'risks, rewards, and pains' of campaigns, the specification, operationalization, and measurement of those factors should be made from an individual-level perspective" (1992, 2).

The Limitations of Ambition Theory

Fowler's recent work makes clear that the various approaches to the study of emergence, though identifying a number of institutional and individual forces that act on the decision to run or not to run, have failed to provide a coherent understanding of the interaction between them (1993, 42). In particular—and somewhat ironically given the preeminence of ambition theory in recent emergence studies—Fowler argues that ambition's role in the decision to seek elective office is not well understood. As noted previously, ambition is simply assumed to be characteristic of all politicians—yet we know little about where it came from or how it develops (Fowler 1993, 42). Moreover, the type of ambition assumed in the literature is what Schlesinger (1966) called "progressive ambition." Progressively ambitious politicians invariably will seek opportunities to work their ways up the political ladder. Other types of ambition, such as "discrete" ambition (characterized by those who hold an office for a time and then leave politics) or "static" ambition (characterized by officeholders who win an office and stay put) receive little mention. Ambition apparently is assumed to be a fixed characteristic, rarely changing even with the evolution of one's life circumstances or political situation (Fowler 1993, 64).

Furthermore, Fowler argues, we see few examples of work that carefully explores the interaction between ambition and context—an exploration that recognizes that "ambition varies with the social and political environment and the individual's relation to that environment" (1993, 65).[8] Indeed, Prewitt argues that ambition should be *defined* as "the ever-so-subtle interplay of shifting self-images interacting with shifting opportunity structures" (1990, 995). The neglect of these interactions is somewhat surprising, for Schlesinger's concept of opportunity structure explicitly recognizes the importance of existing political arrangements and offices as a factor determining when individuals will, or will not, act on their ambitions (Fowler 1993, 56-57).[9]

Of course, recognizing that candidate emergence is more complicated than the ambition theorists have suggested does not imply that decisions about candidacy are nonrational or that such theorists are incorrect about the essentially strategic nature of candidacy. If most of today's political activists are professional politicians operating in a candidate-centered environment, as Ehrenhalt and others have argued, then it should not be surprising that decisions about candidacy are dictated primarily by considerations of winning or losing—in other words, considerations relevant to career advancement. These factors may be paramount in a political system in which barriers to candidacy (such as party selection, racial or gender acceptability, and so on) have weakened, because the decision to run is made by the individual entrepreneur rather than by groups that control access to candidacy.

How are we to know whether the ambition theorists are correct in their emphasis on strategic considerations or, more generally, how ambition and context interact? We need a great deal more information from the field, from the districts in which candidacy decisions are made. Some empirical work has been done, to be sure. Bits and pieces of the institutional environment have been explored, such as the impact of incumbency as a deterrent to prospective congressional challengers (Kazee 1983) and the role of party organizations as recruiters of House candidates (Kazee and Thornberry 1990; Herrnson 1988). Empirically, however, apart from Linda Fowler and Robert McClure's exhaustive study of New York's 30th Congressional District, few efforts have been made to analyze carefully and systematically the impact of various individual and structural factors on the decision to seek office. As Matthews concludes, the initial decision to run "has been little studied ... [f]ormal models of the decision-process have been proposed, but empirical studies are few" (1984, 563).

The absence of such empirical evidence precludes us from answering a variety of important candidate emergence questions. What constellation of factors in a particular district triggers some individuals to run for Congress and others to stay out of the race? Which contextual considerations matter most to potential candidates? Ambition also plays a role in the perception of the district or national context. How often does it distort the objective context, creating a rosy scenario in which unknown contenders see themselves as emerging from the pack to secure upset wins? Research on emergence need also address the phenomenon of "amateur" candidacies, launched by individuals who possess no previous elective experience yet run more frequently and more successfully than ambition theory might predict (Canon 1990a). Knowing little about how potential candidates perceive their political environment, for example, makes it impossible to evaluate Jacobson and Kernell's (1983) strategic politicians theory: do activists pay attention to the national context as they search for the right moment to run for Congress?

Summary

In conclusion, then, it is not that the ambition theorists or the personality theorists or the political sociologists are wrong, for each has contributed important pieces of the emergence puzzle. The sociological approach appropriately emphasizes the key role society plays in defining the universe of activists eligible to seek a House seat. Psychological theories emphasize characteristics of individuals that predispose them to run for public office. Ambition theory brings our attention to the rational basis of candidate decision making. What we lack, however, is a satisfactory synthesis of these perspectives. It is only by going to districts—by talking to candidates, would-be candidates, and district observers—that we can evaluate more clearly the impact of the social and political environment, individual dispositions, and costs/benefits assessments, and to develop a more complete understanding of how they interact.

Ambition and Context in the Emergence Process

We offer in this book an assessment of candidate emergence that recognizes the importance of ambition, but recognizes as well that ambition is more likely to develop in some situations (and districts) than in others.[10] We plan, in short, to do what the ambition theorists have not done—to focus on district-specific factors affecting the development of ambition, and, in turn, to identify and assess the contextual forces that help to determine who runs and who does not.

Ambition

James David Barber's 1965 study of Connecticut legislators noted that any prospective candidacy begins with a simple question: Do I want it? (11-

15). An affirmative answer, however unforgiving the electoral environment might appear to others, increases the likelihood that an individual will become a candidate. More than twenty years later, Fowler and McClure assert that "[a]mbition for a seat in the House, more than any other factor ... is what finally separates a visible, declared candidate for Congress from an unseen one" (1989, 2).

Ambition is defined in this book as a desire to serve in Congress, and a willingness to incur personal and professional costs to fulfill that desire. This definition illustrates why ambition is central to rational-actor theories of candidate emergence. In terms of costs and benefits, the benefits derived from candidacy are largely a function of how much the individual wants the office in question. In the same way, the perception of the costs of running for office are filtered through the screen of ambition.

Ambition is best measured by asking candidates about their past experiences, career goals, and perception of the accommodations political candidacy requires. Answers to these questions must be treated with some caution, of course; as Canon points out, in today's anti-politician environment we might expect few political activists to identify "personal ambition" as the factor that drives their office-seeking behavior (1993, 2). Nonetheless, the alternative to direct contacts with potential candidates—using political career data to draw inferences about ambition (see, for example, Banks and Kiewiet 1989; Jacobson and Kernell 1983)—tells us nothing about individuals who never embark upon a political career, and very little about the impact of ambition on the perception of factors in the political environment.

Conversations with political activists enable us, for example, to determine whether many candidates distort political reality to justify a decision already made. Canon, Schousen, and Sellers (1992, 3) cite the story of L. Sandy Maisel, a Colby College professor who sought unsuccessfully the nomination for Maine's 1st Congressional District. In his book, *From Obscurity to Oblivion,* Maisel describes his conversations with district political observers about his uncertain prospects and his concern about his ability to get elected as a liberal, Jewish college professor from Buffalo. He concludes: "As a practical politician and a knowledgeable student of politics, I knew the analytical questions I had to ask. So I asked them, but I did not really care what the answers were" (Maisel 1982, 19). In another study, one long-shot challenger explained how such candidates reconcile the discouraging reality of an entrenched incumbent and their strong desire to run: "There is a syndrome among sacrificial lamb candidates which I call the 'perhaps' or 'maybe' syndrome. It is a feeling that, despite the odds, perhaps I can beat the incumbent. Even if the odds are fifty to one, perhaps that lightning bolt will strike" (Kazee 1980, 83). Ambition becomes the perceptual screen through which candidates interpret the objective context, much as partisanship screens (and distorts) our perceptions of political candidates and issues.

Contextual Factors

Potential congressional candidates do not live in a world free from personal or political complications. Whether or not they run for office will depend to a great extent on their families and occupational situations, the political environment in their districts, states, and nation, and assessments of their chances of winning the party nominations and the House seats. Ambition notwithstanding, then, contextual factors may encourage candidacies in some districts and discourage them in others. In this sense, the mix of contextual factors in a congressional district affects not only individual decisions, but collectively also may determine the size and composition of the candidate pool.

Context is more complex than the political situation in a particular district at a particular time. District activists are part of a historical, sociological, and institutional environment that establishes a set of constraints on the emergence of candidates. African Americans, for example, could not have considered seriously congressional candidacy throughout much of American history. In the same way, women have only recently seen doors opening to candidacy that for most of two centuries have been formally or informally closed. Structural changes in the political environment, such as redistricting, may kindle political passions previously dampened by recognition of a discouraging party balance in the district. So, a more systematic assessment of the multitude of contextual factors should include explicit recognition of each of these contexts. Six categories of contextual influences have thus been defined for this analysis: eligibility, access, competition, resources, structural, and personal costs.

The Eligibility Context. The sociological approach in the recruitment literature makes clear that eligibility for leadership positions in the United States has been limited primarily to white males of European origin. Changes in law and in prevailing social and cultural mores have opened public office to a wider variety of people, but in many congressional districts candidacy is still not a realistic possibility for individuals of various social, ethnic, and racial groups. African Americans, in particular, have been presented with few opportunities outside the urban North to seek House nominations. Local political culture might imply that women are ineligible to run for office, although recent increases in the number of women holding local and state offices, as well as the dramatic increase in 1992 in the number of women seeking and winning U.S. House seats (150 women sought major party House nominations; 68 percent more women won House seats), suggest that these barriers may be weakening (see especially Darcy, Welch, and Clark 1987). The context of eligibility is ignored if we focus primarily on candidacy as the product of a decision about costs and benefits; ambition may be an irrelevant consideration if candidacy is denied because of an individual's gender, race, or ethnic status.

The Access Context.   Even if one is eligible for consideration as a congressional candidate, the permeability of the environment for declaring one's intentions is an important factor influencing candidacy decisions. At the most fundamental level, this addresses the distinctions between recruitment and emergence. Are self-starting candidacies common in the district, or must an individual be recruited by the party before undertaking a serious candidacy? We know from the literature on emergence that most House candidates are self-starters (Hansen 1991; Seligman, King, Kim, and Smith 1974; Huckshorn and Spencer 1971), but in some districts party organizations have active and effective recruitment operations (Kazee and Thornberry 1990), not to mention the recruitment activities carried out by national party committees (Herrnson 1988; Gibson, Cotter, Bibby, and Huckshorn 1983). Even in the absence of strong parties, must prospective candidates seek the blessing of power brokers—influential, well-heeled political patrons—before a credible candidacy can be launched?

The Competitive Context.   Potential House candidates assess the competitive environment, both locally and nationally, to determine the potential for winning a House nomination or seat. Most fundamentally, is the seat open or is it filled by an incumbent? If the latter, how entrenched is the incumbent? Does he or she have obvious vulnerabilities—perhaps a number of checks overdrawn on the House bank, or a locally unpopular vote on abortion or tax legislation? If the seat is open, who else is considering running? Also part of the competitive environment is the local partisan context, a factor frequently cited as important in determining the quality of emerging candidates (Krasno and Green 1988; Bond, Covington, and Fleisher 1985). How strong have the parties traditionally been in the district? Is the local economy healthy, or is the district dependent on a weakening agricultural or industrial base? What is the media environment in the district: must a candidate try to communicate in multiple television markets extended over a wide area, or is the district essentially coterminous with a single media market? External to the district, a prospective candidate may ask if this is a good year for Republicans or Democrats. How is the national economy performing, and what effect will this have on the campaign and voters' preferences? Is this a presidential election year, and will the national nominees have coattails on which a House candidate might ride?

The Resources Context.   Prospective congressional candidates must estimate their ability to raise funds or attract volunteer support sufficient to mount a credible bid for the House seat. Are funds on hand from a previous campaign? How realistic is the candidate about the amount of money needed to wage a competitive race? How much money has the incumbent spent in previous races? Is the local or national party able to provide resource support? Given the large amount of money necessary to compete (on average, House incumbents in 1992 spent $428,000; Nelson 1993, 107), the prudent candidate must answer these questions before a serious bid for the House can be undertaken.

The Structural Context. Structural factors operate primarily at the district and state levels. For example, the size, shape, and boundaries of the district affect congressional aspirations. Those who may live in less populated areas, distant from the core city or county of the district, may be disadvantaged in winning party nominations or acquiring sufficient name recognition to mount a competitive candidacy. Redistricting may alter substantially existing boundaries, bringing new areas (and potential candidates) into the district and excluding others, or by changing the existing racial or ethnic balance of the district. Furthermore, an unfinished redistricting process creates uncertainty about the final map, adding a variable to the decisional equation that no prospective candidate can evaluate precisely. Related structural concerns include the nature of the state legislature. Is it a professional body that regularly serves as an incubator of congressional candidates, or is it a low-paying, part-time assembly that seldom nurtures hopes for a House seat (Squire 1992; Fowler and McClure 1989; Francis and Baker 1986; Robeck 1982)? More generally, emergence may be shaped by an existing "opportunity structure" of lower-level elective offices or appointive positions (Schlesinger 1966). State election laws, such as those requiring runoff elections for party nominations or the House seat, also may play a role in determining who runs and who does not.

The Personal Costs Context.   Previous research on candidate emergence demonstrates that personal costs may weigh heavily in the calculus of potential House candidates (see especially Kazee 1980).[11] Hansen (1992, 22-23), in a recent essay entitled "The Vanishing American Candidate," painstakingly chronicles the personal burdens of candidacy:

> Running for a high profile office today can mean foregoing personal and family privacy; jeopardizing a promising career; giving up most, if not all, your discretionary time; enduring negative campaign tactics; being separated often and for long periods of time from family and friends; having to raise enormous sums of campaign funds, often alone and at some risk to one's personal integrity; publicly disclosing personal and family economic interests, tax forms, and liabilities; absorbing with equanimity the criticism and abuse of constituents, interest groups, and the press; earning less money; recognizing that you will get little help from local party organizations; understanding that in the final analysis winning and surviving in politics is largely a function of personal wit, skill, indefatigability, and ambition. And when it's all done, you may lose.

Goals of this Book

The question at the center of most previous research on congressional candidate emergence might be stated in this way: "Among ambitious people, why do some run for Congress and others stay on the sidelines?" The answer, the prevailing literature tells us, is that some potential candidates think they can win and some do not. Potential candidates are thus ambitious and strategic, drawing conclusions about candidacy based on rational assessments of the likelihood of winning. This literature, however, does not answer two key questions. Why are some people ambitious and others not? Why do some people think they can win and others think they will lose? The limitations of rational-actor theories thus are both theoretical (the assumption of ambition) and empirical (the absence of contextual evidence).

In this book we assume that potential candidates have widely varying levels of ambition, and that ambition may change as conditions in a district change. Indeed, a major object of the study is to assess the conditions under which individuals of varying ambition decide the time is right to run for Congress. Of course, we cannot provide a complete understanding of the psychological forces that encourage or discourage ambition; it is not our intention to psychoanalyze prospective candidates. However, we can assess the extent to which ambitions are stimulated by what Fowler calls ". . . changes both in the political environment and the individual's relation to that environment" (1993, 88). We also think that contextual considerations are fundamental to understanding candidate emergence, and that those considerations can be identified systematically and evaluated. In short, we can explain more fully why some people think they can win and others do not. Finally, we think that the best way to study candidate emergence—to begin to fathom the complex interactions between ambition and context—is to go to the districts and talk to the activists. The richness and flexibility afforded by personal interviewing and, in particular, the ability to explore in depth the motivations of potential candidates, is absent from much of the recruitment literature.[12] "Soaking and poking" in the district—to use Richard Fenno's (1978) memorable phrase—is the method of choice for those who want to understand more fully how potential candidates perceive the political context within which they operate, and how they process that information in light of their own political ambitions.

The specific goals of the study thus can be summarized as follows:

1. Identify and describe the prospective candidate pool in a number of congressional districts.
2. Evaluate the role ambition plays in affecting perceptions of the political environment and in decisions to run for Congress.
3. Catalog and analyze the impact of individual, district, state, and national factors on the decisions of those aspiring for a House seat.

The Candidate Emergence Project

To reach these goals a group of political scientists set out to identify and interview a large number of potential congressional candidates in a variety of districts during the 1991-1992 election cycle.[13] The Candidate

Emergence Project, as it came to be called, was designed to take advantage of the depth and sensitivity afforded by case studies, yet to do so in a relatively large number of congressional districts and, perhaps most important, to use a common methodology.

In each district, interviewing began in the spring of 1991 and continued until each party had selected congressional candidates—which, in most cases, was in the summer or fall of 1992. Interviews were conducted in person or by telephone, and, when appropriate, follow-up interviews were completed to track the decision-making process over time. Questions addressed a number of topics related to congressional candidacy, including costs of running, what it might take to get an individual to run, the role of parties in the district, potential opposition for the nomination, the impact of issues in congressional campaigns, and an assessment of the incumbent's—if there was one—strengths and weaknesses. In addition, a shorter questionnaire was designed for politically knowledgeable people in each district, persons we termed "informants" (see the appendix for both questionnaires).

Identifying the Candidate Pool

A key to the success of this study was our ability to identify and interview the people whom Fowler and McClure call the "unseen" candidates (1989, 1) as well as those who subsequently decided to seek the congressional nomination. Ideally, prospective candidates would be identified early in an election cycle so that we might evaluate their decision-making process in as contemporaneous a manner as possible. To do this, the researchers in each district began by listing individuals whose prior political activity identified them as potential congressional candidates. Automatically included on each list, for example, were those who held state legislative seats in districts that overlapped with the congressional district. Also included were prominent, locally elected (and sometimes appointed) officials, including mayors, members of city, county, or town councils, district attorneys, and so on. The names of defeated candidates for those positions in recent elections were included as well, with special attention given to those who were once candidates in the primary or general election for the House seat. Our ability to identify political activists in each area was enhanced greatly by our close proximity to the districts included in the study. Indeed, a key assumption of the study from the outset was that participating scholars would select nearby districts for analysis. This not only reduced research costs, but had the more important benefit of increasing the scholar's awareness of each district's political context—including knowledge of idiosyncratic characteristics not apparent to the casual or more distant observer.

Next we contacted "informants," that is, knowledgeable people who could identify elected officials, political activists, and others who might consider running for Congress. These informants were asked a series of detailed questions about people in the district who might someday consider running for the House seat. A number of the people identified by the informants were contacted and interviewed. Although the primary purpose of these interviews was to determine the potential candidates' perception of the contextual and individual factors discussed previously, the interviewees also were treated as informants and were asked to identify other potential candidates in the district. This procedure produced an ever-widening list of informants and activists in each district.

The identification of amateur candidates was of particular concern. By definition, amateurs have built careers or been involved in nonpolitical activities that might make them more difficult to identify before the fact of candidacy. This problem is most significant for amateurs who might mount a credible campaign; we need be little concerned about overlooking unknown, resource-poor amateurs who briefly consider candidacy but decide not to run. The well-known amateurs—local celebrities, sports figures, prominent business people, and so forth—are another matter; as Canon (1990a) has shown, these well-known amateurs win a relatively large number of congressional nominations and House seats. The best way to maximize the probability that such amateurs would be identified, was to locate a wide range of informants and to ask them specific questions about the presence of interested but politically inexperienced individuals in the district.

The methods we adopted to identify the candidate pool produced for most districts a long list of political activists. Interviews were arranged with the individuals deemed to be of greatest theoretical interest—that is, those people who were, for various reasons, most attractive as prospective candidates. For example, special efforts were made to interview the activists whose names were mentioned by more than one interviewee, or who had run for Congress before, or who had substantial name recognition in the district.

Were all of the potential candidates interviewed? Certainly not; the absence of complete information about each district, as well as time and resource constraints, made such a goal unattainable. For our purposes, however, a complete census of prospective candidates was unnecessary. Our objective was to identify a sufficient number of possible candidates in each district to be able to draw empirically well-supported conclusions about the factors individuals weighed as they considered a congressional race. The relatively large number of interviews conducted in each district, as well as the procedure used to identify all potential candidates—tapping, as it did, the key information networks in each area—suggests that the probability of systematically overlooking theoretically interesting individuals is low. Moreover, the lengthy time frame of the study and proximity of the researchers made it possible to return to the districts for follow-up interviews or to meet with individuals not included on the initial district lists.

District Selection

Nine congressional districts were selected for study. Although re-

Table 1-1 Congressional Districts Included in the Candidate Emergence Project (data from 1990)

District	Incumbent	Party	Incumbent percent	Year incumbent first elected
Colorado, 2nd	David Skaggs	Democratic	60.7	1986
Illinois, 9th	Sidney Yates	Democratic	71.2	1948
Iowa, 1st	Jim Leach	Republican	99.8[a]	1976
Iowa, 4th	Neal Smith	Democratic	97.9[a]	1958
North Carolina, 1st	New district			
North Carolina, 9th	J. Alex McMillan	Republican	62.0	1984
Oklahoma, 4th	Dave McCurdy	Democratic	73.6	1980
Texas, 29th	New district			
Virginia, 8th	James Moran	Democratic	51.7	1990

[a] No major party challenger.

source limitations precluded the construction of a sample representative of all district situations, we chose districts that illuminated a variety of emergence contexts (see Table 1-1).[14] Five of the districts, for example, were represented by Democratic incumbents whose percentages in the preceding election (1990) ranged from 51.7 percent to 99.8 percent, and whose seniority reached from Sidney Yates's (D-Ill.) forty-four years in Congress to newcomer James Moran's (D-Va.) two years. Republican incumbents held the House seat in two of the districts, one incumbent winning without opposition in 1990, the other with 62.0 percent of the vote. The former, Jim Leach of Iowa's 1st District, was first elected to the House in 1976. The latter, J. Alex McMillan of North Carolina's 9th District, was elected in 1984. Two of the districts were newly created: North Carolina's 1st District, a Rorschach-test-shaped, black majority district created only after a bitter partisan battle, and Texas's 29th District, also created to elect a minority representative—in this case Hispanic—but that unexpectedly nominated and elected an Anglo Democrat.

Why include so many districts with strong incumbents? First, this is the emergence status quo faced by prospective candidates in most districts. In 1992 incumbents who had won two years earlier with 60 percent or more of the vote ran in more than three-fourths of all House districts (Ornstein, Mann, and Malbin 1992, 61). To focus only on the districts with obvious competition and uncertainty about electoral outcomes might permit us to write about a more competitive set of horse races, but we would surely miss the more important drama being played out in the large majority of congressional districts today. If we are to draw conclusions about the aggregate impact of that process on the American political system, we must look to the type of districts from which most House members come.

Furthermore, the best way to assess widely promoted claims that 1992 was to be the "year of the outsider," a year that would bring an anti-incumbency voter reaction not seen in the modern era, was to focus on districts represented by incumbents of varying levels of seniority and vulnerability. The appearance of a strong set of challengers in these districts would suggest that district activists were responding to forces operating outside the district. A preponderance of weak challengers, however, would indicate, national trends notwithstanding, that emergence is dependent primarily on local factors affecting the competitive environment in each district.[15]

Overview of the Book

What follows is a series of case studies of candidate emergence in nine districts during the 1991-1992 election cycle. The studies are ordered to highlight differences in the competitive context faced by each pool of prospective candidates. In Chapter 2, David Canon, Matthew Schousen, and Pat Sellers illuminate the labyrinthine process that led to the creation of a new black majority district in North Carolina and the election of an African American woman to the U.S. House. In Chapter 3, Douglas Abel and Bruce Oppenheimer show that the law of unintended consequences applies to congressional districting: the 29th Congressional District of Texas, created to increase Hispanic representation in Congress, sent an Anglo male to Washington—an outcome that largely was the result of candidate emergence.

The presence of an incumbent dramatically changes prospective candidate decision making, as Paul Herrnson and Robert Tennant demonstrate in Chapter 4. Although James Moran narrowly won Virginia's 8th District seat in 1990, a favorable redistricting plan and the inability of the Republican party to entice potentially stronger candidates to run left the GOP nomination to a spirited but inexperienced and underfunded challenger. Chapters 5 and 6 consider two districts represented by incumbents in the "expansionist" stage (Fenno 1978) of their careers, Colorado's 2nd District and North Carolina's 9th District. In Colorado, Allen Hertzke analyzes the pool of potential Republican challengers deciding whether to face-off against incumbent David Skaggs. Skaggs won initially in 1986 with 51 percent of the vote, but has since won at least 60 percent of the vote. In North Carolina, Susan Roberts and Thomas Kazee describe the "latent competition" facing Republican J. Alex McMillan, first elected in 1984 by a margin of 321 votes but now seemingly secure.

The obstacles facing aspiring House candidates in districts with presumably entrenched incumbents are detailed in Chapters 7, 8, and 9. In Chapter 7, John Haskell, Kerry Sutten, and Peverill Squire argue that Neal Smith in Iowa's 4th District and Jim Leach in Iowa's 1st District have effectively turned back the threats produced by an unfavorable redistricting plan. The two incumbents thus faced weak opposition in 1992. Gary Copeland concludes in Chapter 8 that Dave McCurdy has so personally dominated Oklahoma's 4th District that local activists have "closed their minds" to the prospect of real competition or alternative representation. In Chapter 9, Anne Layzell and L. Marvin Overby dissect the 9th District of Illinois. In theory, at least, this district should illustrate the full cycle of competitiveness: Sidney Yates was first elected with 55 percent of the vote in 1948, built solid reelection constituencies for four decades, and is now nearing the end of his legislative career. Apparently confirming expectations of a weakened incumbency, Yates attracted a primary opponent in 1990 who spent more than $600,000. Layzell and Overby show how Yates not only beat back that challenge, but appears to have squashed effectively serious opposition in the near future.

In the concluding chapter Thomas Kazee takes stock of what these district stories tell us about candidate emergence. We will see that ambition for the House is alive and well, demonstrated most clearly by the willingness of potential candidates to make substantial personal and professional sacrifices to seek a House seat. The case studies demonstrate also that the pool of prospective candidates, in theory at least, has expanded to admit those previously denied even the right to think about running for Congress—for example, women and African Americans. Moreover, we will see that access to candidacy is largely a matter of motivation and perseverance; congressional candidates are rarely recruited, instead emerging as self-starters whose most important characteristic is an abundance of ambition. It is somewhat ironic, then, that though the doors to candidacy are more open than ever, competition for House seats in many districts has become stultified by an unwillingness to challenge seemingly entrenched incumbents. Prospective candidates do behave strategically—the ambition theorists are right on that score—but their strategic calculations are dictated primarily by local considerations. Factors specific to the district, most notably the presence of an incumbent, usually push potentially strong candidates to the electoral sidelines to wait for a more inviting opportunity. The concluding chapter turns finally to an assessment of the implications of such constrained competition for the future of American politics.

Notes

1. The link between ambition theory and democratic accountability, Prewitt (1970, 210) reminds us, exists only when two conditions are met: elections are the route to office for public officials, and once in office incumbents will wish to remain there. For U.S. House elections, the first condition obviously is met; satisfaction of the second condition is attested to by the large number of incumbents who seek reelection every two years (even as retirement rates have fluctuated over time [Hibbing 1982; Frantzich 1978]). If we accept James Madison's arguments in *The Federalist Papers* about the need for ambitious individuals to press incumbent officeholders, a third condition must be added: that voters have a real choice between incumbents

and challengers. A pattern of declining competition in House elections, traceable to the mid-1960s, suggests that this third condition is not well met. Fowler and Maisel (1991) reported that nearly 20 percent of all House districts were uncontested in 1990—and that nearly three-fourths of all House districts in 1986 and 1988 were noncompetitive, that is, the district was uncontested or the challenger received less than 30 percent of the vote. In addition, the number of challengers with elective office experience declined from 26.7 percent in 1982 to 10.4 percent in 1990 (Jacobson 1993); this finding is particularly significant since experienced challengers tend to do better than those with no experience (Jacobson and Kernell 1983). A variety of studies have suggested that diminished competition may be the result of an emergence process that produces few attractive challengers. Using data from the 1978 National Election Study, several researchers found that House challengers were little known by most voters. Voters were much more likely to report contacts with incumbents than with challengers and were much more likely to rate them positively on a standard thermometer scale (Hinckley 1980; Mann and Wolfinger 1980). One researcher, in fact, referred to challengers as "invisible" candidates (Ragsdale 1981). A study based on interviews with House candidates running in the mid-1970s concluded that challengers viewed incumbents as nearly invulnerable. One challenger declared that "there are two ways you can beat the incumbent. Either shoot him or have your sister seduce him on national TV" (Kazee 1980, 91). Another challenger said, "Getting elected. That's the tough part. . . . Once a guy is elected, that's it. I told my people, 'we get in, they'll never get us out' " (Kazee 1980, 92).

2. The discussion that follows is drawn in part from Fowler's book, which should be consulted by readers interested in more exhaustive critiques of the literature on candidate emergence. Note also Fowler's other work in this area, most notably *Political Ambition* (1989) with Robert McClure.

3. Republican domination of the White House for twenty-eight of the forty years between 1952 and 1992 is, of course, one half of the equation. Various arguments may be advanced to explain GOP dominance at the presidential level, and many of these arguments are rooted in the process by which the Democrats nominate their so-often unsuccessful candidates for the White House.

4. In addition, as Fowler (1993, 14) notes, Arnold's conclusion that House members are motivated by the potential of a strong challenge to take policy positions least likely to engender electoral retribution from angry constituents explicitly recognizes the key role of candidate emergence in congressional policy making.

5. "Emergence" is used here to describe the process by which individuals become congressional candidates, rather than "recruitment." This choice reflects the consistent finding in the literature that few candidates are actually recruited to run for Congress; though party organizations occasionally may recruit candidates, and certainly play a role in the emergence of other candidates (see, for example, Kazee and Thornberry 1990), emergence more accurately describes the range of candidate experiences. For a more detailed discussion of this distinction, see "The Naming of Candidates: Recruitment or Emergence," by Maisel, Fowler, Jones, and Stone (1990).

6. Two of the most exhaustive reviews of the emergence literature, while not using precisely the same terms as Canon, Schousen, and Sellers, identify similar emphases. Czudnowski (1975, 178-209) discusses "social background characteristics" and "motivations," the latter primarily referring to psychological factors. Matthews (1984) uses four categories: "opportunities," which deals largely with social factors that affect access to office (548-556); "motives, incentives, and goals," which includes psychological factors and the rational basis of office-seeking (556-562); "processes," which focuses on factors affecting the decision to run, the role of party organizations in recruitment, and so forth (562-567); and "careers," a body of work

concerned largely with what happens after one gets elected (567-572). Fowler's classification is more detailed; her scheme includes five "paradigms": social, psychological, process, rational actor, and rational/institutional (1993, 44). Common to these categorizations is a recognition of the critical influence of social, institutional, and individual factors on the emergence of candidates.

7. Fowler places Schlesinger's work in her "process" paradigm, arguing that while ambition is central to Schlesinger's work, "the dependent variable in his analysis is not the individual's decision to run, but the presence or absence of processes that permit ambition to follow its course" (1993, 57).

8. The emergence literature has been marked by an absence of empirical information. Commenting on the paucity of research focusing on recruitment as a life-cycle phenomenon, Czudnowski writes: "In the absence of direct evidence, one must rely on tentative theorizing. . . " (1975, 177). This might be said of emergence research as a whole.

9. Moreover, Fowler's discussion of the "rational/institutional" paradigm cites the nearly quarter-century-old works of Schlesinger (1966) and Prewitt (1970), which recognize the importance of situational factors as influences on decisions to seek higher office, and the more recent work of Canon and Sousa (1992) and Banks and Kiewiet (1989) on the factors affecting the emergence of amateurs (Fowler 1993, 66-68).

10. In Schlesinger's words, "The most reasonable assumption is that ambition for office, like most other ambitions, develops with a specific situation. . . " (quoted in Fowler 1993, 56).

11. Personal costs are determined within the context of the situation and are thus properly thought of as contextual considerations. A prospective candidate's family or occupational status are as much elements of his or her environment as the shape of the district or the role parties play in the recruitment of candidates. Moreover, the perception of those costs—and how much weight an aspiring House candidate gives them—is influenced by ambition, much as evaluations of the political context at any given time are colored by ambition.

12. Most of the studies based on direct contacts with candidates, with the exception of Kazee and Thornberry (1990), Fowler and McClure (1989), and Kazee (1980; 1983) use mail questionnaires rather than personal interviews.

13. Under the auspices of the Carl Albert Congressional Research and Studies Center, participants in the project met in February 1991 at the University of Oklahoma to develop a methodology for the study, select districts, and prepare a questionnaire to be used in each district.

14. I initially contacted a number of political scientists in the summer of 1990 to inquire about their willingness to participate in this study. Those who responded affirmatively were then asked to identify congressional districts that might shed light on the process of candidate emergence and that were accessible to them. As noted earlier, accessibility, while reducing research-related costs, also facilitates careful and continuous monitoring of decision making by prospective candidates in each district. It should be noted that the nearest districts were not selected automatically for inclusion in the study. In several cases more distant but nevertheless more theoretically interesting districts were selected. I am indebted to my colleagues for their willingness to assume the costs associated with travel to districts that were not only a considerable distance away, but that were spread over the map in ways only partisan redistricters could devise.

15. A significant omission from our "sample" was one or more open districts (that is, districts without incumbents). Our intent from the outset was to include open districts, but the vicissitudes of politics and the pressures of prior commitments from several scholars originally part of the Emergence Project team conspired to eliminate a number of open districts initially listed for inclusion in the study.

2

A Formula for Uncertainty:
Creating a Black Majority District in North Carolina

David T. Canon, Matthew M. Schousen, and Patrick J. Sellers

The story of North Carolina's 1st District has more intrigue, back-stabbing, and suspense than a mystery novel. The story is about an African American woman, Eva Clayton, who finally won a House seat after initially running nearly a quarter-century ago. This campaign involved ten redistricting plans—one of which was rejected by the U.S. Justice Department—subsequent lawsuits, and two Supreme Court decisions. Players in the story include a twenty-six-year House veteran, Walter Jones, Sr., who planned to retire but died before he could fill out his final term. Next is his son, Walter Jones, Jr., who groomed himself for many years to take his father's seat, only to have that opportunity denied by his own party who punished him for his "independence" through unfavorable redistricting. The cast of characters is rounded out by six other candidates who were enticed to run by the open seat and the new black majority district. The story includes two strategic candidates: an African American contender who some observers claim ran to split the black vote and help elect his white boss's son; and a white candidate, whose sole motivation for running was to split the white vote to help elect an African American. Above all, this is a story of how ambition and self-interest created a collective action problem that almost prevented the African American community from achieving its collective goal of electing a black to Congress (see Canon, Schousen, and Sellers 1993, for an extended discussion of this issue).

This case study supports the recent research that points to the candidate-centered nature of contemporary congressional elections (Jacobson 1992a, 7, 25-30). However, the behavior of candidates in our district contradicts aspects of this recent work and harkens back to Joseph Schlesinger's famous observation that "ambition lies at the heart of politics" (1966, 1). Candidates run because they want to advance their political careers. The ability to finance a campaign, personal and family considerations, party influences, and national tides simply did not influence candidate emergence in the district we observed. Our district also shows how redistricting is a formula for candidate uncertainty and how racial factors influence candidate emergence, both in terms of a direct impact on candidates' decisions and as a filter through which perceptions of the context of the political arena are formed.

Overview of Candidate Emergence in
North Carolina's 1st District

Seven Democrats and one Republican entered their party's primaries to fill the seat vacated by the expected retirement of Walter Jones, Sr. Table 2-1 shows the names, backgrounds, party, race, and percentage of the primary vote for each of the candidates, while Table 2-2 shows the characteristics of their constituencies. Following the methodology outlined in Chapter 1, we interviewed informants, politicians, and candidates to identify potential candidates in the district. This process uncovered nine potential candidates, four of whom ran in the 1st District.

As shown in Table 2-1, Walter Jones, Jr., won the initial primary with 38.1 percent of the vote, falling just short of the 40 percent required for an outright win. Eva Clayton, who came in second with 31.1 percent in the first round, won the runoff election with a unified African American community behind her with 54.8 percent of the vote. The general election was not contested seriously by the Republican nominee, Ted Tyler, who spent only $7,055 in the district and received 32 percent of the vote in the general election.

Redistricting, North Carolina Style

Steady population growth through the 1980s gave North Carolina an additional House seat in the decennial reapportionment process. Some state legislators looked forward to carving a district that would provide an outlet for their progressive ambitions, while U.S. House members hoped to protect their existing turfs, or even make themselves more secure. The state legislature had to work within the confines of a legal constraint (to create at least one black majority district) and a traditional norm (to protect as many Democratic incumbents as possible). The legal constraint is rooted in the 1982 Voting Rights Act Amendment and subsequent Supreme Court decisions. Most central was *Thornburg v. Gingles* (1986), in which the Court held that a minority group can claim a "discriminatory effect" if "its preferred candidates are usually defeated as a result of bloc voting by a white majority" ("Redistricting 1991" 10). The Justice Department cited *Gingles* in mandating the creation of black majority districts through the process of "preclearance" under Section 5 of the 1965 Voting Rights Act.[1]

Creating a black majority district in North Carolina proved to be quite challenging. The African American population in North Carolina is scattered across the state. Only five counties are at least 50 percent black and when added together they are not nearly large enough to compose a single congressional district. However, 22 percent of the state's 6.6 million people are black, encouraging Republicans and some black leaders to argue that two and perhaps even three of the state's twelve House districts should be black majority.

Figure 2-1   North Carolina, 1st and 12th Districts

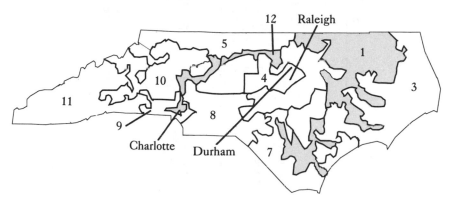

The saga began in earnest in July and August of 1991, when the state House and Senate worked out the details of Redistricting Plan Number 6, which included a single black majority congressional district. The contorted shapes of the new congressional districts provoked immediate controversy. Political commentators poked fun at the shape of the new black-majority district, calling it "a bug splattered on a windshield." In what would be an uneasy alliance, the Republican party and the National Association for the Advancement of Colored People (NAACP) criticized the new plan for serving the interests of congressional incumbents more than the interests of minorities. Republican legislators argued that the Democrats did not create a second black majority congressional seat so that they could preserve as many safe Democratic seats as possible. Under Plan Number 6 the Democrats were likely to win seven of the twelve congressional seats (before redistricting they held seven of eleven).

The Republicans suggested that a second black majority district could be created in the southern part of the state running from Charlotte to Wilmington. The obvious motivation behind this concern for minority representation is the partisan advantage gained by concentrating the traditionally strong Democratic black vote in two districts. By concentrating black voters in two districts, white Democratic incumbents would lose many loyal voters and become vulnerable to Republican challengers. Under this plan, Republicans could have gained a majority of seven to five.

Members of the black community were torn between party loyalty and the desire to increase black representation in Congress. Black state legislators, such as state representative Milton F. "Toby" Fitch, argued that one black majority district would be the best way to increase power for minorities, claiming that a second black congressional seat could isolate blacks on "political reservations." [2] This position, however, was not popular in the black community and as a result black lawmakers kept a low profile in the

Table 2-1 Candidates in the 1st District

Candidate	Background	Party[a]	Race[b]	First-tier?	Identified by informant?	Percent of primary vote	Estimate of expected money	Estimate of needed money	Total receipts
Frank Ballance	State senator, Warrenton	D	B	Yes	Yes	—	—	$350,000	—
Thomas Brandon	Mayor, Williamston	D	W	No	No	5.8	$15,000-$30,000	$15,000-$30,000	$29,883
Eva Clayton	County commissioner, Warren County	D	B	Yes	Yes	31.1	$300,000-$500,000	$300,000-$500,000	$493,341
Toby Fitch	State representative, Wilson	D	B	Yes	Yes	—	—	$200,000	—
Thomas Hardaway	State representative, Enfield	D	B	No	Yes	6.5	"hard to say"	"hard to say"	$43,171
Howard Hunter	State representative, Murfreesboro	D	B	No	Yes	—	—	"not too much"	—
Paul Jones	Attorney, Kinston	D	B	No	Yes	—	—	$400,000-$500,000	—

Walter Jones, Jr.	State representative, Farmville	D	W	Yes	Yes	38.1	$250,000-$300,000	$250,000-$300,000	$226,611
Stacatto Powell	Reverend, Wilson	D	B	No	No	6.7	$150,000-$200,000	$150,000-$200,000	$11,091
Willie Riddick	Legislative aide, Windsor	D	B	Yes	Yes	10.3	$250,000	$250,000	$39,539
Don Smith	House-husband, Stokes	D	W	No	No	1.4	$1,250	$250,000	$1,250
Ted Tyler	Mayor, Rich Square	R	W	No	No	unopposed	$80,000	$300,000	$7,055

Notes: This table does not include Mickey Michaux who was one of the front-runners for the first version of the new district. Michaux ended up running in the new 12th District when Durham was removed from the 1st.

Eva Clayton defeated Walter Jones, Jr., in the runoff 54.8 percent to 45.2 percent and defeated Ted Tyler in the general election 68 percent to 32 percent.

[a] D = Democrat; R = Republican.

[b] B = black; W = white.

Table 2-2 Current Constituencies of Potential and Announced Candidates, Redistricting Plan Number 10

Candidate	Constituency as percentage of 1st District registered voters	Constituency as percentage of 1st District black registered voters	Percentage of registered voters in constituency who are Democratic	Percentage of registered voters in constituency who are black	Vote for Gantt[a] (percentage Democratic)	Vote for Rand[a] (percentage Democratic)
Ballance	33.8	38.2	92.4	57.1	63.1	70.6
Brandon [b]	3.0	2.3	86.4	39.6	46.4	64.5
Clayton [b]	3.8	4.2	94.9	55.2	61.8	71.8
Fitch	13.2	16.7	87.4	64.1	69.9	70.9
Hardaway [b]	12.4	13.3	92.3	54.1	59.5	70.0
Hunter	15.5	16.5	93.2	53.7	60.0	68.7
Jones, P.	4.1	5.0	88.7	61.1	64.8	71.2
Jones, Jr. [b]	13.0	10.5	82.5	40.8	51.5	59.3
Powell [b]	4.9	5.9	86.9	61.3	67.3	69.5
Riddick [b]	53.7	48.1	85.9	45.3	54.9	62.9
Tyler [b]	4.7	4.9	96.6	53.5	60.3	71.6
Overall district totals	100.0	100.0	87.1	50.5	59.9	66.7

Sources: North Carolina General Assembly, Legislative Services Office, *The Broadcasting Yearbook*, 1990.

[a] Harvey Gantt was the Democratic candidate for the U.S. Senate in 1990 and Tony Rand was the Democratic candidate for lieutenant governor in 1988. Their vote totals reflect a range of the normal Democratic vote for the 1st District.

[b] Ran in the 1st District.

debate. The American Civil Liberties Union (ACLU) and NAACP argued that at least two black majority districts should be created, and vowed to fight the plan. Despite this resistance, in September the general assembly finally approved Plan Number 6.

On December 19, 1991, however, just seventeen days before beginning the filing period for congressional elections, the Justice Department refused to "preclear" the North Carolina redistricting plan. The ruling cited the "unusually convoluted" shape of the 1st District and the need for another black majority district.

A special legislative session was called for December 30 to address the Justice Department's decision. Democratic lawmakers knew that a second black majority district in southern North Carolina could deeply hurt their party, so they scrambled to find a less painful alternative. John Merrit, an aide to Rep. Charles Rose (D), proposed a second minority district that was made up of urban blacks in Charlotte and Durham, connected by a thin line that traveled northeast along Interstate 85. Democrats found Merrit's plan appealing because it had the potential of actually adding Democratic seats by protecting the current seven Democratic seats while creating the new black majority district.

Republicans, who had assumed that the second new black district would be in the southern part of the state, were stunned. They complained bitterly about the new I-85 district that was literally half the width of the interstate in some places. At one point the district actually changed lanes, a move that was necessary to keep the 6th District contiguous (without the lane change, the 6th would have been cleanly bisected by the 12th District). Mickey Michaux, who nearly won a House seat several years before, sarcastically quipped, "I love this district. I can drive down I-85 with both car doors open and hit every person in the district" (Greenhouse 1993, A9). Despite these concerns, the general assembly approved Redistricting Plan Number 10, Merrit's I-85 plan, on January 24, 1992, after extending the candidate filing period to February 10.

Democratic leaders were apologetic while Republicans were apoplectic about the plan. House Speaker Blue said, "It is an ugly plan. I will not stand here and tell you these are the most symmetrical, prettiest districts I have ever seen. . . . There are some funny looking districts." But Blue argued that Democrats were forced to make the new plan because of the Justice Department's ruling (Denton 1992, 10A). Republicans called the plan "idiotic" (*News and Observer* 1992a, 5B). They offered an amendment to add a third black majority district, but it was rejected on a party-line vote.

After reviewing Plan Number 10, the U.S. Justice Department accepted it just three days before the beginning of the new filing period, which ran from February 10 to March 2. Republican state party chair Jack Hawke filed a lawsuit against the plan, arguing that the state legislature had created a "government of the Democratic incumbent, by the Democratic incumbent, for the Democratic incumbent." The suit specifically charged that the new plan violated the voters' rights to "freedom of association and to fair and effective representation" and argued that a third black majority district should be created (Ruffin 1992, 1A). When the suit was filed, the court left open the filing deadline for congressional candidates until the case could be heard. At a hearing on March 9, a U.S. district court dismissed the case and ruled that the filing period would close immediately. The Republicans appealed to the Supreme Court, but Chief Justice William Rehnquist rejected the request on March 11. The court challenge, for the moment, was over. When the dust settled, the filing period had ended and the primary campaign was on.[3]

In the final redistricting plan, the general assembly pieced together the new 1st District from parts of four former districts. The new district is more homogenous than the former one. After losing Durham, the coastal areas that rely on tourism, and the military bases, the new district relies largely on farming, with tobacco fields and sheds covering the district. While there is some manufacturing in the new district, many of the available jobs provide low wages. Almost 90 percent of voters in the 1st District are registered Democrats. In addition, the district clearly meets the Justice Department's requirements for minority representation—blacks compose a majority of the total population, voting age population, and registered voters. (See Table 2-2.)

Race and the Collective Action Problem

Race had a direct and indirect impact on the candidate emergence process in our district. The direct effect is caused by bloc voting by white and black voters. If one white candidate and four black candidates run in a black majority district, the white candidate could win the Democratic primary. This situation produces what Mancur Olson (1965) calls a "collective action problem": individuals acting in their own self-interest produce an outcome not in the collective interest. In short, the only way for the African American community to increase their representation in public office is to control the individual ambitions of various politicians.[4] This coordination problem is not easily solved in an era of weak parties and candidate-centered campaigns.

Black leaders in the 1st District recognized the potential problem and acted quickly to try to unify behind a single candidate. The Black Leadership Caucus (BLC), an organization of district black leaders, met on three occasions. However, the process broke down when one candidate, Willie Riddick, was seen by the other candidates as having unfairly manipulated the meetings to his advantage. Two of the leading candidates did not even attend one of the meetings, and others did not have their supporters there. Thus, the process lacked legitimacy and several of the candidates refused to bow out when they did not receive the BLC endorsement.

Four black candidates, Frank Ballance, Howard Hunter, Paul Jones, and Toby Fitch, dropped out to enhance the probability of electing an African American. However, three of these, Hunter, Jones, and Fitch, were pursuing a mixed altruistic and self-interested strategy (Ballance dropped out before the endorsement vote). Fitch was most explicit about this strategy. As co-chair of the redistricting committee, Fitch led the effort to create a black majority district. He believed that the entrance of several black candidates into the race would split the black vote and threaten the election of a black member of Congress. Thus, he did not want to have a part in undermining the election of a black member of Congress, a goal for which he worked a year to achieve. At the same time, Fitch recognized that by dropping out, his political standing in the 1st District black community improved dramatically. If Jones, Jr., defeated the current group of black candidates, Fitch believed the black community would unite behind Fitch in 1994 and turn out the first-term white incumbent.

Hunter and Jones both disputed Fitch's claim that he was the reserve candidate. Jones argued that if Jones, Jr., won, black leaders would choose between Jones, Ballance, and Fitch to produce a consensus candidate for 1994. Hunter added his name to the list and argued strenuously that unity was critical. If Jones, Jr., won, Hunter said he would not enter the race in 1994 unless there was consensus behind him: "I will not be part of another fiasco. We are supposed to be in this together. They [the black candidates who ran] are cutting the throats of every minority in the district. Each one knew that they made it less likely that a minority would win." Later he excused Powell because "he was an amateur and didn't know any better."

Ballance could have been a very strong candidate, with 33.8 percent of the new district within his state Senate district. He bowed out of the race to avoid dividing the black vote as well, but his motivations were slightly different. Ballance was not as ambitious as Fitch, Hunter, Jones, or the candidates who decided to run. He told us that the only reason he ran for the state House in 1982 was that local political leaders drafted him. His run for the state senate was motivated similarly. As the consensus black candidate in his previous elections, Ballance did not like the idea of competing against other quality minority candidates in this congressional election.

Race has an indirect effect on the candidate emergence process by serving as a filter through which subjective assessments of the competitive context are made. Both informants and potential candidates described the election as two separate contests, one black and one white. Much of the black community held a strong suspicion of the white candidates and the white-dominated media (for example, one black informant called the *News and Observer* the "News and Disturber"). In our interviews the black informants and potential candidates, fearing that any leaks would be used to divide and exploit the black community, were much more concerned about our credentials as scholars than were their white counterparts (one candidate openly accused one of us of being a "Republican spy"). One black informant described the tension between wanting to consider candidates regardless of race and wanting to elect a black member of Congress. Many blacks view the latter as a way of achieving the former. Another black county party chair expressed concern that neither the then-current congressional incumbents (Tim Valentine and Walter Jones, Sr.), nor the current white candidates could represent black interests. The white activists we interviewed, however, viewed race-blind evaluation of candidates as the proper short-term and long-term goal; indeed, several were resentful that the new district was created with the goal of electing a black House member. Moreover, in our interviews the white candidates in the 1st District made a strong effort to demonstrate their commitment to blacks and their support in the black community. In downplaying the tensions that exist between the two communities, however, it seemed clear to us that the white candidates were simply ignoring an issue of deep concern to many African Americans in the district.

Despite these conflicts, neither black nor white candidates tried to fan the tensions by adopting racially tinged messages and strategies. The black candidates mostly solicited support in the black community, although Riddick gained some support from the senior Jones's white allies. The white candidates made a stronger effort to appeal to African Americans. Clearly these strategies are the products of different subjective assessments of the district context, assessments that are much influenced by race.

The Context of the Decision to Run

The decision to run for a House seat is influenced by structural, personal, and contextual forces. The nature of the opportunity structure, partisan strength, the absence of an incumbent, race, and redistricting all played a central role in the candidate emergence process in the 1st District.

The Structural Context

Two structural variables at the state level constrain opportunities to run for the House: the size and shape of the opportunity structure. Schlesinger defines the size of the opportunity structure as the number of chances available to run for a given office in a specific period (1966, 20, 37-56). The size of the opportunity structure in North Carolina has been relatively stable for the past sixty years. Between 1931 and 1991 there was an average of exactly one opening per year (sixty openings in sixty years, or two per election cycle). Thus, the average House challenger had to wait for a decade before having the opportunity to run for an open seat or against an incumbent who was vulnerable enough (in retrospect) to be beaten. In our district, the wait was more than twice that long (twenty-six years).

The shape of the opportunity structure, which is defined by the most common path that is followed to higher office, channels the ambitions of potential candidates. States are more likely to produce experienced candidates when such stepping stones to the House are clearly defined. In states in which career paths are less highly structured, amateurs have greater opportunities to run and win. The shape of the career structure in North Carolina is relatively structured: more than half of its forty-six Democratic House members since 1930 (56.5 percent) served in the state legislature. The other common stepping stone is a law enforcement position (judge, district attorney, and so on) that was held by 34.8 percent of the Democrats in the House. An additional 19.6 percent of Democrats were amateurs, which is slightly below the national average. In our district, five of the ten potential Democratic candidates were members of the state legislature. Among Republicans, the career structure is quite different: 35.7 percent of the fourteen members elected since 1930 were amateurs, 28.6 percent came from the state legislature, and *none* of them had law enforcement experience. This reflects the relatively undeveloped nature of the career structure among Republicans, stemming from being the minority party throughout this period.

The nature of the state legislature determines its place in the opportunity structure, that is, the probability that the institution will be used as a stepping stone to higher office. Peverill Squire (1988) categorizes state legislatures as "springboards, career-oriented, or deadend," based on the professionalization of the legislature and the career opportunities beyond the legislature. Squire categorized North Carolina's legislature as a "deadend" institution; however, it scored relatively high in regard to opportunities for advancement (which is consistent with the previous discussion of the opportunity structure).

Electoral law is another state-level structural variable. Whether a state has an open or closed primary has an impact on the probability of producing experienced candidates (Canon, 1990; Tobin, 1975; Tobin and Keynes, 1975), but this variable did not play a role in our district. The runoff provision in the primary, however, played a pivotal role. It is ironic that a recent law that was intended to help black candidates nearly elected white candidate Walter Jones, Jr., who came close to the new 40 percent cutoff required to win the nomination without a runoff. Under the old 50 percent rule, Clayton would have been in no danger of losing the seat. Primaries with no runoff provisions clearly favor candidates of the race that is more successful in solving the collective action problem outlined earlier.

The structural context at the district level also shapes the decision to run. The racial composition of the district, the geographic compactness of the district, and the district's media market all play a role. The black majority in the district removed a constraint for some candidates and added a constraint for others. The black candidates believed that before the current redistricting plan, they did not have a realistic opportunity to win a seat in Congress. As Thomas Hardaway told us, "What we have here is a situation in which blacks have been excluded because whites have written the laws to exclude black participation. They have dammed up the flow to both candidates and voters. Well, the floodgates are open. There are many people who have been waiting for this opportunity."

Clayton said that the most important factor in her decision to enter the race was the possibility of electing a black candidate to Congress. Her attitude was representative of all the black candidates. At the same time, the creation of a black majority district made it more difficult for white candidates such as Jones, Jr., to win the seat. In addition to facing more competitors, Jones, Jr., was less assured of winning a substantial portion of the black community's vote.

The district's geographic dispersion is another important structural constraint on decisions to enter the race. From its eastern-most point to its western-most point, the district measures approximately 150 miles; the north-south distance is almost 170 miles, while the perimeter of the district is 2,039 miles! The limited number of interstates and other major highways complicates travel across the district, particularly in the northwestern counties. Most of the potential candidates live within 50 miles of more than half of the district's twenty-eight counties, but Clayton and Ballance, who live in the northwest, have only seven of the district's counties within 50 miles of their hometowns.

Relying on the media is not any easier than door-to-door campaigning in the new 1st District. Candidates must spread their advertising resources between four separate television markets and ninety-nine radio stations (*The Broadcasting Yearbook* 1990). In contrast, the district created by the first plan had only three markets. Many weekly newspapers cover the district and the *News and Observer* in Raleigh was the most widely mentioned daily newspaper in our interviews. The unwieldy media market did not prevent any candidates from running, but it made their lives more difficult.

The redistricting process provided both the most significant structural constraint and the largest source of uncertainty for candidates in our district. Most obviously, the configuration of the new congressional district plan determined which congressional race a potential candidate could enter. This was true especially for State Representative Michaux (D-Durham), who was a leading candidate in the 1st District race until the Merrit plan switched Durham from the 1st to the 12th District. This change forced Michaux to enter the congressional race in the latter district.[5] Uncertainty about the placement of district lines delayed the initiation of many candidates' campaigns. In our interviews all candidates said that they did not begin organizing their campaigns until after the general assembly's approval of the first redistricting plan, and Thomas Brandon, Don Smith, and Walter Jones, Jr., started their campaigns after the passage of the second plan. Jones, Jr., in particular, expressed his frustration at how the short period between the plan's final approval and the May primary hurt his ability to raise money and set up a campaign organization. However, as we will show, redistricting provided an opportunity as well as a constraint.

The Access Context

Power-brokers, political elites, and parties proved only modestly important as factors in the emergence process in North Carolina's 1st District. In our interviews, none of the candidates mentioned any specific individuals whose support or consent was necessary to run for Congress. The BLC tried to play this role for black candidates, but its success was mixed. Riddick was the only candidate who placed a great deal of emphasis on soliciting and publicizing the support of the BLC. Other candidates, as noted previously, openly questioned the legitimacy of the endorsement votes taken by the BLC.[6] While the candidates were interested in obtaining the black leaders' support, none of the candidates believed that any groups or individuals were active in recruiting candidates for the race. Moreover, the candidates were in unanimous agreement that the Democratic party played little or no role in the recruitment process, which is not surprising given the party's tradition of not involving itself officially in primary elections. One potential access variable that is often central in black majority districts, but played a marginal role in ours (at least in terms of candidate emergence), is the importance of black churches. Stacatto Powell, a black pastor from Wilson, used his church as his organizational and financial base. But Powell realized that the church could not provide him with enough money. Also, he was relatively young and inexperienced and could not extend his base of support.

The Competition Context

The normal vote of our district, defined as the baseline partisan vote that is relatively unaffected by short-term forces, is dominated by the Democrats. This baseline vote is reflected by the 1st District's strong support for Tony Rand, the white Democratic candidate for lieutenant governor in 1988, and for Harvey Gantt, the black Democratic nominee who challenged Jesse Helms in the 1990 senatorial race (see Table 2-2). As in the old South, almost all of the candidate activity is on the Democratic side. Only one weak Republican candidate entered the race and none of the political observers gave him a chance of winning. More important than the district's normal vote, since it is heavily Democratic, is the presence or absence of an incumbent. Though Walter Jones, Sr., finally announced his intention to retire on October 4, 1991, his plans remained unclear until the last minute. A challenge to Jones, Sr., was out of the question, thus prospective candidates engaged in a high-stakes guessing game. Although Jones, Sr., the most senior member of the North Carolina congressional delegation, claimed through the summer and early fall that he was not retiring, most legislators and political elites in the state believed that he would. At 78 years of age at the time, the incumbent suffered from poor health and had to be wheeled around the halls of Congress by an aide. Furthermore, if Jones, Sr., retired by 1993, current law allowed him to convert his $300,000 campaign war chest to personal use.[7]

Although observers had erred in predicting the retirement of Jones, Sr., for the past ten years, the clearest signal to state lawmakers that Jones, Sr., would retire in 1992 was his lack of interest in the redistricting process. One local political reporter saw many congressional staffers at the redistricting meeting, but none from his office. Although Jones, Sr., publicly indicated his displeasure with his new district and never suggested that he planned to retire, one state lawmaker said, "Other congressman were heavily involved in trying to protect their districts, but Mr. Jones made no telephone calls and sent no letters objecting to redistricting proposals" *(News and Observer* 1991a). Others argued that the decision ultimately was made for him by an unfavorable redistricting plan that took away half of his former district. One member of Congress called the treatment of Jones, Sr., by the legislature "humiliating." [8] The probable absence of an incumbent influenced the candidacy decisions of several potential candidates. Brandon challenged Jones, Sr., in 1982 and gained only 18 percent of the primary vote. Citing this experience, Brandon said that he would not have run if Jones had remained in office. Tyler, the Republican candidate, made a similar comment. Mentioning that the staff of Jones, Sr., already had begun searching for new jobs in March, Clayton said she thought from the beginning that Jones, Sr., was going to retire. Ballance claimed that the senior Jones's wavering about retirement was merely an attempt to help the junior Jones, by discouraging others from entering the race.

In a district that stretches into most of the communities in eastern North Carolina, we expected that the lack of name recognition would also be a major deterrent for many candidates. None of the potential candidates claimed they were well known in all parts of the new district, but each spoke of the problem as one that faced all of the candidates. The two candidates with ties to the retiring incumbent (Riddick as a longtime aide and the incumbent's son Jones, Jr.), were more well known than other candidates in the race because the senior Jones's former district represented 53.7 percent of the new district. Five of the other potential candidates were already elected officials, but they represented very few voters in the new district. Hardaway represented 12.4 percent of the district and the next closest candidate, Clayton, represented only 3.8 percent of the congressional district (see Table 2-2).

Four potential candidates who decided not to run said that their decisions had nothing to do with a lack of support in the district. Fitch, who represented 13.2 percent of the district, said that his support was "strong and widespread," citing in particular his strength within the BLC. Ballance, who had the largest constituency overlap, told us that he enjoyed strong support in his senate district and throughout eastern North Carolina.

Hunter and Jones also claimed that they would have had strong support if they had decided to run.

An additional competitive variable is the role of issues in the campaign. T. G. "Sonny Boy" Joyner, the Democratic chair of Northampton County, summarized the role of issues when he said, "Issues won't matter. The candidates will all be about the same and have basically the same platforms." Indeed, all candidates agreed that education and economic issues would be central and there were few differences among candidates' approaches to tackling these problems (Clayton was concerned particularly about equality for women and minorities).

National issues and trends, such as the state of the economy and presidential coattails, which have been the focus of other work (Campbell 1986; Jacobson and Kernell 1983) were simply not relevant in a district that is nearly 90 percent Democratic.

The Resources Context

We also expected campaign finance to influence candidate emergence. Potential candidates in eastern North Carolina faced substantial district-level constraints on their abilities to raise money, largely because of the competition for funds from other races in 1992. Congressional candidates had to compete for a limited pool of money with presidential, U.S. Senate, and gubernatorial candidates, in addition to numerous other candidates for statewide offices. Recession further reduced the total pool of campaign funds. Several candidates linked their fund-raising goals to the difficulties of running a campaign in the new 1st District, another short-term consideration that will change when the district becomes more familiar in subsequent elections. Nonetheless, the difficulties of fund-raising did not prevent anyone from running.

All the potential candidates expressed confidence that they could raise sufficient funds to win the seat. The estimates of amounts necessary for a primary victory ranged from less than $30,000 to as much as $500,000, with the higher estimates generally relating directly to the seriousness of the candidates' campaigns. Brandon offered the lowest estimate ($15,000 to $30,000), arguing that the higher figures were exaggerated and would waste substantial amounts on consultants and other unnecessary expenses. (See Table 2-1.) He believed that he could win the election with a heavy schedule of traveling around the district. The informants and other candidates, however, generally viewed Brandon as a second-tier candidate; in an August 1991 interview, the Democratic party chair in Brandon's home county did not even mention Brandon as a possible candidate.

Hardaway also planned on running a lean campaign. He was uncertain about the exact amount necessary to win because the district was so new. Many informants also categorized Hardaway as a second-tier candidate. Another such candidate, the Republican Tyler, believed that $80,000 would be sufficient for victory, but several Republican consultants had advised him that $300,000 would be a more accurate figure. While he did not believe that he could reach the latter figure, he had received his first contribution ($75) on the day of the interview (March 3), and he hoped that this was a good start toward reaching his goal. Hunter was the least concerned about the cost of running, saying, "I haven't really thought about it, but it wouldn't take too much to win." The final second-tier candidate, Smith, did not spend any money except the $1,250 filing fee, though he estimated a competitive candidate would need to spend at least $250,000.

The other candidates offered estimates of at least $150,000, with Clayton suggesting $300,000 to $500,000, the highest estimate. This was a realistic range, based on what incumbents spent in 1990 in the four districts that make up the 1st District. The amounts spent previously ranged from a low of $111,622 by Jones, Sr., to a high of $499,436 by Martin Lancaster—though David Price spent more than $1 million in defending the old 4th District in 1988. The first-tier candidates (Ballance, Clayton, Fitch, Jones, Jr., and Riddick) seemed confident that they would be able to reach their fund-raising goals. Fitch emphasized that money was not the reason that he decided against running.

Table 2-1 summarizes the amount of money the candidates estimated they could raise, how much they thought they would need, and the total amount received and spent. In actual fund-raising, Brandon, Clayton, Jones, Jr., and Smith were close to their expected spending, while Powell, Riddick, and Tyler missed by wide margins. Thus, while the first-tier candidates had more realistic expectations of what it would take to win, one of them—Riddick—was not able to meet that goal.

The Personal Context

We expected the opinions of friends and family members to influence a potential candidate's decision to run, but much to our surprise, most candidates did not mention families as important factors in their decisions. Only Brandon expressed concern about the burden that a congressional campaign would place on his wife and five children.

Ambition As the Key

While we expected a number of contextual factors to play an important role in the decision to run, we found career aspirations to be the factor that most influenced the decisions of potential candidates. For example, the limited importance of family and friends in the decision-making process may say more about these politician's career goals and personal ambitions than anything else. Most of the candidates had been thinking about running for Congress for ten to twenty years. It is clear that career ambition is the strongest personal factor influencing these potential candidates' decisions to run. Three of the four white candidates had all been waiting for Jones, Sr., to retire before they made their bids (Smith is the exception—he claims to have no political ambitions). Jones, Jr., had been grooming himself to take over his father's seat for many years, saying his main goal was to "take care of the good citizens of eastern North Carolina, just as my father did. State and national issues are important, but constituency service is the most important aspect of a legislator's responsibilities." Brandon also held a long-running ambition to enter Congress, as evidenced by his 1982 campaign against Jones, Sr. Tyler, the Republican nominee, said, "I've wanted to run for a long time. I always said that when Walter Jones retires, I'm going to run. You can't run against an incumbent. They have so many advantages. I've just been waiting for him to retire."

For the black candidates, redistricting was the key factor that turned long suppressed ambition into serious consideration. Each wanted to be in Congress and each believed that the new district represented the best opportunity to win a congressional election. Clayton wanted to be in Congress since her unsuccessful campaign in 1968 against L. H. Fountain, a strongly entrenched incumbent. She saw this election as the first real opportunity for a minority to win a congressional election in eastern North Carolina.

For Hardaway the run for Congress was the logical next step. He served in the state House since 1987 and climbed the ranks to become chair of the Commerce Committee. Hardaway said he helped to shape important legislation and believed that he had achieved all he could in Raleigh. He also said that he was tired of being a part-time lawmaker and part-time lawyer, so a run for Congress was his best opportunity to achieve his goal to be a full-time politician.

Four black candidates who decided not to run also were influenced by career considerations. For example, Ballance recognized the existence of a career ladder in which politicians start out in the state House, as he did in 1982, then move up to the state Senate, as he did in 1988. According to Ballance, the next step on the ladder is the U.S. House, and he said he gave "very serious" consideration to running. Paul Jones, the attorney from Kinston, decided that he should gain some experience in lower office before attempting a House race, and thus decided to run for county commissioner instead.

Other Potential Candidates

Though our district was overflowing with ambitious politicians and potential candidates, to understand the motivations of those who decided not to run we interviewed eight state legislators who were not mentioned by informants and had expressed no interest in running. By virtue of their positions in the opportunity structure, these politicians were situated similarly to many of the candidates who decided to run. However, a variety of factors prevented them from entering the fray.

Two white Democrats cited the creation of the black majority district as their main reason for not running. One said, "The 1st District was created to elect a minority candidate and I think that is a good thing. I would not want to stand in the way of that. I would never consider running in the 1st, not now or in the future." The other also said that she did "not want to step on toes" in the new district, but also was blunt in recognizing she would not be able to win because she is white. Two other state House members, one white and one black, wanted to establish their careers in state politics before thinking about higher office (both were serving in their first terms). At the other extreme, one Republican state House member cited his age (then 62) and health as the main reasons for not running. He also noted that a Republican would not have much chance in the new district anyway. Mary McCallister, an ambitious state representative from Fayetteville, said that the uncertainty of the redistricting process and urban-rural tensions prevented her from running:

> Had Fayetteville been in the new district from the get go, I would have run. By the time we were added to the district it was an "us versus them" thing [urban vs. rural]. They did not want us to participate. Fayetteville is a pivotal part of the 1st District as it is drawn up now, but they didn't want us in it. . . . It was a rural district and they wanted to keep it rural, but the present 1st isn't so rural any more . . . they didn't want to give up the power.

Finally, one state senator said he did not run because he knew he could not win, while another said he had "absolutely no interest in running for Congress" and "wouldn't serve if I was appointed." Thus seven of our eight unseen candidates support David Rohde's assumption that politicians would accept higher office if it were offered to them without cost or risk (1979). What separates these seven from the candidates who ran, then, is limited ambition, bad timing, or a sense that they could not win.

Strategic Behavior

Most contextual factors in any congressional district are fixed; even highly ambitious potential candidates can do little about a disadvantageous opportunity structure, multiple media markets, or a faltering national economy. Other elements, however, are open to influence. The most noteworthy target for manipulation is the redistricting process. The general assembly is filled with "wanna-be" House members, and many members try to use institutional positions, such as membership on the redistricting committee, to help fulfill those ambitions.[9] As with many legislative committees, much of the redistricting work was performed in informal, behind-the-scenes settings, with limited publicity. As a consequence, it is difficult to uncover the candidates' efforts to draw the district lines in ways that furthered their electoral interests (especially because candidates would not readily admit to self-serving strategic behavior).

Jones, Jr., provided one account of conflict over the drawing of district lines. Because of his "independent" record in the state House (in 1988 he had joined a group of Republicans and maverick Democrats in overturning the House leadership), Jones, Jr., believed that he had been punished in the drawing of state House lines. His old district was split in half, making it much more difficult for him to win reelection. Jones, Jr., also had problems with the congressional redistricting. His hometown in Farmville was in the 1st District in the initial versions of the plan, but it was excluded in the final plan. Just before the final committee vote, Jones, Jr., introduced an amendment to return Farmville to the 1st District. The amendment passed with the approval of all nine committee Republicans and several blacks on the committee, who, according to Jones, Jr., were criticized later by others in the black community. When the redistricting plan reached the House floor a black representative introduced an amendment to take Farmville back out of the 1st District. The amendment was defeated, but the vote had definite racial overtones. Jones, Jr., was very bitter and said that the general assembly had treated "his people" and his father unfairly.

Congressional incumbents also were actively involved in the redistricting process. One House member acknowledged that "we all had people at the redistricting meetings, and we all made suggestions concerning our districts." Private memoranda that later were made public describe proposals to swap parts of counties to enhance incumbency safety (*News and Observer* 1991b, 6C). Most significant, the staff of U.S. Rep. Charlie Rose (D) of the 7th District played an important role in the formulation of the final redistricting plan that the Justice Department approved.

Interaction between the various candidates also influenced candidacy decisions. For example, Ballance deferred to Clayton's abilities as a candidate and a potential representative and decided not to run. A more uncertain relationship existed between Jones, Sr., his son, and Riddick. Both candidates claimed to be the rightful successor of the elder Jones. Jones, Jr., acknowledged their competing claims to the seat and said that he encouraged Riddick to run (indeed, as we will argue in following sections, it was in his interest to have Riddick split the black vote). Jones, Sr., offered conflicting signals about which of the two he supported. In November he openly endorsed Riddick, but three days later, he qualified his support, saying that he had only been saying "nice things" about Riddick. During this same period Jones, Jr., actively was considering running for state auditor or lieutenant governor. He later decided to run in the 1st District congressional race. Jones, Sr., did not officially endorse either one. One local commentator speculated that the two candidates would simply divide the senior Jones's support and organization, largely along racial lines, though the commentator added that each candidate could expect some support from the other race.

An intriguing interpretation of this relationship was that Riddick was running to split the black vote and help Jones, Jr., get elected. At first we discounted this story because the initial source was one of the other black candidates in the race. But later we had independent confirmation from three other reliable sources (one claimed it was "common knowledge"). One state representative, when asked about Riddick's campaign, nearly exploded:

> That man! He prostituted himself for a job. He was never a serious candidate. All he wanted to do was help Jones, Jr., win. I don't believe in giving the district to one person and then handing it down to his son. It's wrong. The district was created to help elect a black American and he is trying to help Jones.

Another source heard through the junior Jones's press secretary that Riddick offered to drop out of the race if Jones, Jr., would give him a job. But Jones, Jr., according to the source, convinced Riddick that Riddick would do him more good if he stayed in the race and hinted that he would get a job if he so cooperated. This source also claimed that Riddick was part of the Jones machine and pointed out that Riddick boycotted a last-minute meeting called by Clayton to get the black community behind a single candidate. Even if this story was false, and we continue to question its veracity, a substantial proportion of the black leaders we interviewed saw Riddick as a traitor. Thus perception, in this case, is as important as reality.

Perhaps even more interesting is the chain of events and strategic behavior surrounding the most unlikely of the candidates, Don Smith. Smith entered the race because of an article he read in his local paper, *The Daily Reflector,* that led him to believe that Jones, Jr., was the only white candidate in the race (Smith thought that Brandon was black). This struck Smith as unfair because the district was created to elect a black and he thought that Jones, Jr., would win. Smith's candidacy was "an attempt to level the playing field" and so if Jones, Jr., were to win, "he would have to earn it fairly in a one-on-one runoff" rather than by splitting the black vote. At one of the election rallies, Smith met Brandon's campaign manager, Otis Carter, who is black. This reinforced Smith's impression that Brandon was black. Smith was in for a surprise the first time he met Brandon at a candidate forum; Brandon and his campaign manager encouraged Smith to stay in the race to split the junior Jones's vote. As it turned out, Smith did not affect the outcome of the race; he only received 1.4 percent of the vote while Jones, Jr., missed winning the election by 1.9 percent. Nonetheless, Smith considered it a well-spent $1,250 (the filing fee), and said that the experience "gave me a good education in politics, and for much cheaper than I could have gotten at Duke!"

Conclusion

The candidate emergence process is shaped by a host of political, structural, and strategic factors. Among district-level elements, the redistricting process was extremely influential in candidacy decisions. Political ambition was the key, ultimately, to understanding who ran and who did not. Counter to expectations, the potential candidates' name recognition, fund-raising abilities, family, and friends were not very important. Strategic influences were crucial as candidates manipulated the redistricting process, influenced the decision-making process of other potential candidates, and attempted to divide votes along racial lines. Finally, while the racial makeup of the district influenced the decisions of all candidates, white candidates deemphasized the question of race while black candidates focused on the importance of electing a minority candidate to Congress. Though the political ambitions of individual black politicians prevented them from solving their collective action problem, the runoff primary preserved African American representation in the newly created black majority district.

Race also entered the strategic equation in an unexpected way. The North Carolina experience rejects the common wisdom concerning the consequences of the unlikely alliance between Republicans and African Americans to increase minority representation in the House.[10] Rather than concentrating Democratic strength in relatively few districts and opening up opportunities for the Republican party, the Democratically controlled legislature protected and expanded their turf by devising a plan that would have made Elbridge Gerry (source of the term "gerrymander") proud. The redistricting currently is being challenged in court, but for now it appears that the Democrats staged a major coup.[11]

Notes

1. Under Section 5, southern states with a history of past discrimination must submit their redistricting plans to the federal government for approval. Plans may either be "precleared" by the Justice Department, or approved by the federal district court for the District of Columbia. Most states use the preclearance option because the judicial route is more time consuming and costly.
2. This debate rages in the academic literature. Carol Swain echoes Blue's sentiment: "In 1991 seven congressional districts ranged from 66 to 90 percent black. The result was wasted black votes and influence" (1993, 210).
3. On October 5, 1992, the Supreme Court voted 8 to 1 to uphold a lower court's decision to dismiss another Republican suit that claimed the Democratic plan "is the most egregiously convoluted and contorted in the nation" (*News and Observer* 1992c, 2B). However, the Court reversed itself on June 28, 1993, in *Shaw v. Reno*, holding that the North Carolina redistricting plan potentially discriminated against white voters. By ordering the district court to rehear the case, the Supreme Court left many other states' plans open to challenge (Greenhouse 1993, A1).
4. Our focus on the collective good provided by black representation is largely through symbolic and collective representation rather than selective benefits. There are clear differences within the African American community in the 1st District, thus

one cannot assume that a single black member of Congress will represent all those interests any more than a white member would.

5. Many candidates stood to gain from this last-minute change. Michaux himself may have encouraged the move because our interviews in eastern North Carolina revealed that he did not enjoy extensive support in the rural areas of the new 1st District. In addition, the other 1st District candidates may have preferred not to run against Michaux, who was described by several informants as a "formidable" candidate despite his weak support in rural parts of the district. A reporter told us that State Rep. Thomas Hardaway, one of the black candidates from eastern North Carolina, was a strong proponent of the I-85 district (indeed, one unconfirmed report placed Hardaway as the original source of the Merrit plan). Other candidates also expressed relief about not having to run against Michaux. Michaux eventually lost in the Democratic primary for the newly created 12th District House seat to Mel Watt, also an African American candidate.

6. One potential candidate who did not enter the race pointed out that Jones, Sr., made Riddick his liaison to the BLC. Riddick attended many BLC meetings and was a very visible participant, thus the charge that the BLC vote was rigged for Riddick has some plausibility.

7. As it turned out, Jones, Sr., was the only incumbent (of the forty who were eligible) who announced that he was going to convert his campaign funds into personal use (*News and Observer* 1992b, 2B).

8. Walter Jones, Sr., died on September 15, 1992. By state law, a special election to fill out the last two months of Jones' term in the old 1st District was held on November 3. There was speculation for several weeks that Jones, Sr.'s, wife Elizabeth or Jones, Jr., would run to fill out the term. However, they both declined to run and Eva Clayton won the special election by a margin of 57 percent to 41 percent over the Republican nominee, Ted Tyler. This additional two months of tenure gave Clayton an important seniority advantage over the rest of the huge first-term class in the 103rd Congress (not to mention an extra $21,500 in pay).

9. All the potential candidates in the general assembly served on the redistricting committees. Ballance was a member of the Senate committee. On the House side, Fitch was a co-chair of the committee, and Michaux was a vice-chair. Hardaway, Hunter, and Jones, Jr., were also committee members.

10. However, Brace, Grofman, and Handley note, "[E]ven where white Democratic voters are proximate to black Democrats, it is sometimes possible by creative cartography to create new black Democratic districts while holding constant (or even increasing) the total number of districts held by Democrats of either race" (1987, 183). The North Carolina legislators certainly were masters of "creative cartography"!

11. In remanding the case to federal district court, the Supreme Court demanded that North Carolina demonstrate a compelling state interest in addition to the overriding concern with race. Immediately following the *Shaw v. Reno* decision (see endnote 3), U.S. Rep. Mel Watt said, "I think, ultimately, we will prevail in this litigation. It's unfortunate that they've put some more procedural hoops in our way." *Durham Herald Sun,* June 29, 1993, B1.

   The federal district court in Raleigh started hearing arguments in the remanded case, *Shaw v. Hunt,* on March 28, 1994. A decision is expected sometime early in the summer, but most observers expect the case to make its way back to the Supreme Court. Mike Easley, the attorney general of North Carolina, blamed the ambiguity of *Shaw v. Reno* for the protracted legal struggle. Easley said, "This case is going to continue to be appealed until someone gets a definitive answer from the Supreme Court. Right now, they haven't told us what to do they've only said 'this won't work.' It's kind of like the monkey who can only classify the light bulb as a non-coconut." *New York Times,* March 28, 1994, A9.

3

Candidate Emergence in a Majority Hispanic District: The 29th District in Texas

Douglas D. Abel and Bruce I. Oppenheimer

Political events often result in ironic outcomes. Unanticipated consequences of changes or reforms tend to overshadow the anticipated ones. Frequently these events lack closure—they are stories without endings. The story of candidate emergence in the newly created 29th District in Texas is a good example. In this case, a district designed to maximize the probability of electing the first Hispanic from the Houston area to the U.S. House of Representatives resulted in the elimination of Hispanic candidates in the Democratic and Republican primaries. The general election campaign featured an Anglo Democrat running against an African American Republican to represent a 60-percent Hispanic district.

Yet it is clear that the story of candidate emergence in the 29th District does not end in 1992 with the election of an incumbent capable of discouraging serious challengers and making the district a politically safe one for his reelection in 1994. Instead, some of those defeated in 1992, and perhaps some who did not consider running, were evaluating candidacies for 1994 even before the 1992 election was complete.

In addition to telling part of the story of the race for the new House seat, we intend to address a series of questions about candidate emergence. To what extent are potential candidates ambitious politicians who pursue strategically elective office? Are they self-starters, recruits, or carefully groomed apprentices? How much are their decisions based on personal considerations and to what degree do national issues play a role? Do election results accurately reflect the level of competitiveness or do they ignore an important part of the selection process?

Two features of the 29th District enable us to examine candidate emergence in particular contexts. First, because it is a new district, the 29th District had no incumbent or former incumbent to condition the emergence of candidates. We normally might expect that such conditions would lend themselves to a highly competitive environment and invite a large candidate field. Yet as we shall see the field was a modest one and only a few candidates were given any chance of winning. Second, because it was created as a Hispanic majority district, the 29th offers the chance to study candidate emergence within a community that previously had not experienced congressional representation from a member of their own community. We begin our analysis with descriptions of the candidates who emerged.

The Democratic Candidates

Gene Green

At age 44, at the time of the election, Gene Green was a veteran state legislator, having served seven terms as a state representative and completing his second term in the state senate. He was on the Texas Senate Subcommittee on Legislative Districts. About half of the 29th District was composed of Green's multiethnic senate district. He was the only Anglo candidate in either primary. His anti-abortion position (which he switched to pro-choice during the campaign) and his sponsorship of a bill in the state legislature allowing "law abiding" citizens to carry concealed hand guns made this otherwise moderate candidate controversial, especially with liberal white voters. Although he announced his candidacy just two months before the first primary, Green had been involved actively in campaign-related activities for several months before.

Ben Reyes

The last of the Democratic candidates to enter the race, Ben Reyes, then 45 years old, was the first Hispanic elected from Houston to the state legislature. As the first and, until 1992, the only Hispanic to serve on the Houston City Council, Reyes was the best known candidate in the race. His council district, with a high proportion of Hispanics, comprised less than 40 percent of the 29th District. Having been reelected to his council seat in November 1991 and being embroiled in controversies including bankruptcy, failure to pay school district and city property taxes, and being the subject of several investigations (one of which resulted in a probated misdemeanor conviction), Reyes's entry was somewhat surprising and occurred only after he persuaded his protégé, State Rep. Roman Martinez, to drop out of the race and run instead for a state senate seat that overlapped considerably with the 29th District.

Al Luna

After five terms in the state legislature, Al Luna, then 41 years old, did not seek reelection in 1990 and instead enrolled in law school. Originally a protégé of Reyes's (the two still reside directly across the street from each other), whom he succeeded in the legislature, Luna split with him over the selection of a candidate for a new state representative seat. Later Reyes backed an unsuccessful opponent to Luna in a bitter 1988 campaign, and they feuded in a subsequent constable race when they backed

Figure 3-1   Texas, 29th District

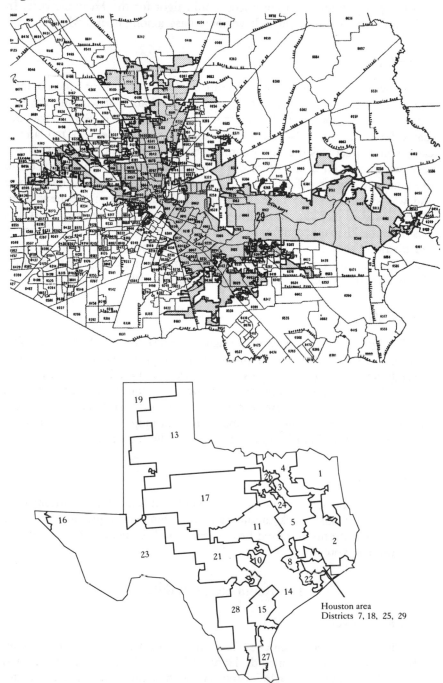

Houston area
Districts 7, 18, 25, 29

competing candidates. Until Martinez's exit from the race, it was assumed that Reyes's two former apprentices would fight for the Hispanic vote. In addition, Luna was thought to have some base among liberal whites.

Sylvia Garcia

Chief Municipal Judge Sylvia Garcia had never run for office before, and at age 41, was not thought to have much chance of winning the primary. When Mayor Kathy Whitmire, who had appointed Garcia, was defeated for reelection in November 1991, it was clearly a setback to Garcia's campaign. Garcia was the first to announce an intention of running for the seat, which she did even before the boundaries were known. Because she lived near Martinez, who headed the state house redistricting committee and was sure to include himself within the boundaries of the new 29th, Garcia felt sure that she would live in the district. Her base of support was less from the Hispanic community, and she said that she would have run "if the district was only 40 percent Hispanic." Although free from the controversies that surrounded the other candidates, as a newcomer to politics, Garcia faced the problem of not being taken seriously.

Roman Martinez

By age 33, Yale educated Roman Martinez already had served five terms in the state house. As the prime operative in the redistricting effort in the state house of representatives, it was always assumed that he would run in the 29th District. He withdrew from the U.S. House race, however, and instead ran in the state senate primary, a race he ultimately lost to an Anglo candidate after a Republican-dominated federal judge panel substituted its own senate district map for the one drawn by the legislature.

Andrew Burks, Jr.

Andrew Burks, Jr., then 41, a preacher and telecommunications consultant, was the sole black candidate in the Democratic primary field. He received little attention, raised little money, and received only 2.6 percent of the primary vote.

The Republican Candidates

Clark Kent Ervin

Clark Kent Ervin, then age 32, is an African American, pro-choice Republican. His credentials include Harvard Law, a Rhodes Scholarship, and three years in the Bush administration; he had never run previously for elective office. Despite the Democratic dominance in the district, Ervin, who announced his candidacy on September 24, was able to raise more than $100,000 prior to January 1—more than any other candidate at that time.

Freddy Rios

Freddy Rios, then 44, a Hispanic businessperson with a history of activity in Republican politics and community service, announced his candidacy on January 7, making him the last to enter the race. Rios received encouragement and backing from Rep. Jack Fields (R-Texas), a quarter of whose former district was included in the 29th. Rios entered only after failing to find another Hispanic Republican willing to run.

The Birth of a Hispanic Congressional District

Texans knew that their state, one of the fastest growing in the nation, would gain two or three new U.S. House seats after the 1990 census was tabulated. Hispanics argued that at least one of the new districts should be a Hispanic majority since much of the population growth during the past decade was concentrated in the Hispanic community. Hispanics had begun to flex their political muscles with the election of Henry Cisneros as mayor of San Antonio and Dan Morales as state attorney general—the first Hispanic to win statewide office. Moreover, the number of Hispanics in the Texas congressional delegation had increased from two to four.

Hopes for a Hispanic seat rose when it was announced that Texas indeed would get a third new seat. Hispanic leaders in Harris County, which includes Houston, were optimistic that the state legislature would create a new district in their area since two members of the Harris County delegation, Senator Green and Representative Martinez, served on the state senate and house redistricting committees; as it turned out, both had congressional ambitions of their own.

Drawing a majority Hispanic district in the Houston area was complicated by the dispersion of the Hispanic community, which made it more difficult to create a district consistent with federal goals about compactness and contiguity. In addition, those Hispanics who were citizens (many were not) had low rates of voter registration and turnout. Perhaps the most significant obstacles, however, were the aspirations of Green and Martinez. Martinez, for example, produced a plan that left Green's home outside the district, as well as certain Hispanic areas that were within Green's state senate district (Ratcliffe 1991).

Using computerized redistricting technology, Martinez, in particular, was able to fine-tune a district to his liking. As one consultant said, "drawing districts is like playing Pac-Man. Just find census blocks with high percentages of Spanish surnames on your computer screen and gobble 'em up" (Burka 1992). Green observed:

> We could have drawn a pretty contiguous district at 54 percent. Then it
> got to be a game between me and Roman Martinez. We would inch it up
> [another] half a percent because under the federal [Voting Rights Act],
> whoever has the most minority population is the one that they go with,
> no matter what neighborhoods you've got (Fleck 1992).

The new 29th District, which snakes its way through Harris County, is approximately 61 percent Hispanic, 10 percent black, and 28 percent Anglo. Its estimated voting-age population in 1992 was 55 percent Hispanic, 10 percent black, and 33 percent Anglo. However, only 46 percent of the voting age population was registered to vote at the time; of those registered, 31 percent had Spanish surnames, 10 percent were black, and 58 percent were Anglo (Bernstein and Simmon 1991).

The apparent Anglo voting majority is a bit misleading. Although Hispanics made up only 31 percent of the registered voters, it was expected that they would exceed 40 percent of the Democratic primary vote. Few Hispanics would vote in the Republican primary, which would be composed of mainly Anglo voters. Also, efforts to register new Hispanic voters and liberal Texas registration laws (including postcard registration) were expected to increase considerably Hispanic registration. Reyes told us: "I expect that we will have registered 30,000 new households by February 10." Finally, there was an expectation that the creation of this new district would stimulate the participation of Hispanics.

The plan finally adopted for the new 29th District was heavily Democratic: the precincts comprising the district cast 60 percent of their votes for Michael Dukakis in the 1988 presidential election. The district included much of Green's state senatorial district, a substantial part of Martinez's state house district, and most of Reyes's city council district.

Overview of the Campaign

The formal race for the 29th District actually began with the announcement that Green and Martinez had come to an agreement on the boundaries of the new district (Ratcliffe 1991). As various candidates entered the race, the only real surprise was the late entry of Reyes. He had been involved in a race for his city council seat and, most observers assumed, was a Martinez supporter. Councilperson Reyes told us that he had been shown a poll that had been commissioned for Martinez, which Martinez assumed would convince Reyes not to run. Contrary to Martinez's expectations, Reyes was encouraged by what he saw in terms of his name recognition and the fact that his negatives, although quite high, were lower than he had expected. Reyes apparently was able to convince Martinez he could not win, so Martinez withdrew from the congressional race and filed for a state senate contest.

The campaign for the first primary was decidedly low key and "retail" (in other words, aimed at individuals or small groups of voters, largely through direct contacts). Only in the last ten days of the primary campaign did Garcia use a television advertising campaign to attack Green—an expensive strategy because the television market in Houston covers more than five congressional districts. Polls indicated that Green and Reyes were headed for a runoff, despite endorsements of Garcia by the *Houston Chronicle* and several prominent women's groups, and of Luna by the *Houston Post*. Luna was never able to raise enough money for a serious effort, however. On the Republican side, Ervin was very well funded and mounted a formidable campaign. Rios, by entering late and relying primarily on contributions from within the district, had trouble raising sufficient money and had to adjust his campaign accordingly.

The first round of elections saw Reyes coming in first among the Democrats with 34 percent of the vote, followed by Green's 28 percent. Garcia received 21 percent, Luna received 15 percent, and Burks received 3 percent. On the Republican side, Ervin won the contest outright with 55 percent compared to Rios's 45 percent. Turnout in the first primary was very low. With more than 175,000 registered voters in the district, fewer than 32,000 voted in the Democratic primary and fewer than 6,500 voted in the Republican primary.

The runoff between Reyes and Green, held five weeks later, featured Green's criticisms of Reyes' various financial and legal problems. One of Green's advisors claims that Green was reluctant to go on the attack until he was told, "you have two choices, you can go negative or you can go back to practicing law." Green chose to go negative. Green benefited also from the unwillingness of Garcia and Luna to make a formal endorsement in the runoff; Garcia claimed that as a judge it would be inappropriate for her to do so, while Luna assisted Green's efforts to publicize Reyes' difficulties.

When the votes were counted on April 14, Green appeared to have won the runoff by 180 votes, but it soon came to light that some 430 Republican voters from the first primary had crossed over to vote in the Democratic runoff. Reyes claimed that the practice, illegal in Texas, invalidated the runoff and asked to be declared the winner or to have a new runoff held. After a much publicized and expensive trial the judge threw out the results of the runoff and called for a second runoff on July 28. Green appealed the decision but was unsuccessful.

The attention generated by the trial and the more visible, more media-oriented campaign for the second runoff resulted in a 20 percent increase in voter turnout, concentrated primarily in Anglo precincts, and a victory for Green, who won with 51.5 percent of the vote. The vote was polarized, with Anglos heavily supporting Green and Hispanics heavily supporting Reyes, though Green was able to capture 15 to 20 percent of the Hispanic vote. A bitter Reyes subsequently endorsed and supported Republican Ervin in the general election.

Factors Affecting Candidate Emergence

The key to understanding why some ran and some did not in the 29th District is appreciating the preeminent role of personal political ambition. With one exception, every candidate in this race was a self-starter. Moreover, most clearly had envisioned running for a long time. All of the candidates had devised a scenario, however improbable, for victory in the new district. The comments of four of the candidates illustrate that this ambition in several cases preexisted the creation of the district:

> Green: I thought about it both in '81 and '91 while I was involved with redistricting in the legislature. I had no real desire to run in '81. I think everyone in public office thinks about running for Congress. I started to seriously consider it in the spring of the legislative session when I looked at the new area and went to the public hearings. Some people were actually pushing me to run in '85 against Jack Fields. Hopefully, I'm more realistic than that.

> Garcia: Yes, in a general sense I thought that I would like to run some day. It was a dream in my mind.

> Martinez: This has always been a dream of mine. My goal has been to be in Washington. When I graduated from high school I got a letter from Barbara Jordan. She is a big role model of mine. In the back of my mind I always thought that some day there would be a Hispanic district that I could run in. That this current district would exist seemed more realistic about two or three years ago. I started looking at population trends and growth in the Hispanic community, and I knew that if we had a successful census campaign the numbers would warrant a Hispanic district.

> Ervin: I've always wanted to run for office. I had no real interest in the state or local level, however. I thought that the time to go for this was in '92. I figured on a new seat after redistricting so I would have no incumbent problems. I guess I've really thought seriously about it since 1988.

As mentioned previously, only Rios was recruited to run. When first approached in March 1991, Rios declined to run but agreed to recruit someone else. His efforts among Hispanic Republicans were unsuccessful. He even talked with Garcia to convince her to run as a Republican. (Garcia confirms this and indicated that Rios was an intermediary for Houston-area Republican Rep. Jack Fields. She rejected the offer to switch and told Rios that she was a Democrat.) In November 1991, Rios says he met with high-level members of the national Republican party and "agreed to run because no one else would."

With Rios as the exception, there is no indication that anyone was actively involved in urging candidates to enter the race, no mention of national, state, or local party organizations being active in the process.

Many of the candidates did consult with others, including elected officials, other potential candidates, and various other players. But the initiative in every case came from the candidate. Our research lends little support to Paul Herrnson's (1988) findings about the growing involvement of national party organizations in candidate recruitment. Whether this is an indication of the candidate emergence process in open districts or the reluctance of party organizations to be active in what they perceive as safe districts cannot be determined.

At least two of the candidates were openly critical of the failure of state and local Democratic party officials to influence the process of candidate emergence. Both complained that the party had a responsibility to discourage Green from running for a "Hispanic seat." One argued: "This is a Hispanic seat, created for that purpose. The party should have done something to ensure it for Hispanics. . . . The party should have leaned on Green. . . . It should have been recruiting a Hispanic to run . . . encourage them. . . . If it were a new black district that would have happened." Another candidate claimed that elsewhere in the country, party and labor leaders had been more active in preserving Hispanic majority districts for Hispanic candidates.

Although not agreeing with these contentions, Green substantiates the claim that no one tried to persuade him not to run for the seat. Having represented a multiethnic legislative district, Green did not feel he should have been precluded from running. In addition, he says that no one raised the issue with him before he announced his candidacy and that it only was raised during the campaign by his opponents or their supporters. Green further denied speculation that he had considered dropping out after his unsuccessful appeal of the court decision ordering a new runoff election.

Nearly as absent as party influence in decisions about candidacy was discussion of national political conditions. All the Democratic candidates viewed the district as safely Democratic, regardless of the success of the Bush campaign. Only Ervin mentioned the national campaign in his calculations for winning. During our interview in late November 1991, Ervin argued:

> I'm depending somewhat on presidential coattails which I think will be larger than most people believe. . . . The past ten years have proven that Democrats will vote for a Republican president who represents their interest. I think we can count on the Democrats picking a liberal Democrat like Tsongas or Harkin to head their ticket and then a lot of the conservative Democrats will be back in our corner because the Republicans represent them better on the hot button issues. We are just more mainstream.

Although events related to the campaign improved Ervin's chances, his expectations about national politics were clearly not among them. The unpredictability of national political events and the volatility of the American electorate may suggest that there is little evidence supporting Jacobson and Kernell's (1983) theory about strategic candidacies. Decisions on candidacy often are made so early that it is, as Ervin's comments attest, nearly impossible to estimate what national partisan trends will be at the time of the election.

How important is ambition as a factor affecting perceptions of the political context? Each candidate believed that he or she could win and had developed a scenario whereby that would occur. For the Democrats their scenarios involved how they would win the Democratic primary, which each believed was tantamount to winning the seat. For the two Republicans their scenarios focused on how the Democratic primary would produce a vulnerable candidate in the general election and how they would be assisted by a successful Bush reelection campaign. Each candidate had a self-fulfilling conception of the district's ethnic and partisan composition, the likely registration and turnout of various groups, and the strengths and weaknesses of the other candidates. In not one instance was there a hint that a candidate was undertaking the race without hope of winning but rather to further a future political career. A sampling of the victory scenarios illustrates the interaction between ambition and context.

Luna believed there would be a runoff, Green would be in it, and that he could attract sufficient support from liberal whites to defeat Green. Part of this calculation was based on his belief that the candidates would receive substantial press scrutiny. Luna was certain that Martinez and Reyes could not survive questions of personal ethics and integrity. He believed that he had sufficient strength in the Hispanic community, combined with support from liberal Anglos, to make the runoff. In the runoff he believed he would have consolidated support among Hispanics and have had sufficient crossover backing from Anglo voters for whom Green was too conservative.

Garcia compared herself to another Hispanic woman, Gracie Seanz, who had just unexpectedly won a seat on the Houston city council and categorized her campaign as "an underdog story." Garcia saw the Democratic primary as the main race and getting into the runoff with Green as the main goal. But her approach to all of the candidates was to paint them as incumbents and run against their records both door-to-door and through the media.

Reyes's scenario for victory was predicated on substantial increases in voter registration. He felt that people do not register because they do not feel they have any say in the process. His goal, therefore, was to make the people believe the system would work for them and to get them involved. While others might run high-technology campaigns using sophisticated targeting techniques and formulas, Reyes was concentrating on registering 30,000 new Hispanic households and working to turn them out on election day. He also planned to identify the voters 65-years-old or older who did not vote, presumably because they found it hard to get to the polls. These potential voters either would be sent ballots by mail or taken to the polls during the early voting period.

For Green the key to success was a low-turnout primary, low participation among Hispanics, and the presence of several Hispanic candidates splitting the vote. He was viewed as the favorite and was not concerned about his ability to raise sufficient money. In addition, he believed that he would garner some support from Hispanics who had voted for him in other elections and whom he had represented effectively in the state legislature.

Ervin, the candidate with one of the worst chances of winning in November, had the most detailed plan, one year out, for doing so. Ervin had calculated his Republican base to be 35 percent in the district, meaning that he only needed another 15 percent. "The key to this race," Ervin told us, "is Hispanics and turnout. Currently the 18th Congressional District has the lowest turnout in Harris County, but the 29th will be half of the turnout of the 18th. By my count it will only take 7500 people (from the Democrats) to be elected in this district. I think I can attract that many." Ervin discounted the effect of voter registration drives because, he argued, "I don't think you can turn a culture on a dime." Ervin believed he could win conservative Democrats in the district and argued that Anglo voters "are ideologues first and partisans second."

Though we talked to Rios in April, one month after his defeat in the primary, he still had ideas about how he could have won and how the Republican Ervin could win in November. His scenario for victory in the primary was to distinguish himself from Ervin as being more like the average district resident—in other words, not an Ivy-League educated, big law firm attorney. If he had started earlier and raised more money, Rios believed that his strategy would have worked in the primary. In the general election Rios felt "since Anglo voters make up about 65 percent of the district and minorities are 35 percent, and the number of Anglo Republicans and Democrats are about equal, there is definitely a chance if the Republican can pull the Hispanic vote over Green."

Even after they changed strategies and even in defeat, the candidates adjusted their explanations about how they were going to win. At one point following the New Hampshire presidential primary, Reyes argued that conservative Anglo Democrats would be voting in the Republican primary in Texas so that they could support David Duke and Pat Buchanan, thus undercutting Green's base in the Democratic primary. Garcia believed that her sister was correct when she said that all they needed was "twenty more days and $20,000" to have won.

The Personal Context

We asked candidates about how their families reacted to their decisions to run and what personal sacrifices they expected in the campaign. In every case some sort of personal factor was considered by the candidate but, if it created a conflict, the candidate was able to make adjustments. Both Garcia and Ervin are unmarried and have no children. They discussed their entries with family (siblings and parents), but it had little bearing on their decisions. Martinez, who was married at the time but whose spouse lived outside Texas, confined his comments mainly to his parents: "[They] never made it past the second or third grade so most of the decisions about my life have been left up to me. They always thought I knew what was best for me. The first time my family voted was in my first election."

Luna saw his family as "very supportive" of his decision to run, but still saw the personal sacrifices of running primarily in family terms:

> No family life. No free time. All of your time is spent at functions or planning. The campaign consumes your whole life. My wife's been through it many times before, but my daughter is at an age where she needs more attention. This is a problem. You are delaying your future [Luna is in his third year of law school] and incurring financial sacrifices.

Reyes viewed the campaign for the 29th District as having a positive effect on his family:

> I have talked mostly with my wife. This is a strange thing. She has never been involved in any of my campaigns. She's never worked the polls, gone to fund-raisers, nothing. But this time she got excited about the race. We basically made this decision together, which is the first time that's ever happened where politics is concerned. This is the best part of this election.

Only Rios admitted that family considerations had delayed his decision to run. At first, his family was opposed:

> Originally, they were not supportive of the idea because they were protective of me. They didn't want me going through all that. I have been able to keep them away from the campaign so their lives wouldn't be disrupted.

Except for time commitments, insufficient time left for family, and in Luna's case a delay in completing law school, the candidates' discussions of personal sacrifices was limited. Only Garcia—the only candidate other than Rios who had not previously run for office—elaborated substantially on personal sacrifices:

> To campaign full time . . . I've taken a leave of absence without pay from the judgeship. . . . I'm not rich . . . not much more than J.P.s get paid. But I have trouble with holding one office while running for another. I didn't want to do that. I'm not required to take the leave of absence, but I felt I should run on my own time not the taxpayers. . . . It's a short campaign so I can manage on my savings account. But I'm not rich and my family's not. . . . Time, it just takes so much time. I'm up working by 7:00 until 11:00 or 12:00 at night. And I have the normal things to do. I have to take the dog to the vet. It needs a bath. I don't

have time to go to the movies with a friend. I've always been a private
person. Media consultants want to know everything about you. I have a
clean-desk policy, and the campaign people have a messy-desk policy.
They go through my files and ask me more questions. . . .

Another potential personal sacrifice that only Garcia discussed—but
that may have been on the minds of others as well—was the impact of
losing. She had been advised that losing is "like a death in the family. You
have to be emotionally prepared. . . . If I make a decent showing, everyone
will respect that . . . but I just couldn't handle a big loss." By comparison,
when asked about the effects of losing, the other candidates either were
unconcerned or talked primarily about their future political careers.

Contextual Considerations

Aside from the individual judgments of those who remained on the
sidelines, we found important contextual factors contributed to the decision
to run. Probably the most important factor was redistricting, which created
several problems for potential congressional candidates. Unlike an existing
congressional seat in which a candidate can build support from a small base
over a two-year period, there was uncertainty about the district and its
boundaries until the late summer of 1991. Even then there were questions
about whether the new districts would pass Department of Justice scrutiny.
Also, the congressional primaries were scheduled early, March 10, the
same day as the presidential primaries. In addition, a hotly contested may-
oral contest in Houston did not conclude until December 7, and the holidays followed shortly thereafter. No one paid much attention to the March
primary contests until after the New Year. In effect, the campaign in the
first primary in the 29th District lasted sixty days. Thus, a viable candidate
had to have the ability to organize in a very short period of time. In this
regard it is important to note that all the Democratic candidates, with the
exception of Garcia, were experienced campaigners who had some organizational capabilities.

The redistricting process also created structural complexities for candidates. The dispersion of the Hispanic population and the resulting strange
shape of the district meant a candidate known in one part of the district
would not necessarily be known in another part. The problems of becoming
known were sizeable: the candidates had to decide where to place billboards, what radio stations to use, where to walk neighborhoods, how to
organize volunteers, what zip codes to include in mailings, and so on.

These factors combined to make it extremely difficult for a relative
unknown to have a realistic chance, at least in the Democratic primary. A
poll conducted in early March suggests the problem of building name identification, even for the major candidates. Responses to the question "Have
you read or heard a great deal, something, only a little, or nothing at all

Table 3-1   Survey Responses: Amount Read or Heard about the
Candidates (percentages)

Candidate [a]	"Great deal"	"Something"	"A little"	"Nothing"	"Not applicable"
Luna	24	24	27	25	1
Green	35	21	21	22	1
Reyes	76	16	4	2	2
Garcia	18	26	28	26	3
Burks	1	7	13	78	4

[a] Candidates appear in the same order as on the survey.

about (candidate name)?" are shown in Table 3-1. Aside from Reyes, who had been the subject of media attention on a range of matters over the years, the other major candidates had only modest recognition. (Although Garcia had never run for office before, she may have benefited from the fact that a Republican of the same name previously had run for office.)

The short campaign, the city elections, and the holidays also affected the ability of the candidates to raise money. According to Federal Election Commission (FEC) reports, as of the March 10 primary, not counting self-contributions, Green had raised $166,802; Reyes $122,400; Garcia $75,641; Luna $5,500; Burks $1,400; Ervin $123,997; and Rios $33,750.

As longtime officeholders in the Houston area and as favorites to make the runoff, Green and Reyes were in the best positions to raise money. Aside from individual contributions, Green had success in raising money from a range of political action committees (PACs), especially from labor organizations and the National Rifle Association (NRA). Reyes, although relying less on PAC money, did well among those who had contact with him in his role as a city councilperson—after all, he would continue in that capacity if his bid for Congress was unsuccessful. Garcia became somewhat competitive in this race, in part because of money she raised from various national women's groups (Emily's List, National Organization for Women, National Women's Political Caucus) and from the individual contributions she received from women. Without an elective office as a base and not considered a favorite in the race, Luna never raised sufficient money to compete. Ervin raised much of his money from attorneys in major Houston law firms, traditional Republican sources of funds in the Houston area, and a range of business PACs. His lead on Rios in tapping these sources seems to have been crucial. When Rios raised only a third of his $100,000 budget, he only had money enough to do a mailing to two-thirds of the likely Republican voters in the district.

Even in a retail politics campaign, having sufficient money was crucial to being competitive. It is important to note that the population of the district is not a wealthy one. Ervin, Garcia, Green, and Reyes were able to raise much of their money from outside the district. Still, by the standards set in other congressional primaries in the Houston area in 1992, the candidates in the 29th District were unsuccessful in raising money. In the neighboring 25th District, for example, a Republican primary was held to select a candidate to challenge incumbent Democrat Mike Andrews. Although the contest occurred before there was any indication that Andrews had House bank overdrafts, the district was safely Democratic in its composition, and the chances of a Republican victory were more remote than in the 29th District, the two Republican contenders raised funds far in excess of any candidate in the 29th District. The FEC reporting for the first quarter of 1992 alone shows that these two Republicans raised more than $350,000 and $208,000 (*Roll Call* 1992).

Deciding Not to Run

The context of the 29th District contest, indeed, was one that limited candidate emergence. With a relatively small number of visible Hispanic officeholders—many of them owing their political success to a key Hispanic leader, with many potential Anglo candidates conceding that the district should be represented by a Hispanic, with a Republican given little or no chance of winning, with a geographically dispersed district, and with limited financial resources available in the district, the field of candidates was bound to be limited. Only two of those candidates were given a chance of winning the seat.

Why did not more activists enter the race? What contextual factors influenced their decisions? For several well-known, Anglo potential Democratic candidates, the ethnic composition of the district was a key constraint. As noted earlier, many believed that the 29th District was drawn to be a Hispanic district. This factor, coupled with the realization that there was not room for more than one Anglo candidate, and the understanding that Green's state senate seat gave him the strongest base among the district's Anglo voters, precluded the entry of several potential candidates. For Houston City Councilperson Jim Greenwood, for example, who ran unsuccessfully as the Democratic candidate in 1970 for the congressional seat left vacant by George Bush, the design of the district and some personal considerations overrode any serious thoughts about running:

> It's designed for a Hispanic candidate. I believe in representative assistance. . . . It would have been hypocritical for me to run. . . . Hispanics are entitled to the seat. It was crafted for Hispanics. I don't know what would happen if a good opportunity came open. I'm a Democrat, and I live on the west side of Houston so there are limitations on that. In addition, my wife has a successful business, and it would be difficult for us if I were in D.C. I'm more likely to run for County Judge or mayor. I

could be drawn into a congressional race. I have the name i.d. and the money if someone like Mike Andrews gave up his seat.

Another possible Anglo candidate, City Councilperson Dale Gorczynski, entered the primary for a vacant justice of the peace position instead of the congressional primary. The mayor of the industrial suburb of Pasadena (part of which was included in the 29th District) John Ray Harrison, who had run in the Democratic primary for the 22nd District in 1982, thought about running, but chose to remain local. In Harrison's case, several factors entered into his decision not to run. He said that he wanted to see how the district lines finally would be drawn. Being from a Houston suburb, Harrison was not as concerned about the ethnicity of the district as he was that enough of "his territory" was included. He claimed that if the lines had been drawn north-south rather than east-west he might have run. Harrison attributes the small candidate field to the drawing of the district because "they've drawn the lines where the people (politicians) don't live." Other considerations in Harrison's decision were his advancing age and the fact that he would have to give up being mayor of Pasadena. He indicated that he just did not think that he wanted to start all over again in a new office. Finally, he noted that a federal office was not as attractive to him now as it once was because "too many people are just looking for someone to blame." Green had spoken with both Gorczynski and Harrison, potential candidates whom he described as "definitely looking at making the race" before announcing his candidacy. Of course, Green's influence in designing the district gave him an important strategic edge over any of the other potential Anglo candidates.

The pool of potential Hispanic Democratic candidates for the 29th District seat was limited as well. Relatively few Hispanics had held elective office in the Houston area and thus few had a base on which to run. Until the fall 1991 election, Reyes was the only Hispanic on the sixteen-member Houston City Council. There were no Hispanic state senators in the area. The Hispanic state representatives from the Houston area included Martinez and Mario Gallegos, who succeeded Luna. When asked about the likelihood of his running for the seat, Gallegos simply replied, "I don't feel like it's my time."

To a significant degree, many lesser known Hispanic politicians were indebted to Reyes for their political successes, and as Martinez's withdrawal suggests, they were unwilling to challenge Reyes or his designee. Many other Hispanic officeholders were either linked to Reyes or to Luna or were too new in politics to make the race. Put simply, there were few Hispanic Democrats in the Houston area with a base of support independent of Reyes, although that is beginning to change.

One observer of Hispanic politics in the area remarked:

> I don't see any saviors in the current group of Hispanic politicians. I think the people in the state legislature will be the new corps of His-

panic leaders. However, there are a lot of youngsters who are getting involved in politics, and they are the future of Hispanic politics.

Given the bleak prospects for a Republican winning the district, the fact that there was a primary contest was described by one observer as "remarkable." One Democratic observer whom we interviewed in November 1991 assessed Ervin's prospects: "He couldn't even win with a million dollars. This is a solid Democratic seat. The Democratic candidate would have to get caught raping a four-year-old for a Republican to win this district." Although a number of Hispanic Republicans were mentioned in our efforts to uncover potential candidates, Rios's efforts to find a Hispanic Republican willing to make the race, and our conversations with a variety of observers indicate that none of them could be persuaded. Most frequently mentioned was Vidal Martinez, a prominent Houston attorney and an active Republican, but Rios was unable to induce him to run.

Elimination of the Hispanic Candidates

Although the defeat of the Hispanic candidate in the Republican primary can be explained easily, the analysis of the Democratic primary result is far more complex. Ervin defeated Rios for many of the traditional reasons one candidate defeats another in a primary contest. Ervin started his campaign, obtained commitments, and raised money before Rios even agreed to run. And Rios was not a highly visible Hispanic politician. Potentially stronger Hispanic Republicans refused to make the race. Without the ability to buy name identification among likely Republican primary voters, Rios's local ties in a small part of the district were insufficient to overcome Ervin's links to downtown Houston's business and legal community. In addition, few Hispanics in the 29th District vote in the Republican primary.

The victory Green achieved over Reyes, like most close contests, can be attributed to a number of factors. One of the most important appears to have been the low levels of registration among Hispanics, a situation Houston's Hispanic leaders have worked hard to change, seeing this as an important key in the empowerment of Hispanics and in the success of Hispanic candidates. Moreover, it was believed that the appearance of Hispanic candidates would serve as a catalyst for these registration efforts. All of the Hispanic candidates with whom we spoke agreed that the registration of more Hispanics in the 29th District was crucial for a Hispanic to defeat Green. Over the course of the campaign we heard estimates that 15,000 to 30,000 new Hispanic voters would be registered for the March 10 primary. If this were the case, it would mean an increase in total Hispanic registration of 30 to 60 percent and would mean that there would likely be more Hispanics voting in the Democratic primary than Anglos.

Our analysis of the available data suggests that the increase in Hispanic registration in the 29th District fell considerably short of those goals.

When the district was drawn, it was estimated that it had a population of 566,217, of whom 377,217 were of voting age. It was estimated further that 46 percent of the voting age population was registered. Based on those figures there would have been approximately 175,500 registered voters in the district. At the time of the April runoff, the actual registration was 177,015 (registration figures were not available for March 10). By the second runoff on July 28, 183,766 persons were registered. Unless the legislative estimates were substantially incorrect, it appears that the impact of the registration efforts was exaggerated.

In addition, when we examined the changes in the number of voters registered in thirteen selected precincts in the 29th District with boundaries largely unchanged between 1990 and 1992 (redistricting had changed the boundaries of many precincts) and having more than 50 percent Hispanic registrants in 1990, again there is little evidence of extraordinary increases in voter registration. Registered voters in these sample precincts increased by 6.9 percent (20,888 to 22,326) between 1990 and the April 1992 runoff. By the second runoff only 169 additional voters had been registered. When we examine the registration changes for all thirty-five sample precincts, the increase from 1990 to 1992 was 8.4 percent (54,359 to 58,904).

Why is there a discrepancy between claims about registration increases and our estimates of the increases? One explanation is that our figures only look at the net change in district registration. Some of the people who are being registered merely may have moved from one residence in the district to another. Their registrations are new, but the registrants themselves are not. In addition, although the purging of voting lists is a slow process, the net figures understate the actual number of new registrants because clearly some of those listed in 1990 were no longer registered in 1992. Even with these qualifications, it seems clear that a continuous registration effort has not produced dramatic increases among Harris County Hispanics.

An analysis of the vote in the three primary elections provides another indication of why a Hispanic candidate did not win the 29th District. Reyes led the field after the March 10 primary with 6,487 votes (34 percent) to Green's 4,661 votes (28 percent). Garcia received 21 percent and Luna received 15 percent. Under such circumstances, it appeared that Reyes was in a strong position to win the runoff. Not only was he leading, but the two eliminated Hispanic candidates shared nearly 36 percent of the vote. If Reyes had split the Garcia and Luna supporters with Green, he would have been assured of victory. Many factors, such as Green's negative campaign, the dispute over the runoff outcome, and the increased turnout for the second runoff, played important roles. But it is the failure of Reyes to win sufficient support from voters willing to vote for another Hispanic candidate in the first primary that proved crucial in his loss to Green.

Table 3-2, which presents data from the three primaries for our three groupings of sample precincts, illustrates the problem. In the group of

Table 3-2   Support for Candidates in Sample Precincts
(percentages)

Precinct breakdown	Primary		First runoff		Second runoff	
Ten precincts with less	Green	53.1	Green	78.3	Green	78.6
than 20% Hispanic	Reyes	18.3	Reyes	21.7	Reyes	21.4
registered voters	Garcia	14.4				
	Luna	12.2				
	Burks	2.2				
Twelve precincts with	Green	23.7	Green	46.4	Green	48.1
20 to 50% Hispanic	Reyes	37.2	Reyes	53.7	Reyes	52.0
registered voters	Garcia	20.9				
	Luna	16.3				
	Burks	1.8				
Thirteen precincts with	Green	6.2	Green	20.1	Green	18.4
more than 50% Hispanic	Reyes	50.3	Reyes	79.9	Reyes	81.6
registered voters	Garcia	17.0				
	Luna	26.0				
	Burks	.6				

precincts with more than 50 percent Hispanic registrants, Reyes increased
his percentage of the vote from 50.3 percent in the first primary to 79.9
percent in the first runoff to 81.6 percent in the second runoff. Green, who
did have some support among Hispanics, went from 6.2 percent to 20.1
percent to 18.4 percent. It appears that two-thirds or more of the support
for Luna and Garcia in these precincts may have gone to Reyes, despite
Luna's opposition to Reyes's and Garcia's decisions not to endorse either
candidate in the runoff. In the middle group of precincts (those with 20 to
50 percent Hispanic registered voters) the results are mixed. Green appears to have improved his position more than Reyes between the first
primary and the runoffs. Where the election was lost for Reyes, however, is
demonstrated by results from the sample precincts in which Hispanics comprised less than 20 percent of the registrants. Reyes's percentage of the
vote in these precincts goes only from 18.3 percent to 21.7 percent to 21.4
percent across the three elections, while Green's percentage jumps from
53.1 percent to more than 78 percent in the two runoffs. Put simply, Reyes
was unable to attract the support that Garcia and Luna had received in
more heavily Anglo precincts. (Of course, we recognize that many of the
Luna and Garcia voters may have chosen not to vote in the runoffs and that
Green may have benefited in part from increases in Anglo turnout in the
runoffs.)

Even though Green may have been successful in winning as much as
15 to 20 percent of the Hispanic vote in the runoffs, Reyes was pleased by

his own performance. He contended, "I conceded Green 15 percent of the Hispanic vote, and he only got 12." What hurt Reyes's chances more than the loss of Hispanic support was his failure to have much crossover appeal among Anglo voters. Yet many Anglo voters showed a willingness to support a Hispanic candidate in the first primary.

Candidate Emergence and Election Outcomes

Two features about candidate emergence in the 29th District had significant impact on the probability that a Hispanic candidate would win. The first was the decision of Democratic party officials and other important institutional and individual elites *not* to involve themselves directly in the candidate emergence process. As a result, emergence was largely a decision of the candidates themselves. If, in fact, the major criterion in the design of the 29th District was to produce a district that would maximize the chances for the election of a Hispanic, there was no effort by national, state, or local Democratic party officials to reinforce that likelihood. We found no one who suggested to Green that he not run or who offered him an alternative in the pursuit of his continued career in politics. More than any other single factor, Green's decision to run influenced the outcome in the 29th District.

More subtle and only slightly less important is the process through which Hispanic candidates emerge. Though Reyes disputes it, it generally is held by district observers that he was the only Hispanic candidate who could have lost to Green in a runoff. Although not having Reyes's level of visibility or intensity of following among Hispanic voters, Garcia, Luna, or (perhaps) Martinez would have been better able to consolidate support among Hispanics. In addition, they would have had substantial crossover appeal among Anglo voters. The poll conducted prior to the March primary, as we previously have stated, showed that Reyes was the best known of the candidates. It also showed that he had by far the highest negative evaluation, with 34 percent of those surveyed rating him "unfavorable." Among Anglo respondents 44 percent gave him an "unfavorable" rating and only 31 percent gave him a "favorable" rating. No other candidate exceeded a 12 percent "unfavorable" rating. Yet Reyes was able to persuade Martinez not to run, to lead in the first primary, and to out-distance Garcia and Luna easily. He clearly had the strongest base within the Hispanic community, despite some negatives there as well.

This leads us to speculate about the process that surrounds the creation of new minority legislative districts. The goal of those involved in designing such districts is to maximize the opportunity for a member of the minority group to win the district (see Swain 1989; Bullock and MacManus 1987; Davidson 1984). The strategy normally relies, as it did in the 29th District, in maximizing the minority population of the district. However, this strategy may have other consequences. It may favor a minority candidate who relies almost exclusively for support from the minority community at the expense of minority candidates who have less intense support in the minority community but are better able to appeal to other voters. In fact, this may be precisely why candidates like Reyes are vulnerable to defeat in a runoff primary or in a general election by a candidate who is not a member of the minority group. In addition, this is the type of candidate who needs the highest percentage of minority voters in the district to succeed. Put another way, raising the percentage of the minority population beyond a certain limit decreases the chances for the emergence and success of minority candidates who have crossover appeal. Yet these are precisely the candidates who are able to win such districts without extraordinarily high percentages of minority population. Although in some senses such candidates may not represent the minority community as well as the candidate with the strongest base there, these candidates may help to maximize overall representation of the minority group in the legislative body in virtual terms. Applied to the 29th District, this means that Garcia or Luna might have stood a better chance against Reyes in a district that had a lower percentage of Hispanics than the 29th District, that Reyes emerged as the Hispanic front-runner in part because of the effort to concentrate Hispanics in the district, and yet Reyes may have been the only Democratic Hispanic candidate who could have been defeated in the 29th District.

Postscript: Candidate Emergence Continues

As many predicted, Green easily defeated Ervin in the general election, winning more than 65 percent of the vote. Ervin was far more competitive in terms of raising money, with total receipts of more than $500,000 compared to Green's $700,000 (*Campaigns and Elections* 1993). Well before the election, however, there were already discussions about the 1994 election. The consensus among observers was that whether Green or Ervin won the seat, the incumbent would be vulnerable to a Hispanic challenger in 1994. The changing demographics of the district will make the district increasingly more favorable for a Hispanic candidate. The Hispanic population in the district and Hispanic voter registration are both increasing. Green, even as an incumbent, will find the context of a Democratic primary more unfavorable in years to come. It is ironic that had Reyes won the seat he might well have been unbeatable for years to come. Potential Hispanic candidates would be most likely to emerge to contest for other offices. In this sense Reyes's defeat opened an opportunity for Hispanic candidates who would not have fared well in the 1992 contest for the 29th District.

Given this analysis, it was surprising that new candidates did not emerge in 1994. Reyes again challenged Green. Despite his loss in 1992, Reyes remained sufficiently formidable that other potential Hispanic candidates stayed out of the race. Garcia, who months after her 1992 loss had not removed her campaign sticker from her car and was considering running again, did not enter the 1994 primary. Neither did any other Hispanic candidate. Martinez and Gallegos competed for a newly redistricted state senate seat. They were joined by Yolanda Flores, one of two Hispanic women elected to state representative seats in 1992 from the Houston area. Without an open split among Hispanic candidates and with two years to increase Hispanic voter registration, it would seem Reyes's chances would improve.

By 1994 Green had the mantle of incumbency with its advantages (staff, a record of casework service, and fund-raising abilities) and its potential disadvantages (a voting record including votes against the popular Brady Bill and the North American Free Trade Agreement).

The 1994 primary outcome largely was unchanged, however. Green won again, albeit with a somewhat more comfortable 55 percent of the vote. Two of the major factors that affected the 1992 outcome were still critical in 1994. First, Hispanic participation, although increasing, remained low. Unofficial totals indicate that Reyes received more than 20 percent fewer votes in 1994 then in the second runoff in 1992. (Green's total was lower as well.) Second, Reyes continued to suffer from a lack of appeal to Anglo voters.

The 1994 results offer only a brief respite for Green, however. New Hispanic candidates are likely to emerge in 1996. They may not possess the intensity of support that Reyes enjoys in the Hispanic community, but perhaps they will be better positioned to win a larger share of the Anglo vote.

4

Running for Congress under the Shadow of the Capitol Dome: The Race for Virginia's 8th District

Paul S. Herrnson and Robert M. Tennant

L ocal politicians should have viewed the election for Virginia's 8th District House seat as a target of opportunity in 1992. The incumbent,
Democrat James Moran, had first been elected two years earlier with a
mere 52 percent of the vote. A weak economy, congressional scandal, widespread voter alienation—all seemed to promise that 1992 would be a bad
year indeed for incumbents. Moreover, the 8th District is virtually in Washington, D.C.'s backyard; the Republican party, in particular, might have
placed a high premium on the recruitment of an able challenger to carry
the fight against Moran.

Instead, the best known, most experienced candidates (of both parties) opted to stay out of the race. Perhaps it is not surprising that the
Democrats maintained solidarity behind their incumbent. The Republican
story is more complicated: a redrawn congressional district, an incumbent
who labored to improve his image and serve the district, and career and
family concerns of the potential candidates all conspired to keep the strongest candidates out of the race. In short, it was the story of an ostensibly
vulnerable incumbent whose seat is becoming safe—largely as a result of
the unwillingness of quality candidates to oppose him. As such, it illuminates the critical role candidate emergence plays in understanding House
election outcomes.

Geography, Demographics, and Political Profile

Virginia's 8th District is in a suburban area located south of Washington, D.C., with a total population in 1990 of almost 750,000. The district
includes historic Alexandria, portions of Fairfax and Prince William counties, and under the new redistricting plan, the city of Arlington and the
Mount Vernon corridor located in Fairfax County. The new district is
largely white and upper-middle-class, although it contains a substantial minority population and some families living below the poverty line. It is also
more heavily Democratic than the old 8th District. The new district is
typical of many drawn for first-term members whose party controls both
chambers of the state legislature and the governorship. Its composition was
designed to improve Moran's prospects by adding heavily Democratic sec-

tions of the city of Arlington and Fairfax County to an already Democratic-leaning constituency.

Alexandria is the cultural and political heart of the district and carries with it about 20 percent of the electorate. The population in Alexandria is composed mostly of young white professionals, with African Americans comprising about 20 percent and isolated at the fringes of the city. What sets Alexandria apart from most cities is its astounding opulence. The median income in this city is the second highest in the nation at more than $22,000. Many candidates for higher office, including Moran, have emerged from the ranks of its local government, which is viewed by many as the natural stepping stone for other statewide or national offices.

While Alexandria has experienced moderate population growth in the past years, Fairfax and Prince William counties have been booming. The bulk of the 8th District electorate now comes from Fairfax. In the past, the vast majority of residents in Fairfax were white, but an influx of African Americans, Asians, and Hispanics accounts for most of the new growth in the county. Fairfax County had been a Republican bastion in years past, but Democrat Moran was able to wrest the county away from Stan Parris by a 50 to 47 percent margin.

The proximity of the district to the seat of national power has had a number of effects on congressional campaigns in the 8th District. Races in the district tend to get heavy media coverage because national reporters find it easier to cover races in their own backyards than across the country. Campaign appearances by President Bush, Vice President Quayle, or GOP cabinet members on behalf of Republican House candidates were fairly common, resulting in media exposure for the entire GOP ticket. As one Republican activist stated, "It is much easier and cheaper to get the President to 'cross the bridge' than to move him across the country."

Being under the shadow of the Capitol dome brings with it certain sources of campaign assistance that are not as readily available in other parts of the country. To begin with, candidates can obtain top-quality campaign consulting services at discount rates because many consultants are located in the immediate area and offer less expensive rates to local candidates. Joe Trippi, a well known Washington political consultant, for example, prepared Moran's pro-choice television advertisements very inexpensively.

In addition, a wide array of individuals and groups provide important "in-kind" campaign services. For example, Capitol Hill staff members, civil servants, and representatives of federal unions provided issue research to the Moran campaign during the 1990 election. Democratic staff members from the House Banking Committee disclosed some of Parris's weaknesses and liabilities. These sources of assistance are available routinely to candidates who run in Virginia's 8th District or the other districts located in the Washington suburbs.

Figure 4-1   Virginia, 8th District

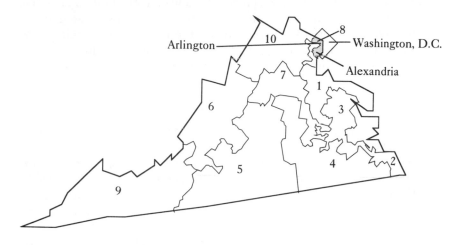

Candidates, Parties, Interests, and Issues in 1992

What would the ideal candidate for Virginia's 8th District be like? One Democratic activist felt that it would be most advantageous for a candidate to have an old-line Southern background and to have lived in the district for his or her entire life. The candidate also should have been active in local charity and civic groups, and enjoyed some success in local politics. Democrats also felt that the ideal candidate would be liberal on social issues, a male who is sympathetic to women's issues, and knowledgeable about issues of concern to federal workers. The candidate also would have a strong understanding of district-based concerns, including transportation, federal government development, and urban growth.

GOP activists believed that it was useful, but not essential, for the ideal candidate to have previous experience in government. Conservative activists asserted that the candidate should be opposed to abortion rights, while moderates felt that a pro-choice position was needed to win the seat. Representatives of both wings of the party believed a conservative position on economic concerns would be mandatory. Republicans also maintained that the ideal candidate would focus on local issues.

Perhaps most important, perhaps, the ideal candidates for both parties would have to be excellent fund-raisers. Washington, D.C., is one of the nation's most expensive media markets, and candidates must contend with exorbitant advertising costs. Although local papers, such as the *Alexandria Gazette-Packet,* have reasonable rates, candidates must use the mass media, including television, radio, and newspaper advertisements in the *Washington Post* and the *Washington Times* in order to reach the entire 8th District.

This is both very costly and inefficient because the media market includes almost four million individuals spread over a wide metropolitan area. The need to hire some of the premier political consultants located in the Washington, D.C., area further drives up the cost of campaigning, even though, as already mentioned, many offer local candidates discount rates. The costs of running make a bid for the House prohibitive for some would-be challengers.

Political parties do not have great influence in the candidate recruitment process in the 8th District. Local political elites told us that ambitious people are the individuals who generally decide to run. As one Democrat stated, "The local parties are not particularly strong in northern Virginia; it usually is a matter of who can best put their organizations together—in terms of volunteers and fund raising. There are no party bosses in the old style."

For Democrats who wish to serve in Congress there is a long ladder of succession. The only way to become a Democratic nominee is to climb each rung of the ladder. One must start out posting signs and working for other candidates, volunteer in local civic groups, and get elected to local offices before attempting any run for the state legislature or Congress.

A small group of Democratic activists, based primarily in the Alexandria area, are the principal architects of Democratic politics in the district. Many ambitious and experienced political activists and government employees live in the district. This has contributed to the development of a sophisticated brand of insider politics. Local elites resist outside interference in candidate recruitment and other local political matters. These insiders usually line up in support of the best prospects for the party during the primary and form the organizational foundation for the general election campaign once the candidate is selected. This selection process—though informal, is well established—virtually assures that the party will nominate someone who is well connected, and at the same time excludes party outsiders.

For the GOP, the process of candidate recruitment is quite different. Attractive candidates can come forward at any time, post their $250, and run for office. The comparative openness of the GOP's nomination process reflects the relative weakness of the local Republican party. The local party has a shallow candidate pool, has been ineffective in candidate recruitment, and has only modestly helped its nominees wage their general election campaigns.

Neither the national nor the state parties have been heavily involved in recruiting candidates for the 8th District. Such involvement would be viewed as interference by the district's sophisticated party elites. Once the nomination campaigns are over, however, the parties step in and provide campaign assistance (Herrnson 1988). They help recruit campaign volunteers and provide technical assistance. The parties' congressional campaign committees furnish issue research, mailing lists, and polling information. The most important function they assume is helping the candidates raise money.

Although the ideal career ladders of the two parties' candidates differ, the political coalitions both are expected to build are similar. Local civic associations, recreational groups, and grass roots organizations are considered important elements of a winning coalition by both parties. The condominium association appears to be the new force in northern Virginia politics, a development that has not yet taken hold across the nation.

The business community is much involved in northern Virginia politics, especially in the funding of election campaigns. The Chambers of Commerce wield considerable power, as do Rotary Clubs and the Knights of Columbus. Specifically singled out for help by both Democrats and Republicans are real estate developers, who are very active at all levels of electoral politics and need to be cultivated by all serious candidates. Bankers, primarily those with real estate interests, are also important. Despite the fact that the district is not heavily unionized, labor groups do have some impact in the 8th District; Moran received a great deal of money from these traditional Democratic supporters in 1990 and 1992. Nevertheless, those interviewed stressed that candidates usually are not promoted by any specific interest group. Rather, candidates typically make the contacts needed to run for Congress by becoming involved in civic associations, community groups, party committees, and by getting elected to local office.

The African American community accounts for approximately 10 percent of the population of the district, but it has not been particularly successful in influencing congressional politics. A number of local activists suggested that African Americans would be more influential if they were less fragmented, but so far they have been unable to transform their numbers into political leverage.

Despite its proximity to the seat of national government, local issues tend to dominate the political agenda of the 8th District; national concerns are largely of secondary importance. Transportation and the decline in federal transfer payments are typical of the local problems that are addressed by candidates. Also, sharp federal budget cuts, especially in defense, have hurt the 8th District economy.

National issues important in the 8th District include abortion, crime, and drugs. The drug-related violence rampant in the District of Columbia is a perennial issue, as is the crime spillover from Washington to the suburbs, though these issues were less important in 1992 than were such traditional issues as the state of the economy and joblessness.

The Democrats: The Beginning of the Moran Legacy?

James Moran's personal and political history is both tenacious and stormy. In 1979, he was elected to the Alexandria City Council; in 1982 he became the city's vice mayor. His political star fell almost as rapidly as it had risen when in 1984 he had to resign from the office of vice mayor after pleading no contest to conflict of interest charges.

In 1985, just when it seemed Moran might fade from the political scene, he defeated Democratic incumbent Charles Beatley in the general election for mayor of Alexandria. His victory as an independent candidate provided evidence of his impressive political base. As mayor, however, Moran ran into difficulties with some Alexandria residents as a result of his approach to social problems. Complaints were lodged against him when he directed police to evict from public housing the families of suspected drug users, most of whom were African Americans.

The 1990 congressional race between Moran and Parris was one of the most scrutinized around the country. It pitted a moderate Democrat against a feisty, hard-line conservative Republican. Both campaigns were extremely well financed, and there was certainly no love lost between the challenger and the incumbent. Realizing that northern Virginia voters were solidly pro-choice, Moran hammered away at Parris's vehement opposition to abortion rights and stressed his (Moran's) support for a woman's right to choose. Planned Parenthood purchased independent advertisements in the local newspapers criticizing Parris on the issue. Moran's use of the issue of abortion, one of the most politically divisive in the nation, was crucial to his 1990 victory.

Money also played a key role; the Moran-Parris contest was the third costliest House race in the nation at that time. Prior to Moran, the previous three Democratic candidates ran low-budget campaigns. They used no television advertising and each lost decisively. Moran, by contrast, spent more than $883,000 to portray himself in the mold of the late president John F. Kennedy and to characterize Parris as a doddering, old, grandfather-type. Parris, who spent more than $982,000, could never overcome his image problem. Moran, the rare example of a quality challenger overcoming the advantages of incumbency, won the election with 52 percent, compared with Parris's 45 percent.

An Uncontested Nomination

To those pondering a bid for Virginia's 8th District in 1992, the political and financial advantages of a congressional incumbent proved to be especially strong disincentives. Moran worked hard to bolster his strengths and reduce his liabilities, and, at the same time, Democrats involved in the state's redistricting process helped to strengthen his hand.

Moran labored to solidify his hold on the district early in the 1992 election cycle. He had $257,000 in his campaign war chest by early July, and had plans to raise considerably more by the fall. Moreover, by most accounts Moran has solid political instincts. He was correct that 1990 was the time to challenge a ten-year incumbent who held positions that may have been out of step with the district. He also was able to raise close to $900,000 to run against an incumbent, an impressive feat for any challenger. One Democrat candidly stated, "If he can keep his hands in his own pockets, he will be around [in Congress] for many years."

Despite the many accolades, Moran has some political liabilities. His abrasive style and tendency to speak before considering the consequences are considered his most important personal disadvantages. One Democratic activist stated, "Jim has the worst case of foot in mouth disease I've ever seen . . . and is not the most thoughtful or reflective politician." Republican activists generally focused more on the content of Moran's politics, criticizing his credibility, ethics, and congressional votes. His flip-flop on the Persian Gulf War was viewed as a possible weak point.[1] He also was criticized for bashing Parris for being on the House Banking Committee and then "sneaking" on to it himself.

For many, Moran's biggest liability was his questionable personal integrity. Informants cited his plea bargain while he was a member of the Alexandria City Council and subsequent resignation as vice mayor. They also mentioned his accepting a $10,000 donation from a real estate developer during the 1990 campaign and then returning it when the issue threatened to torpedo the campaign.

His potential weaknesses notwithstanding, Moran remained unchallenged for the Democratic nomination in 1992. One reason for the absence of party competition is teamwork. This term refers to the fact that the party actively supports a strong incumbent and just as actively discourages potential primary opponents. Campaign resources such as volunteers, campaign expertise, legal assistance, and financial support are put at the disposal of the incumbent, decreasing the likelihood that other Democrats could challenge effectively. Teamwork has been viewed as essential to political success in northern Virginia, and teamwork was considered important in enabling Moran to defeat Parris in 1990. Having wrested the seat from the Republicans, the Democrats were not going to risk it by splintering their support.

While there were no individuals who officially stepped forward to contest the nomination, several were mentioned by party activists as possible challengers. Patricia Ticer, the current mayor of Alexandria, was considered by some to be a potential congressional candidate, but it would have surprised many if she left the safe haven of local politics. While seen as the "warm consensus" type, Ticer was viewed by many local Democrats as indecisive on key issues and not a particularly strong political leader. One informant candidly suggested that she may be a little too old to run for Congress, stating "Ticer would be great if you wanted a grandmother in Congress!"

One potential candidate who had not planned to run in 1992 but has strong congressional aspirations is Mark Warner. According to a number of Democratic leaders in the district, Warner could have made things very tough for the incumbent. Respected by many in the local hierarchy, Warner was described by one Democrat as "articulate, likeable, from a nice family, an American dream story." Warner, a 36-year-old lawyer and president of his own cellular telephone company, is, as one informant stated, "Dying to get to Congress!" He unabashedly proclaims his ambition to hold a seat in the House or Senate, stating he could easily run in Virginia's 7th, 8th, or 11th Districts because he owns homes in Alexandria and Fredericksburg.

Warner, a millionaire and head of one of the largest communications companies in the Washington area, has been very active in statewide Virginia politics. He was a key player on Douglas Wilder's gubernatorial campaign and transition team, and most recently served as treasurer of Wilder's presidential campaign committee. Warner's main weakness appears to be his lack of local political involvement. As one informant suggested, Warner has yet to pay his dues in local civic associations or politics. Some resent his plan to vault over others who have been working their ways up the political ladder.

Warner's strength as a candidate, however, is such that several district activists told us that he would have won the seat had he run in 1990; Moran preempted him by announcing his candidacy first. Warner seems likely to run for Congress in the not-too-distant future. Asked what would happen should Moran decide not to seek reelection, Warner replied, "Pass me the sheet and I'll sign up and go out and raise $250,000 in twenty-four hours."

Another young political star in the 8th District is Kerry Donley. In his mid-30s, Donley is a vice president of Crestar Bank and a member of the Alexandria City Council. His parents came to the Washington area from South Dakota in 1962 to work for then newly elected Sen. George McGovern. Characterized as "young, smart, committed, and a quintessentially active guy," Donley is viewed quite favorably by fellow Democrats. They identified his solid ties to the community and praised his combination of community activism and fiscal responsibility. Similar to Ticer and Warner, Donley was content to work for Moran's reelection rather than challenge the incumbent's hold over the 8th District. This is not to say, however, that Donley does not harbor further political aspirations. He views his political career as "episodic and to be advanced one step at a time." He projected that he would try to move "from city council to mayor and then perhaps to Congress, depending on the specific opportunities that present themselves."

Many of the possible Democratic candidates mentioned that there would be high personal costs to run for Congress. Donley, for example, jokingly suggested that his family "would probably shoot him" should he decide to run. He discussed the personal and financial implications of running a campaign, and mentioned the fact that family privacy would be lost. Growing up in a family that worked for Senator McGovern, he witnessed firsthand the diminishment of a senator's personal and family life. Another local Democrat concurred, stating that "even a trip to Safeway [a grocery store] for milk turns into a campaign excursion. You have no time to breathe because you are always campaigning and everything you do is visible." However, some noted that holding a seat so close to the capital means that you could continue living in the district and commute into the city, instead of having to set up two households.

Although many other highly talented Democratic politicians lived in the district, and all recognized Moran's shortcomings, Democratic activists indicated that there were three reasons why no legitimate party member would challenge him for the nomination. First, from a candidate's point of view, in order to run successfully for the nomination an individual would need the support of Moran's people. The volunteers and activists that form Moran's core supporters are an essential part of any viable Democratic coalition. Second, Democratic loyalists worked extremely hard to help Moran wrest the seat from Parris and would react negatively to any challenge to Moran. Third, potential rivals recognized that a successful Democratic candidate would have to be well known in the local community, have strong political and social ties, and be a superior fund-raiser. Moran has all these qualities and as a consequence was viewed by many as virtually unbeatable.

The Republican Heavyweights Sit Out the Race

While the Democrats easily united behind their strongest candidate, the Republicans were unable to get some of their best potential candidates to run. Former 8th District Rep. Stan Parris, U.S. District Attorney Henry Hudson, and congressional aide Mark Strand opted not to enter the primary. Three less qualified individuals were left to contest the race: Bill Cleveland, a Capitol Hill police officer and Alexandria's vice mayor; Joe Vasipoli, a multicareer federal employee; and Kyle McSlarrow, an attorney practicing environmental law.

The Republican Bystanders

Strand would have been one of the most experienced and promising challengers the GOP could have fielded against Moran, but he abandoned thoughts of a candidacy when legislators in Richmond drew an 8th District that did not include his Prince William County home. Strand, who became California Rep. Bill Lowery's administrative assistant after Parris's defeat, would have made a formidable challenger. As Parris's most important assistant, he ran the campaign in 1990 and publicly debated Moran more times than did his boss. He is an excellent speaker, knows the issues, and knows Capitol Hill. Strand's major strength is also a liability, however. Best known as Parris's sidekick, he would possibly have had to shed that image to have a chance to win. Strand was also not considered as being well versed on local issues. Once the legislature sent its redistricting plan to the governor, Strand said he knew his candidacy was "out and it was time to focus on Bill Lowery's reelection."

A second powerful Republican who decided against challenging Moran was Hudson, the U.S. attorney general for the Eastern District of the country. Many viewed this position as an excellent stepping stone for higher office. He was born and raised in Arlington, Virginia, and attended the American University School of Law in Washington, D.C. In addition, he received a great deal of local media exposure while serving as county attorney for Arlington. As of December 1991, Hudson had begun some informal scouting and had opened a private legal practice, a move many interpreted as preparation for a run at Moran's seat.

At that time, Hudson appeared to be the best possibility for a strong Republican candidate. With Moran's liabilities, especially his handling of the Gulf War vote and his past scandals, Hudson's law-and-order conservatism would have been attractive to many voters. But Hudson chose not to run. Instead, he accepted an appointment in September 1991 to be head of the U.S. Marshal's Office. The redistricting plan that gave the 8th District more Democratic strongholds, the huge war chest Moran had accumulated, and the prestigious position Hudson was offered all encouraged him to bypass a confrontation with Moran.

A third name mentioned as a potential candidate was the former incumbent, Parris. He had been highly successful at fund raising in the past and several Republican activists believed that $400,000 had been earmarked for a Parris war chest prior to the race. Yet, Parris's candidacy also was not to be. Parris was appointed to the St. Lawrence Seaway Commission by the Bush administration soon after his 1990 defeat and appeared to have little motivation to campaign again. Most believed that he would stay out of the 1992 race, except for some back-room politicking and perhaps some fund-raising for other Republicans.

The Republican Candidates

Cleveland portrayed himself as an insider politician, but more properly he should be viewed as an outsider. He received the largest number of votes in the race for Alexandria City Council, a feat that awarded him the position of vice mayor. While this post is largely ceremonial, particularly now that the present mayor is a Democrat, it raised Cleveland's name recognition and carried with it the impression of increased public responsibility. Cleveland calls himself "An elected official with a proven record of public service." In support of this claim, he cites his record of military service during the Vietnam War and his position as a U.S. Capitol police officer since 1974. He continues to be a full-time officer on the force.

What set Cleveland apart from the others were his stands on abortion and gun control. Cleveland had stated that while "his personal choice is life," he supported a woman's right to choose. Cleveland also endorsed the Brady Bill, legislation that established a nationwide requirement that all prospective gun owners wait five business days before purchasing firearms.

His position on gun control fell outside the official posture of the Republican party, yet it was in tune with district voters.

Cleveland, however, did face certain problems going into the primary. Several political observers suggested that many white Virginia voters would refuse to vote for a black candidate. He also faced opposition from blacks. Many in the African American community viewed Cleveland as a sellout—a politician who turned his back on his people by running as a Republican. Moreover, the majority of African Americans in the district are registered Democrats and could not participate in the Republican primary.

Some Republican activists claimed that Cleveland was unprepared intellectually for office. Local Republican official Lysander Hitlowe was quoted as saying "It's a large jump from the City Council to the House of Representatives. . . . I do not believe that he [Cleveland] understands the complexities that face the average congressman" (Capute 1992a). One informant very candidly stated that he did not believe Cleveland was bright enough to be a member of Congress.

Why did Cleveland decide to run? Officially Cleveland contends that "the state of the economy, inner-city problems, and a lack of accountability in Congress" convinced him that his voice was needed. One activist interviewed before the primary confided that the Cleveland candidacy was an indication of the lack of talent available to the Republican party. He called Cleveland's judgment into question, stating that even if Cleveland could win the Republican nomination, he would surely get "swamped" in November.

While Cleveland appeared to be highly issue-motivated, other factors helped drive his candidacy. Some informants have suggested he may have aspirations beyond 1992 that involve further runs for Congress or perhaps mayor of Alexandria. Running for the House of Representatives would increase his visibility among voters and party members.

Joe Vasipoli has a penchant for comparing politics to golf. "Golf is pure skill. . . . There is no favoritism, no back stabbing, and no cronyism, it's the total opposite of politics" (Capute 1992a). This criticism of a profession that he has chosen to pursue suggests that Vasipoli, like many other politicians running for Congress in 1992, attempted to portray himself as a political outsider. Then a 39-year-old lawyer, Vasipoli has worked in the Washington area since 1977. He is the son of an Asian mother and a white father, a heritage some stated might bode well with the minorities in the district. In terms of social policy, Vasipoli is on the left of the Republican spectrum. He supports abortion rights and takes a strong stand on protecting the environment. These atypical Republican policy stands might have earned him votes with the relatively liberal 8th District voters, but they certainly cost him support among Republican activists. Vasipoli's strengths include a proven ability to raise funds (Capute 1992a).

If there was a front-runner on the Republican side, it no doubt was McSlarrow. This then 31-year-old environmental lawyer had some strong qualifications and attributes, but also some negatives. He enjoyed a close rapport with the conservative element within the Republican party. He was endorsed strongly by former Representative Parris. Parris stated "Kyle is right on the issues that are important to many Republicans and to the 8th District . . . he is the only one of these three candidates that I believe has the ability and knowledge to go toe-to-toe with Jim Moran in debates and win." This was no minor endorsement, for Parris had been one of the conservative Republicans' favorite sons, a position that usually brings with it access to large amounts of campaign money.

McSlarrow strongly opposed gun control, professed anti-abortion views, and aimed his economic program at stimulating the economy by leaving business alone. He labeled the breakdown of the American family as the key cause of drug abuse, crime, and poverty. These positions endeared him to conservative Republicans in the district, a particularly important factor during the primary election because turnout rates in primaries are notoriously low. Solidly organized candidates with ideologically charged electoral bases almost always have the upper hand in low turnout elections (Crotty and Jackson 1984). Ideological fervor can be a powerful force in an election, especially in fund-raising and in constructing a campaign organization.

One of McSlarrow's major drawbacks was that he had never been elected to public office. In 1992, however, this may not have been quite as strong a negative as it was in previous years. Cleveland's experience in local politics normally would have given him an edge in the primary, but the rampant anti-incumbent mood may have given McSlarrow some advantage.

Of the three candidates, McSlarrow was by far the best fund-raiser. By March 30, 1992, he had raised $50,209 compared to Vasipoli's $42,256 and Cleveland's $21,590. By the end of the primary season McSlarrow, perhaps reaping the benefits of Parris's endorsement, had raised an impressive $108,296.[2] Cleveland was able to almost triple his earlier total, raising $61,236, while Vasipoli's campaign failed to ignite in the latter stages of the campaign, adding just more than $3,000 for a total of $45,380. As expected, McSlarrow easily defeated his two opponents in the June 9 primary. He received 54 percent of the vote to Cleveland's 28 percent and Vasipoli's 18 percent. Turnout was low; only about 17,000 votes were cast in the primary.

The 1992 Election and Beyond

Some contended that McSlarrow would run as the proverbial sacrificial lamb in November's general election. Others viewed the 1992 contest as one with future implications. A "good loss" for McSlarrow, in which he captured at least 40 percent of the vote, might set him up for a more legitimate shot at the seat or another office some time down the road. In the end, Moran defeated McSlarrow by a 57 to 42 percent margin, with independent candidate Alvin O. West receiving the remaining 1 percent of the vote. While Moran received significantly more votes than he did in 1990, McSlarrow performed much better than many had expected.

The two waged a vicious and negative campaign, similar in tone to the 1990 race between Moran and Parris. Moran recycled advertisements and campaign themes, stressing the differences between himself and McSlarrow on the issues of abortion, women's rights, and health care (Baker 1992). McSlarrow countered with charges that Moran had defended, in House Banking Committee hearings, the directors of a failed bank who had donated to his campaign (Simpson 1992).

There were two other issues that unexpectedly came to the forefront of the campaign. First was the issue of drug use by the candidates. During a televised debate in October, Moran admitted that he had twice experimented with drugs while he was a college student. McSlarrow also admitted to drug use as a youth, but Moran contended he had evidence that McSlarrow had "continued to use drugs into his twenties" (Baker 1992). The second issue—the proposed move of the Washington Redskins football team from RFK Stadium in Washington to a new stadium to be built at Potomac Yard in Alexandria—was probably a more significant factor in Moran's victory. Moran, who strongly opposed the building of the new stadium, was one of the leading spokespersons on the issue. McSlarrow, who originally supported the building of the stadium, later altered his position to support a new stadium "somewhere in Northern Virginia" (Capute 1992b). Eventually, Redskins owner Jack Kent Cooke and Virginia's Governor Wilder abandoned their plans to build the stadium. Moran, who claimed credit for this outcome received considerable media exposure for his stand and attracted increased electoral support in Alexandria.

Conclusion

The political environment that preceded the election should have encouraged more politicians to challenge Moran. Given that 1992 was widely proclaimed to be the "year of the outsider," one might have expected a stampede of qualified primary candidates to Virginia's 8th District. A one-term incumbent who had committed a major ethical transgression in the recent past, cast some difficult roll call votes during his first year, and appears to have a tendency to speak without thinking, could have encouraged many talented politicians of both parties to seek the nomination. A district that is home to many politically ambitious individuals and that could have provided them with easy access to the resources needed to wage a congressional campaign could have also produced a strong field of challengers.

What happened was markedly different—the strongest candidates decided to sit out the race. Moran was able to solidify his hold over the district long before the primary season even began as a result of his own efforts and those of some of his Democratic allies. First, Moran was highly successful in cultivating support from within his own party in the district. Potential Democratic challengers refused to contest the primary, saying they were biding their time until Moran retired or committed a major mistake. Others considered running in a different district or positioning themselves to run for some other office. Second, redistricting situated heavily Democratic areas of northern Virginia in the 8th District. This discouraged potentially strong GOP challengers from coming forward to contest the nomination. Third, Moran expanded his base of support during his first term in Congress, softened his image, and toned down his harsh rhetoric. Fourth, Moran began to build up his campaign war chest for 1992 almost immediately after the 1990 election. Fifth, Moran continued to take advantage of the considerable political expertise and consulting services available in the Washington area.

These factors, combined with personal and family considerations, discouraged challenges from within Moran's own party. They also combined with career concerns to discourage potentially strong Republican candidates from running for the seat. None came forward to take advantage of the rich political resources available in the local community or across the Potomac River in the nation's capital. Instead, only three lesser GOP candidates sought the opportunity to challenge Moran.

The experience of the 1992 congressional election in Virginia's 8th District has mixed implications for the roles of political ambition and political parties in candidate emergence. In the case of the Republicans, the party was too weak to encourage a number of strategically inclined politicians to turn down what appeared to be safe jobs in the Bush administration for a chance to run for the House. In the case of the Democrats, there was enough solidarity among local politicians for them to put the party's interests ahead of their own ambitions and to leave Moran unchallenged for the nomination.

The general discontent with government that was sweeping the nation may have encouraged an abundance of highly qualified challengers to run for Congress in 1992, and contributed to the election of 110 new House members, but this trend did not find its way to Virginia's 8th District. Representative Moran faced no competition for the Democratic nomination and faced only moderate opposition in the general election. It is a common story: an incumbent who narrowly won the first time out surged to a more comfortable victory as a sophomore. In the process, a once competitive seat becomes safe in the future. Most important, the self-fulfilling prophecy of incumbent invulnerability discourages potentially strong opposition in future elections.

Notes

1. Moran had stated publicly that he would support the resolution calling for force to be used to remove the Iraqis from Kuwait. After deciding, however, that U.S. casualties might be too high, he voted against the resolution. Moran's Gulf War vote was a discussion point for virtually all informants early in the interviewing process. However, once the primary season got under way the Gulf War issue no longer appeared to be as salient.
2. McSlarrow received contributions from a variety of sources. In addition to individual contributors, several influential political action committees (PACs) supported his candidacy, including the Free Congress PAC, National Right to Life PAC, Ruff PAC, and GOPAC. He also donated $15,000 of his own money to the campaign and collected $1,000 from both of his parents.

5

Vanishing Candidates in the 2nd District of Colorado

Allen D. Hertzke

Represented for three terms by Democratic incumbent David Skaggs, the 2nd District in Colorado was targeted by Republicans in 1992 as a seat they could capture with the right candidate and circumstances. Weakened by the House banking scandal and several local controversies, Skaggs appeared vulnerable at a time of increasing anti-incumbent sentiment. Moreover, state and national party officials targeted the district early, working with the Republican-controlled legislature to draw favorable new district boundaries and actively recruiting candidates on the basis of an ideal profile that emerged from polling.

In the end, however, none of the potential Republican candidates touted as the most competitive emerged to challenge Skaggs. Indeed, the two candidates who contested the Republican primary were not even among the twenty-five individuals mentioned at least once by district insiders as possible candidates. Moreover, the primary winner was a genuine political novice, a conservative Baptist minister who could not have been further from the party's "ideal profile." Though Reverend Brian Day ran a respectable general election race against Skaggs—in a campaign the *New York Times* depicted as an electoral test of the Religious Right (Clymer 1992)—the incumbent Democrat won handily with nearly 61 percent of the vote. Because the *Times* focused on the general election contest, it missed a number of key points. By examining the process of candidate emergence prior to the general election we can better understand why the Republican party offered a candidate so ill-fitted to the district.

The story of Republican candidate emergence in the 2nd District is a confusing tale of odd twists and turns, complete with a long redistricting fight, court edicts that took one candidate off the ballot, an aggressive but unsuccessful recruitment effort by the state party, a search for the "right women" candidates and a close, bitter primary that revealed deep divisions within the GOP over abortion. We can begin making sense of such diverse and seemingly idiosyncratic circumstances by focusing on the key problem that emerges in this study: the "vanishing candidates." Though a host of different reasons kept potentially strong candidates out of the hunt, they collectively point to a dilemma in what is clearly an unforgiving contemporary political environment. The real pool of viable candidates—those who combine the right mix of previous experience, conducive family situations,

Figure 5-1   Colorado, 2nd District

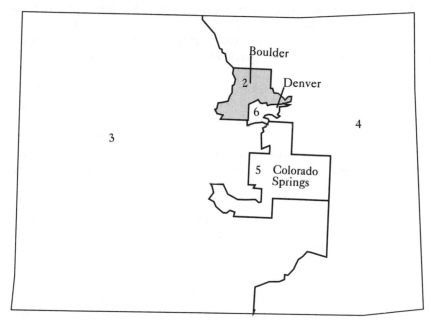

career flexibility, psychological makeups, and luck—is, in fact, inevitably very small. Competitive congressional elections, therefore, may depend on relatively rare and fortuitous circumstances.

Since competitive elections are at the heart of representative government, this dearth of candidates willing or able to make the run should cause us concern regardless of partisan loyalties. Thus if the narrative that follows conveys a sense of regret at the outcome, this should not be interpreted to imply that Skaggs did not deserve to be reelected, or that Day would not have been a worthy leader. Rather, this story of vanishing candidates is intended to offer a sober appraisal of a real dilemma in American politics today.

Colorado Political Geography and the 2nd District

A western spirit of independence is touted as a characteristic of Colorado politics, and the state's voters often send mixed political signals. For two decades the Democrats have owned the governor's office while Republicans dominated both houses of the state legislature. Colorado was also one of the first states in the nation to liberalize its abortion laws, yet it recently passed an anti-gay-rights measure that sparked a threatened boycott by Hollywood mavens of its storied ski resorts.

The state is also unique it its approach to party politics. Candidates for all offices are selected through a two-stage system that provides a role for both party insiders and the mass electorate. In order to be listed on the ballot for the primary, prospective candidates must gain threshold support (30 percent) of convention delegates selected through a system of precinct caucuses. One of the virtues of the Colorado system is that it weeds out less serious candidates. It is impossible, of course, for more than three candidates to gain the necessary 30 percent to be listed on the primary ballot, with two candidates far more likely. Moreover, a strong candidate has the potential of eliminating any primary opposition by keeping opponents below the threshold. The process for nominating congressional candidates begins in mid-April with precinct caucuses, followed by conventions at the end of May and party primaries in August.

The vast majority of Colorado's 3.3 million people live along the Front Range, a narrow corridor on the east slope of the Rocky Mountains that runs from Fort Collins in the north through Denver in the middle, and on to Colorado Springs in the south. Colorado's 2nd District lies right in the middle, encompassing all of Boulder County, portions of adjacent Denver suburbs in Adams and Jefferson counties, and two sparsely populated mountain counties just to the west of Boulder. The district is anchored by the city of Boulder, home of the University of Colorado (CU) and an upscale, well educated, and politically liberal citizenry. Alternative bookstores and vegetarian restaurants blend with expensive ski shops and clothing stores on the fabled downtown mall in Boulder, where guitar players still jam. Wealthy, hip, and politically correct to a fault, the city is home to the likes of Beat poet Allen Ginsberg and is decidedly inhospitable to conservative Republicans. Boulder enjoys a well deserved reputation for political liberalism, especially on social issues. It was one of the three Colorado municipalities to pass gay rights ordinances that were overturned in the much-publicized 1992 state referendum. A pro-choice position on abortion, moreover, is *de rigueur* for activists in both parties. Thus one could hardly imagine a candidate less suited to this town than 1992 Republican congressional nominee Day, an evangelical minister who abhors homosexuality and believes that the women's movement was deceived by the Devil into embracing abortion on demand.

Despite Boulder's strong Democratic tilt, the 2nd District is still viewed as one of the most competitive in the state. Beyond liberal Boulder the district shades Republican in the affluent Jefferson County suburbs west of Denver and among working-class ethnics in the towns of Longmont, Louisville, and Lafayette, where a fervent pro-life constituency coalesces. While the district also includes some working-class Democratic suburbs in Adams County north of Denver, redistricting reduced that population somewhat and added more residents of Republican Jefferson County, making the district slightly less favorable to Democrats.

Education is a major industry in the district, with CU's 20,000-plus students and 1,200 faculty. Successful candidates must be able to speak intelligently to education issues. But the district also has emerged "as a Rocky Mountain version of California's Silicon valley" (Duncan 1991). Large companies such as IBM, AT&T, Hewlett Packard, and Bell Aerospace operate major plants from Boulder to Longmont, producing a constituency for certain kinds of pro-business, entrepreneurial Republicanism.

For many years the district was represented by Tim Wirth, a "Watergate baby" elected in 1974 who typified the new class of entrepreneurial politicians that transformed Congress in the 1970s and 1980s. Through aggressive constituent service and campaigning Wirth kept his seat in what was clearly a competitive, swing district. Republican party leaders spoke with grudging admiration for the "Wirth Machine" that beat a number of strong Republican challengers. When Wirth vacated the seat in 1986 to run for the U.S. Senate, his protégé and former administrative assistant, Skaggs, was a natural choice to make the run. As a high school valedictorian, a captain in the U.S. Marine Corps in Vietnam, Yale Law School graduate, and three-term state legislator, Skaggs had excellent credentials. Moreover, he had the strong backing of Wirth's organization, now activated to support Wirth's U.S. Senate race. In his maiden congressional campaign Skaggs barely defeated Republican Mike Norton, who had run a tight race against Wirth in 1984. But by copying Wirth's pattern of assiduous constituent work, Skaggs breezed to victories in the next two elections. He enjoyed a moderate image, a loyal following in his home town of Boulder, and a district with a Democratic edge in voter registration.

By 1992, however, Skaggs was viewed by Republicans as the most vulnerable of the three incumbent Democrats in the Colorado delegation (both Pat Schroeder of Denver and Ben Nighthorse Campbell on the Western Slope were viewed as unbeatable). Steel workers at the Rocky Flats nuclear weapons facility were angry at Skaggs for his perceived role in allowing the plant, a huge employer in the district, to be phased out by the Department of Energy. Some Adams County officials held Skaggs partly responsible for their losing out in the competition with Denver for the new international airport. The extent of his vulnerability, however, was not revealed until late in the candidate emergence process. The issue that no one predicted, of course, was the House banking scandal. First reports suggested that Skaggs had bounced only a couple of checks. But then it was revealed in March that he was on record for fifty-seven overdrafts. Equally embarrassing, Skaggs had voted not to release all of the names of members who had bounced checks. Prospective Republican candidates also began criticizing his vote for the congressional pay raise and his "knee jerk" loyalty to the House Democratic leadership. Said one insider, "He has a moderate image, but whenever Speaker Foley says jump, he says how high."

All this baggage, some felt, would hurt Skaggs in a political year in which hostility toward conventional politicians was rising. Jerry Brown's protest candidacy, for example, received 47 percent of the presidential primary vote in Boulder, and Ross Perot's independent candidacy surged in the state. Clearly unpredictable forces were at play that gave reason for incumbents to run scared. Skaggs enjoyed a number of advantages, of course. He could raise huge sums of money as a member of the Appropriations Committee, and as an incumbent representative he could blanket the district with constituent mail. But Republicans felt that with the right kind of candidate they could tap the anti-incumbent mood and turn Skaggs's incumbent advantages against him. Surveys conducted by the party in the spring revealed a weakening favorability rating for Skaggs that the right candidate could exploit.

Just what the "right candidate" would be like was stated in remarkably specific terms by almost all party insiders. The ideal Republican to oppose Skaggs would be a moderate, well educated, pro-choice woman from Boulder with proven vote-getting capacity. Who better than a woman could represent unconventional politics in a year of disgust with politics as usual, the party professionals felt. Moreover, a pro-choice Republican woman could cut into Skaggs's Democratic stronghold in feminist Boulder, and would have broad appeal elsewhere (national polls in 1992 showed that voters saw women as more trustworthy and committed to domestic issues). Living in the 2nd District were a number of potential candidates who approximated the ideal profile. An unusual number of Republican women serve in elected positions in the state, a pool from which congressional candidates can be drawn. In 1992 women held 37 percent of the seats in the state house and 23 percent in the senate, with slightly more than half of them Republicans. Alan Ehrenhalt (1991) suggests two reasons for this strong female Republican presence. First, low pay for what amounts to a full-time job makes legislative representation, in some districts, "women's work." Many legislators are women whose husbands have jobs that enable them to campaign full-time and work for part-time wages. Second, well-educated women in the communities along the Front Range, many of them Republicans, form the backbone of voluntary community groups, parent-teacher associations, and party organizations. These women know their communities well and are natural campaigners in the suburban context.

Republicans thus began the election cycle with reason for optimism. They had a pool of potential candidates on which to draw, the year looked bad for incumbents, and redistricting might have given them a boost in the 2nd District. A big problem, however, was that the redistricting struggle dragged on so long that the race did not crystalize until very late in the spring, thus delaying the organizing required to unseat an incumbent. Redistricting, then, was the first major factor that figured into the calculations of prospective candidates and took some of them out of contention. It added more uncertainty to an already murky process for prospective candidates.

Redistricting Uncertainty

On the eve of the 1992 election, the Colorado delegation to the U.S. House of Representatives was split evenly, with each party holding three seats. The Republican-dominated state legislature sparred with Democratic Governor Roy Romer over redistricting plans. All of the early legislative proposals would have given the Republican party a strong advantage in five of the six districts, while leaving only the Denver district, held by Representative Schroeder, safely Democratic. Governor Romer blocked these redistricting attempts, producing court challenges and a protracted struggle between the branches.

Redistricting delayed the process for all candidates, but the various proposals had different impacts. For example, an early plan considered by the Republican legislature was viewed as a snub to Jason Lewis, who had run against Skaggs as the Republican nominee in 1990. Lewis, who won 39 percent of the vote against Skaggs, was thinking about running a second time and viewed redistricting as a tremendous opportunity to make the district more competitive. An early plan considered by the legislature, however, was drawn to include in the 2nd District the Western Slope town of Glenwood Springs, the home of Scott McInnis, popular state house majority leader.[1] Lewis viewed it as a direct snub to him as a potential candidate from the current district and felt that the Republicans had lost the opportunity to craft the district in such a way that would both seem reasonable and make it more competitive for the Republicans (which would have helped his candidacy).

Ultimately, however, Governor Romer and the legislature could not reach an agreement on any plan, and a court-appointed mediator had to be employed to negotiate the final map. That plan was not approved until mid-March, barely in time for county officials to prepare for April precinct caucuses. The 2nd District lines slightly reduced the Democratic advantage in registration from about 10,000 to about 4,000. But the Skaggs organization still viewed the result as highly favorable, in part because it belied the strong tendency of registered Independents in Boulder to vote Democratic. For risk-averse Republican candidates, therefore, needed redistricting advantages did not materialize.

Why They Did Not Run: A Catalog of the Vanishing Candidates

We have seen already how the politics of redistricting affected Lewis, and how uncertainty held others back. But redistricting per se did not emerge as a dominant influence in candidate calculations. A variety of other factors, such as electoral defeat, timing, and family considerations, kept potential candidates out of contention.

Cut Down: Potential Candidates Who Lost Lower Races

Several prominent political figures in the district apparently did not seriously consider a run for Congress. Three of them, it turned out, lost their own reelections for local or state legislative races in the fall, indicating that they had serious political liabilities that would have undermined a congressional bid. Most notable of these was Ted Strickland, Adams County state senator, president of the Colorado Senate, and two-time Republican nominee for governor. As leader of the Republican majority in the state senate, he would have been a formidable presence in any Republican primary, but never seriously considered it, according to those who know him. "Ted is beat up politically," according to Bruce Benson, state party chair, as a result of two bruising and unsuccessful gubernatorial races. Moreover, it would have been hard for him to "go back down" after running for governor and leading the state senate to become a first-time representative among 435 House members, and in the minority party at that. In 1992 redistricting hurt Strickland in his own state senate district, and with the accumulated baggage of years of battles, he lost in the general election.

Rich Ferdinanson, a commissioner from Jefferson County, was mentioned by a number of informants as ambitious for higher office. But he suffered from some bad personal publicity and he lost his reelection race. State Sen. Bonnie Allison from Jefferson County, whose name emerged along with other prominent women in the district, got caught in the undertow of the party's surging anti-abortion wing. Allison, a pro-choice legislator, was defeated in the Republican primary by a pro-life challenger, who then went on to lose to the Democrat in the general election.

These stories provide lessons in candidate viability. Any list of potential candidates for Congress will include those holding lower offices, but not all of them are "high quality individuals," as one party leader put it. Elected officials can bring baggage from previous battles, and they may be humanly arrogant, lazy, corrupt, or just plain tired. Thus the viable candidate pool shrinks.

Moreover, contemporary politics is terribly unforgiving. Republican former State Rep. Cathy Williams from Adams County was mentioned by several informants as a tough campaigner, and she might have been a contender in 1992. But in 1990 she lost her seat to the Democratic challenger. Though some urged her to run for Congress in 1992, it would have been difficult for her to make her case when she had lost at the lower level. Lynn Ellins, a liberal Republican and former CU regent, also was urged to run by some party people. Elected as a regent for the University of Colorado from the 2nd, he had shown himself a proven Republican vote-getter in a Democratic district. But Ellins lost his seat in a reelection bid. Once again, the loss may well be explained by bad circumstances in a given year, but it inevitably led to the retort, "He couldn't win his own regent seat in the District, how can he run for Congress?" There is also the case of David Leeds. Selected by the party committee to fill a vacated state senate seat in Boulder County, Leeds, then 34-years-old, was touted by some as an up-and-comer in the party, a person "grooming" himself for higher office.

Leeds mentioned that he had not ruled out the possibility of a run in 1994. But first, of course, he had to face the electorate in 1992, to be elected to his own term in the seat he inherited from the party insiders. Perhaps over confident, Leeds lost by a bare 377 votes out of nearly 45,000 cast in the general election.

Candidate Readiness: Not the Right Year

For some prospective candidates the timing was just not right. Michelle Lawrence, a state representative from Jefferson County, was mentioned as a possible candidate. But as a one-term representative she felt it was premature for her to make a bid for the seat—and unfair to her constituents. Feeling she needed more seasoning, she opted out of 1992, but then began planning for a run in 1994.

Ellins, a "Rockefeller Republican" from New York, also noted the role of timing: "Often when you are ready the political circumstances may not be right, and when the circumstances are right you may not be ready." Ellins had considered running in 1986 when it was an open seat, but that was not an option because the party "owed" Norton another shot at the seat after he "fell on the sword" against Wirth in 1984. Then in 1988 Ellins claimed that the nomination was "mine if I wanted it," but at the time he would have had to give up a lucrative job as counsel for J.C. Penneys in Denver to make the run. By 1992 Ellins had retired and was free to run when party people approached him, but he concluded that a successful race against Skaggs was highly unlikely and would be costly. "If Skaggs dropped out I'd be in there." The most pessimistic of all potential candidates interviewed, he recounted horror stories of the consequences of soft-headed political ambition. "I have seen a lot of people go into debt running in the 2nd District. . . . I know someone who went $60,000 in debt just for the primary." He estimated that it would take an incredible $2 million to run an effective race, twice the figure mentioned by anyone else. Before he took the plunge, he said, he would want to see "real negatives on Skaggs" in surveys. Consequently, the pattern of a risk-averse individual that emerges here is of a person who has just enough ambition to want to run under the best of circumstances, but not enough otherwise. Since the best of circumstances rarely converge for a given individual, such proclivities take one out of contention.

The claim of bad timing thus may belie a risk-averse individual who may never feel ready. Faye Flemming, a ten-year veteran of the state house, considered running, and in her case family considerations did not deter. Her children were grown and her family was supportive. But she evinced a strongly risk-averse makeup. Sounding a lot like Ellins, she was not convinced that Skaggs could be beaten and felt that it would take at least two years to accomplish the task plus $1 million in threshold funding. She also said she would consider a run against Skaggs in 1994 only if a thorough analysis of his record showed true vulnerability.

One individual who more clearly stressed the role of timing was Boulder County Commissioner Sandy Hume. Hume was viewed by party insiders as one of their most formidable candidates. A longtime resident of the district and former state senator, he stepped down halfway through his four-year senate term to run for the Commission (which, unlike the state senate, pays a decent wage). His race gained him a lot of stature because "he cleaned house" against an incumbent Democrat to become the only Republican on the commission. Moreover, since Boulder County comprises about 43 percent of the voting-age population in the 2nd District, Hume emerged as a proven vote-getter in nearly half of the district, and the most heavily Democratic portion at that.

But, primarily for family reasons, 1992 was not the right year for Hume. When asked why he did not run, he stated that his daughter was the first and last reason. Recently divorced, Hume held joint custody, along with his former wife Gwenne, of their 15-year-old daughter. He spoke of how he enjoyed a special relationship with his daughter, and just "couldn't do it"—run for Congress and threaten that relationship. Sandy Hume also spoke frankly about the pitfalls and challenges of running for Congress. He was concerned that a pro-choice candidate like him would have to spend $25,000 in the primary against a very committed group of right-to-life voters in the district. He noted how "you have to wreck your life" to run for Congress. Other informants speculated that if conditions had been more favorable, Sandy Hume might have overcome family considerations to make a race. But the important element for Sandy Hume himself was that he just was not ready in 1992. Though he said he would like to run for Congress someday, Sandy Hume acknowledged a hard political fact: "This was my year. Destiny works that way. . . . It may be that my time is passed."

Family: How Commitment to Children
May Keep Potential Candidates Out of Congress

As we saw with Sandy Hume, family considerations represent a major impediment to candidate availability. Cynics scoff that politicians are renowned for wanting to spend more time with their families when faced with imminent defeat at the polls. But in 1992 family concern emerged as a major reason why three of the top potential candidates chose not to run.

Of all the candidates recruited by state and national party officials, none was as sought-after as Gwenne Hume, former wife of Sandy Hume. Well educated (with a doctorate degree), pro-choice, and a proven vote-getter from Boulder County, she fit the ideal profile, as her former husband approvingly noted. But more than fitting some abstract profile, Gwenne Hume was viewed by many as the strongest possible candidate against Skaggs because she was a quality candidate, period. While Benson, state party chair, said that Sandy Hume *"could* have beaten Skaggs," he said that "Gwenne *would* have beaten Skaggs." Others referred to her as "smart," "attractive," and "the best." She describes herself as a New England Republican, libertarian on social issues but fiscally conservative—a combination party insiders thought would play well in the district. "A tenacious and committed campaigner," as one other candidate observed, she had served in the Colorado legislature from Boulder from 1976 to 1982, racking up large margins in a Democratic district. Her then-husband Sandy took the seat when she stepped down, and it is not implausible that each has helped maintain the other's name recognition. Though she has not served for a decade in the legislature, people still recognize her, refer to her as a state representative, and express great loyalty to her. A friend of Gwenne's campaigning in Longmont once told her that a voter asked pointedly, "Are you running against Gwenne Hume?" She speculated that she kept the high name recognition because she made an impression early on, and that because her husband has "a female sounding name" people associate the two of them. Though she never seriously considered running until 1992, she had been approached and urged to run "every two years" since 1976. She described the process thus:

> The morning it [the House banking scandal] broke about Skaggs, I told the guy at the front desk of my office building, "I'm so disgusted I'm going to run for Congress," and I called a couple of friends at the Capitol. And then supporters and party people said "have we got a deal for you."

Not only did Benson recruit her, but so did Kay Riddle of GOPAC, a national Republican organization. Gwenne Hume thought it would take $1 million to win, and wanted to know up front that at least $500,000 would be there. She was assured by various party committees that it would be. Her own analysis suggested that she could win bipartisan support, that there was a great level of frustration among voters over the ineffectiveness of government, and a considerable disenchantment with Skaggs. She conveyed that it was "as flattering as can be to be asked to run." Finally, she also was interested in running to check a faction of the Religious Right that she feared was threatening to take over the party.

With so much going for her, why did Gwenne Hume decide not to run? When asked, she walked over to her desk and picked up a photograph of her daughter. Her daughter was concerned about the prospect of her mother running for Congress, especially because a victory would have meant a disruption of the amicable joint custody her parents had worked out, and the prospect of long periods of separation from her mother. Gwenne Hume, picking her words carefully, tried to convey that it was not, as some friends and supporters thought, that she was letting her daughter run her life. Rather, it was that "this was the first significant pull between career and family I had faced. I knew that I would be pulled in both directions. So it wasn't just for my daughter, but it was for me too." Admitting there are moments when she wishes she had run, Gwenne Hume reflected that she was able to devote a lot of time to her daughter instead. "I was there when she came home from school," Gwenne said, a simple statement that eloquently expresses the poignant trade-offs of a political career. Like Sandy Hume, she expressed an awareness that while *she* might be ready two or four years in the future, the opportunity might have passed.

The other candidate who expressed clear family reasons for not running was Les Fowler, a former twenty-year-veteran of the state senate. Having recently retired from his insurance agency, the then 68-year-old Fowler was free to run in a way that he had not been before. Described as well liked and well known in the district, Fowler might have been able to mount a Perot-like attack on Skaggs, articulating his gruff disgust with professional politicians.

When asked why he did not run, he stated flatly that his "wife didn't want to go—that was the decisive factor." Still, he also expressed some hesitancy about the race from a strategic standpoint. Ideally, he felt, one should spend eighteen months running against an incumbent, not the eight or nine months he had available when recruited in the spring. He said the state party people were enthusiastic, but he was concerned about the short time frame, and wanted assurances that he would not go into debt. Thus he evinced an aversion to risk: "Those who say full speed ahead litter the road with bodies." Still, he said that he was willing to take the risk if not for his wife.

The Role of the State Party: Too Much Micromanagement?

In an era of weakening parties, Colorado presents what appears to be a contrary trend. All of the local party informants and all of the prospective candidates agreed that the state party played an aggressive role in recruitment. Indeed, not only did Benson, state party chair, actively seek candidates he viewed as strong, he actively discouraged those he felt were weak or not suited to the district. And he did so on the combined basis of his assessment of the district electorate and the candidate's strengths and weaknesses. This meant, in short, that he encouraged moderate candidates and discouraged conservative pro-life ones. Benson's active and powerful role, which critics describe as meddling, arises from his longevity and his role as a fund-raiser for candidates. Like his predecessor Bo Calloway, Bruce Benson served six years as state party chair, making him senior to all but two or three state chairs in the country. This longevity is especially useful in fund-raising and in making contacts with national party leaders and contributors. "What I represent is money." He spoke of running the state on a $3.5 million budget each election cycle, of personally raising hundreds of thousands of dollars for candidates, and of loosening up the purse strings of national party committees. Without this kind of state and national party support, congressional challengers cannot usually raise the threshold quarter of a million dollars or so necessary to make a credible race for Congress. Benson was the gatekeeper for this money, though he worked in tandem with such figures as Calloway, then national coordinator of GOPAC, who also played an active recruitment role. Thus when Benson told certain candidates that they were not right for the district, they had to take that judgment seriously as an indication that state and even national financial support would not be there. Thus, several ambitious individuals became "vanishing candidates" directly as a result of the state party's role.

One of those, as we have seen, was former congressional candidate Lewis. Lewis felt that the 40 percent base he built in 1990, if combined in 1992 with strong party support, would produce a viable second campaign. But the support was not there: "I had already started having coffees, but the party was cool." He stated flatly that if the party had been supportive he would have run. He understood that the party leaders' lack of support was the result of his political identity: he was a conservative from Jefferson County and did not fit their profile. But he took issue with the conventional thinking. As a young, "William F. Buckley conservative," Lewis argued that effective campaigns sharpen issues rather than blur them. The state party did not buy the argument.

Another individual who seriously considered running was Tom Tancredo, regional officer for the National Department of Education. A former state legislator, he served as a political appointee in the Reagan and Bush administrations in the Denver regional office of the federal government. Tancredo apparently was favored by some local party officials, and as late as the end of April was still considering a run. The decisive factor was a call from Benson. Aware that the party was sponsoring a poll of the district's voters, Tancredo had submitted earlier some questions relevant to his potential candidacy for Benson to include in the survey. As Tancredo recounted the story, Benson called him with the results of the poll. Sensing the bad news, Tancredo said "Let me guess, I can win if unopposed." Benson told Tancredo that the worst factor was that he was a ten-year federal bureaucrat. It did not matter, Benson noted, that as a political appointee Tancredo worked with Secretaries Bennett and Alexander to shake up the bureaucracy. To be a federal bureaucrat in 1992 was a serious liability, not to mention the fact that Tancredo was "male, conservative, and pro-life."

As is often the case, however, Tancredo had other reasons not to run. He expressed some relief that the numbers showed he could not win, noting that a life in the House would only be worthwhile as a stepping stone to the Senate. He spoke freely of the enormous sacrifices a congressional campaign entailed, and noted the loss of privacy, the threat to his job, and his wife's reticence. Moreover, he admitted that he never asked Benson to see the actual numbers, and he even speculated that "They may have told me that just to get me out." He harbored little resentment, however, stating that he had fulfilled his obligation to the party without sacrificing his family.

Although Tancredo was resigned, some local party officials resented Benson's role in dissuading him. One local official recalled a meeting toward the end of April in which the chairs of the five counties were to meet with Tancredo. But she ruefully noted that did not materialize when "Benson told him he did not fit the profile." That the "state party intruded as it did," she argued, "was wrong."

Benson remained unapologetic about his role in every candidate's ultimate decision making except one, the amazing case of the on-again, off-again, on-again recruitment of Jim Martin. With the district convention scheduled for late May, and with the only announced candidate the Reverend Day, state party efforts intensified in mid-April. By that time Sandy Hume, Gwenne Hume, Faye Flemming, Michelle Lawrence, Cathy Williams, Lynn Ellins, and Les Fowler, among others, had taken themselves out of the running. Candidates were vanishing fast and the party was threatened with a takeover by a candidate associated with the religious right. As the campaign manager for Sandy Hume's successful county commissioner race, Jim Martin, then a 42-year-old lawyer with high political aspirations, began to test the waters. A longtime resident of Boulder, Martin remembers having Washington political ambitions since high school, when he was student body president. As a professional he had worked for IBM, then owned his own business while returning to law school. Owning his own business, he suggested, gave him the flexibility to finally pursue his political aspirations. He first flirted with office in 1988 when he allowed his name to be put before the party's vacancy committee to fill Sandy Hume's senate seat. He lost to Leeds in that effort, in part because he "refused to sell out to the anti-abortion crowd." Decidedly on the liberal side of the party, he explored his options in 1992, considering a statewide race for regent of the University of Colorado. Because of that exploration, he was brought into contact with Kathy Arnold, executive director of the Colorado Republican party, and others at the state level. He was aware that the party was "out searching" and actively had recruited Sandy and Gwenne Hume in March. He was impressed that Benson was willing that early "to put state money behind Gwenne and money from Washington." He noted that "there was a lot more commitment early to her than any one else." When both she and Sandy dropped out, Martin was approached by Benson. "They knew of my interest for public office" because of the regent exploration.

Though the state was less committed to Jim Martin than Gwenne Hume, things heated up in the spring. As Martin recounts it, in mid-April he spent an intense two-week period lining up the necessary support for a congressional announcement. "During that two-week time frame it was like sitting at the control panels at Cape Kennedy and all the lights are turning green for go." Everything looked good, including his selection of a seasoned campaign manager, Carol Taylor-Little, a former state representative from Jefferson County. Taylor-Little had served eight years in the state house before stepping down and moving to Texas with her husband early in 1991. Her marriage broke up and she returned to the district in the spring of 1992. Martin said he met with Taylor-Little five times in preparation for an announcement of his congressional race. "So I was down to this last green light. We had prepared announcement plans with specific places in mind. Then at the end of April I called her and she said, 'Jim, I can't. . . . I think I want to run myself.' " Martin claims that he was convinced that she did not meet the residency requirements, having moved back into the district after the required sixty-day deadline prior to the mid-April precinct caucuses. He recalled saying, "Carol, I wasn't trying to preempt you. You didn't meet the residency requirements." Taylor-Little's response, according to Martin, was "We're re-looking at that."

This announcement struck Martin like a thunderbolt. "If she changed her mind, I thought, it represented a breach of trust by the state party." While courting him they simultaneously had undercut his bid by recruiting Taylor-Little. Martin fumed for a week, concerned about the commitment of the state party. Then the state party executive committee met and decided that Taylor-Little's candidacy could pass muster, contrary to the advice of Republican Colorado Secretary of State Natalie Meyer. "I'd read the statute and I knew no way. This was the second message from the state party that they gave their blessing" to Taylor-Little. But Martin acknowledged his own role: by working with Taylor-Little, he felt he probably "got her enthusiastically involved. Gave her a new sense of possibility."

The party may have cooled to Martin in part because of a news story appearing in Boulder on April 14. Martin was quoted as saying that "David Skaggs is a noble individual with a lot integrity, but we need new people who can get results in Washington" (Pochna 1992). This statement was flagged by an employee in the state Republican party office and sent to Benson, who was concerned about the potential use of such a statement in a campaign against an incumbent who had overdrawn his House checking account. Martin claimed that he knew what he was doing. "I try to elevate the electoral process to as high a level as possible. Knowing Skaggs's constituency, I wasn't going to take him on personally. I wasn't going to use the check writing scandal as a challenge to his integrity. I was not going to attack his integrity." Told by Benson that he was not to make such statements in the future, Martin blew up and said he would say what he wanted to say. "I won't be censored."

Smarting from the rebuff by the state party, Martin decided to plan his response. "I knew they would draft me because Carol Taylor-Little could not get on the ballot." So, Martin "outfoxed them" by announcing his candidacy for the regent's seat—which he went on to win—the day before Meyer ruled that Taylor-Little was ineligible, sparking a month-and-a-half legal battle in both state and federal courts. Before the battle was over,

Taylor-Little had dropped out of the race, then reentered on the eve of the district convention, then dropped out again. In the meantime, state party officials came back to Martin, as he predicted, and tried to draft him: "After Taylor-Little was disqualified [by a state judge affirming Meyer's decision], they came back to me the day before the convention," on May 28. National party people were in town for the district and state conventions, so Martin was invited to a hotel room to discuss the race. "Draft Martin" stickers had been printed, and the delegation included Dick Bond and Robert Mosbacher of the Republican National Committee, Kay Riddle and Bo Calloway of GOPAC, along with Bruce Benson and Kathy Arnold of the state party. Dick Bond told a poignant story of how George Bush and he visited Lee Atwater on his death bed, and Atwater made the plea to Bush, "Make Bond the Chair." Bush selected William Bennett instead, and Bond left Washington to start a new life, hurt and dejected. But he related how he got a call late one night to take over the party. "I wasn't the number one pick. I knew that." The moral of the story was that Martin should accept that they had made a mistake and run. Though flattered, Martin ultimately decided against it, criticizing the "micromanagement" of district recruitment by Benson. Benson himself admitted that he made a mistake in initially abandoning Martin for Taylor-Little. But he claims that his lawyers cited precedents that would allow the state party to decide if Taylor-Little met their criteria. Given her strong credentials, he and others felt that she was worth the risk.

The "Right Woman" Hits a New Glass Ceiling

Though we explored earlier how family considerations implode on congressional ambition, the story of Taylor-Little's candidacy illustrates as well the cost of mobility. As a veteran state legislator from Arvada with a number of awards to her credit, and as a pro-choice, moderate woman, Taylor-Little looked like the closest thing to the "ideal profile" available to the party in May. She burst on the scene with a flurry of favorable publicity, including laudatory columns in the *Denver Post*. A longtime resident of the district, she was aware of the possibilities that might open up to her in what was being dubbed the "Year of the Woman." Moreover, her time was right. She had considered running four years earlier, but was convinced that if she won the seat she would lose her marriage and jeapordize her family. In 1992, however, her children were grown, and she was divorced. Most important in her decision to run, though, was the fact that she is a personal crusader who thrives on politics and public policy issues.

Yet, as one *Denver Post* columnist put it, "she hit the new glass ceiling" that faces a woman who follows her husband to a new state (Ewegen 1992). Had Taylor-Little not moved to Texas, she would have had no difficulty meeting eligibility requirements and would likely have won the Republican House nomination. She was a quality candidate in the right district at the right time, and had well-placed friends: Bruce Benson pushed her nomination, as did Joe Coors of the fabled brewery family, who signed on to serve as fund-raising chair and made the nominating speech for her at the convention. Although she was a victim, perhaps, of what one insider called "bad legal advice," Taylor-Little would not have been in that position had she not put family considerations first and moved out of the district.

Taylor-Little initially had dropped out of the race after a ruling that she was ineligible by the secretary of state was upheld in state court. In a last minute search for an alternative to Day, Benson called Taylor-Little on the eve of the district convention, imploring her to reconsider. Having been given fresh assurances by party lawyers that they would take the case to federal court this time, she arrived at the convention with no literature, after calling as many of her delegates as possible the night before to urge them to attend. In spite of these adverse circumstances, she captured 44 percent of the vote to Day's 50 percent, apparently earning a place on the primary ballot. However, her candidacy ended for good in mid-June when a federal court upheld the ruling of the secretary of state: Taylor-Little indeed was ineligible to run in the 2nd District.

This did not end the search for the right candidate, however, and for a change the local party took the initiative. The Republican Executive Committee of the 2nd District met to designate a candidate to replace Taylor-Little, a move Day argued was unnecessary because the party had a candidate on the ballot—him. But the nine members of the committee ignored him and selected one of their own county chairs, Sharon Klusman, who lacked the name recognition of Gwenne Hume or Carol Taylor-Little, but was willing to run against Brian Day.

Why Did Brian Day Capture the Nomination?

The Reverend Day must have felt like an unwelcome relative at a family reunion. He watched as both state and local party officials engaged in frantic, down-to-the wire efforts to recruit an alternative to his candidacy. Incredulous party leaders just could not imagine a conservative Baptist minister as their nominee. Thus when Representative Skaggs earlier told Martin he would love to run against Day, Martin retorted, "There's no way we [Republicans] would do that!"

Yet Day went on to win the primary by a razor-thin margin against Klusman. Why did Skaggs get his wish? One reason is that Day, unlike so many erstwhile candidates, was simply willing to run. Part of that willingness stemmed from the self-confidence of an entrepreneurial minister. He started his current parish (800 members in 1992) in his living room, and he developed his own local religious television program. Day also felt relatively unencumbered. He did not have to resign to run, his family was used to shifts in their fortunes, and he viewed public service as flowing from his ministerial role. But faced with such strong opposition among party leaders, Day also demonstrated a boldness and uncalculating ambition derived from a simple motive: deep conviction. Day recalled that since high school he has entertained the idea of running for Congress. But what propelled him were his passionate views about abortion, the state of American culture, and the federal debt. He interpreted his political foray as a calling from God.

But Day did not capture the Republican nomination entirely by default. Klusman ran a vigorous primary campaign against him. Day overcame her challenge because he activated a strong local right-to-life network, along with a resurgent Christian conservative political movement led by Pat Robertson's Christian Coalition, which actively supported him. While Klusman blasted Day's anti-abortion position on the radio, right-to-life forces blanketed the churches in the district with flyers on the Sunday before the primary. Thus Day's candidacy represents another manifestation of the cultural division in the GOP between establishment Republicans and insurgent religious conservatives. The Religious Right will retain its clout in the Republican party, however, because it combines two attributes of a social movement: (1) its members are highly motivated by their deep discontent with the status quo; and (2) they increasingly have resources— money, education, church networks—to channel that energy and commitment (Hertzke 1993). Day's candidacy, therefore, foreshadows a changing blend in the Republican candidate pool. Animated by a sense of cultural crisis, other Christian conservatives will run for office, and some are likely to prevail in districts more hospitable than Colorado's 2nd.

In the general election, Day ran an unexpectedly aggressive and creative campaign, one that deemphasized abortion. When asked if he was a one-issue candidate he responded, "Yes, the Congress is broke and it needs to be fixed." He hammered away at the deficit, the debt, and the mortgaging of the children's future. State and national party officials were impressed enough to invest real money in his long-shot candidacy. *Congressional Quarterly Weekly Report* declared the race a competitive one in September, and the *New York Times* featured an article on it in the fall. With all this attention Day and his backers began to feel confidence that they actually could win against Skaggs. They probably only had a prayer. Benson said he told Day, "You would be a good candidate in Colorado Springs, but not in Boulder." He was probably right. But Benson suspected that the abortion issue alone did not doom Day's candidacy. Rather, he suspected that many voters in the 2nd District were not ready to elect a minister to Congress. In November Day garnered only 32 percent of the vote to Skaggs's 61 percent, while the remaining 7 percent went to an independent candidate and a Perot-follower, Vern Tharp. The late emergence of a third-party candidate seemed a fitting cap to a crazy season.

Summary Lessons

Contrary to the large number of potential candidates that may be listed for a congressional district, the realistic pool is extremely small, diminished by family concerns, risk-averse behavior, and career considerations.

In their fine book on political ambition, Linda Fowler and Robert McClure (1989) noted how a multitude of reasons kept otherwise viable people out of a congressional race. In Colorado's 2nd District we also see how family factors, bad timing, miscalculations, satisfaction with current positions, lack of complete information, and lack of party support all combine to winnow the field. But the pattern we witnessed in the 2nd District cries out for more general lessons. What does it mean when not one of the prominent figures chooses to run for Congress? What does it portend for representative government?

Fowler and McClure hinted at these problems, but they ended without fully addressing two possibilities: (1) that ambition alone may not be sufficient to ensure competitive elections, especially since calculating ambition plays the odds and thus may be lacking in some years; and (2) that political representation is affected by the kind of people who can or will make the run. What was lacking in the 2nd District perhaps was not ambition per se (several "vanishing candidates" nursed strong ambitions), but a rarer kind of driving ambition willing to take enormous risks, even to the point of jeopardizing loved ones. I am led to believe, consequently, that in our unforgiving candidate-centered environment, many politicians who decide not to run may be more balanced, thoughtful, and rooted than those who have the driven single-mindedness required of congressional candidates.

Our polity indeed might benefit from the different perspective—the leaven if you will—provided by such people as Gwenne Hume, who stepped away from a possible congressional seat for the sake of her daughter. Such perspectives do not receive full representation in Congress because the people who could represent them do not get there. The perspective disenfranchises itself. One might have the same complaint about the host of White House aides, congressional staff members, and lobbyists, many of whom lead lives detached from the real-world problems of parents, children, and neighborhoods. By circumstance, those who are willing to forgo glory for their children or their local communities are underrepresented in the halls of power. To an extent, of course, all this is merely the human condition. But that should not deter us from exploring those impediments to candidacy that exaggerate the problem. What kind of person becomes a successful candidate? Perhaps a person less like the rest of us than we think or hope.

Note

1. It is ironic that the Republicans did not know at the time that Democratic Representative Campbell would jump into the U.S. Senate race (with Wirth's decision not to run for reelection), leaving the Western Slope seat open. McInnis was thus able to make a run for Congress in the 3rd District, gaining a seat for the Republicans and producing a 4 to 2 edge in the 103rd Congress.

6

Challenging a "Safe" Incumbent: Latent Competition in North Carolina's 9th District

Thomas A. Kazee and Susan L. Roberts

North Carolina's 9th Congressional District is typical of many districts around the country. It is represented by a popular incumbent who seems to have little serious opposition in the district. Even in the midst of the apparent anti-incumbent fervor of the 1991-1992 election cycle, in which the *Charlotte Observer* carried as standard fare interviews with citizens "who had lost faith in politicians," most voters in the district had not lost faith in J. Alex McMillan (Funk and Morell 1992). Indeed, when asked in October 1992 by the *Charlotte Observer* whether they would "vote against someone mainly because he or she is a current member of Congress," 60 percent of those polled responded "not likely"; only 16 percent said it was "very likely" they would do so (Funk and Morell 1992).

Despite the absence of an inviting electoral environment, however, the pool of quality candidates, both Democratic and Republican, was surprisingly deep and ambitions were deceptively muted. Numerous potential candidates, many of whom had previous elected experience, kept an eye on McMillan's House seat. As our interviews revealed, this is a district rich in latent competition.

The Political Geography of the 9th District

State legislators and politicians frequently call Charlotte and its environs "The Great State of Mecklenburg," referring to the preeminence of Charlotte, in the county of Mecklenburg, in population, prosperity, and economic growth compared with the rest of the state. The 9th District has been dominated by Mecklenburg County since the 91st Congress. Following the 1980 census, 75 percent of the district's population came from Mecklenburg County. Iredell County, Lincoln County, and parts of Yadkin County composed the remainder of the district. The 9th District has voted Republican in presidential elections since 1980, with the district voting overwhelmingly for Ronald Reagan in 1984 (65 percent) and George Bush in 1988 (61 percent). In 1992 Bush (43.5 percent) narrowly defeated Bill Clinton (42.7 percent) in the three-way race with Ross Perot (13.6 percent). Mecklenburg County experienced a record turnout, topping by 59,000 votes a record set in 1988.

Since 1952 voters in the 9th District have elected Republicans to Congress. Charles Jonas served from 1952 to 1972, winning percentages ranging from 52 percent to 72 percent during his ten elections and running without opposition in 1970. James Martin, a chemistry professor and former member of the Mecklenburg County Commission, succeeded Jonas in 1972 and served until 1984. He won his first term with 59 percent of the vote and defended his seat five times against a series of undistinguished challengers.

In 1983, Martin declared his intention to run for the governorship, triggering high-profile congressional primary fights in both parties. Two prominent Republicans, Harris-Teeter supermarket executive J. Alex Mc-Millan and local conservative activist Carl Horn, III, vigorously sought their party's nomination. McMillan won the primary by 58 percent to 42 percent. On the Democratic side three attractive would-be nominees emerged: Susan Green, a neighborhood activist and Mecklenburg county commissioner; Ben Tyson, a member of the North Carolina House of Representatives; and D. G. Martin (no relation to the incumbent), a prominent local attorney and community activist. Green finished first and Martin finished second in the primary, setting up a runoff for the nomination. Martin won the nomination, and subsequently lost to McMillan in the general election by only 321 votes. The amount spent by the candidates in the open seat race was nearly as even as the outcome: Martin (who made a campaign issue of his refusal to accept contributions from political action committees) spent $686,495; McMillan spent $686,247. McMillan faced Martin again in 1986, with McMillan—despite losing the city of Charlotte—winning 51 percent of the district-wide vote. He has not faced significant opposition since then, winning in 1988 and 1990 against little known and underfinanced Democratic challengers.

McMillan's opponent in 1992, pharmacist Rory Blake, was perhaps even less well connected politically than his Democratic predecessors. The absence of a serious challenge to McMillan in 1992 was underscored by the *Charlotte Observer* when the newspaper endorsed McMillan in the 9th District, while also endorsing incumbent Democrats Bill Hefner for the 8th District and Mel Watt for the newly created 12th District. The paper's editors noted that "party is always a factor in congressional elections, and we endorsed the Democratic presidential nominee. But while Mr. Blake carries the party standard, he's not prepared for Congress" (*Charlotte Observer* 1992). The McMillan-Blake contest received virtually no attention from the local press or media. McMillan outpaced Blake in campaign receipts almost 35 to 1. Neither candidate purchased television advertising. With heavy turnout in Mecklenburg County as well as the remainder of the 9th District, McMillan easily defeated Blake 66 percent to 34 percent.

The Political Environment of the 9th District

As a boom town in the past several decades, Charlotte has seen the influx of newcomers both from inside and outside the state. As a result, the

Figure 6-1   North Carolina, 9th District

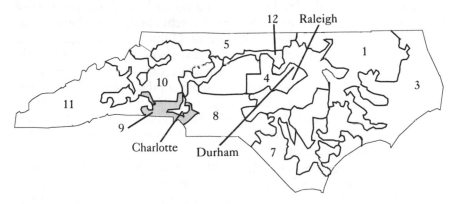

community of political activists includes young and old, male and female, liberal and conservative, black and white. Liz Hair, longtime Democratic activist and former county commissioner, said, "Charlotte is ready to accept newcomers who want to achieve." Michael Daisley, frequently mentioned as a "comer" and potential congressional candidate, echoed this sentiment, emphasizing that "if you want to get involved, people will pull you in. No one cares that I didn't go to Country Day" (Charlotte's leading private school). Rod Autrey, former member of the Board of County Commissioners and a potential Republican congressional candidate, described Charlotte and the 9th District as "a Camelot cocoon . . . where we are still more interested in visions of Camelot, of what could be right about this place." Mayor Richard Vinroot characterized the district as an "open meritocracy" and "a community of doers."

One perceived requirement of viable candidates reverberated throughout our interviews: a demonstration of commitment to visible and energetic community service. Luther Moore, long associated with local Democratic party affairs, said that an ideal candidate would have extensive community involvement: "you have to be 'out there.' " Peter Keber, a Republican activist and former member of the Board of County Commissioners stated, "this town really revolves around community service. It's the mark of a member of the 'in crowd' instead of a 'good ole boy' or party network." Carla DuPuy, also a former member of the Board of County Commissioners and frequently mentioned as a potential Republican congressional candidate, views Charlotte's civic priority as somewhat unique, with community service as "the mark of being able to deal with both parties."

Given the preeminence of Charlotte as a center of commerce and banking, it is not surprising that several interviewees suggested that acceptability to the Charlotte business community was essential. Ray Farris, a Charlotte attorney, told us that a strong candidate must be "a successful professional or business person . . . you have to represent business." Farris,

Moore, and several other interviewees noted that someone considering running for Congress in the 9th District would do well to call on members of the prominent business elite such as Ed Crutchfield of First Union Bank, Hugh McColl of NationsBank, Bill Lee of Duke Power Company, and John Belk of Belk Department Stores. These people appear to play little role in candidate recruitment, but prospective candidates must measure their support, if for no other reason than to ensure that their wealth will not be used to support an opponent. Other interviewees said that a strong candidate must be acceptable to southeast Charlotte, an area of upper-middle-class and wealthy Charlotteans, to whom one would presumably look for funds to run a campaign.

Finally, the 9th District of the 1980s had an additional characteristic that has been minimized in the redistricted 9th of 1992—the necessity of strong ties to the black community. Though a white candidate, D. G. Martin's nearly successful run in 1984 owed much to his support from African American voters in the district; his high profile and popularity in the black community was largely a result of his work with local black churches.

The New 9th and the Newer 12th: The 1992 Redistricting Struggle

The 1990 census resulted in an additional district for North Carolina, and the U.S. Department of Justice made it clear that the new congressional district map produced by the state legislature must reflect the 22 percent black population of the state. An initial congressional districting map drew favorable comments from many Democrats in the old 9th District because it removed from the district a number of areas outside Mecklenburg County. Indeed, Democrat Martin won a majority in his race against McMillan in the areas of the old 9th that were placed in the redistricted 9th; this map, however, which created a black majority district in the eastern part of the state, was thrown out by the Justice Department because it said it should have included a second black majority district.

The Democratic-dominated legislature, after much delay and Republican criticism, produced a new map that created a second black majority district by piecing together black neighborhoods running from the Raleigh-Durham area in the north central part of the state to the Charlotte-Gastonia area in the southwestern part of the state. After its final approval, the second black majority district attracted national attention. The *Wall Street Journal* (1992) labeled the map "political pornography," describing the district as "a long snake that winds its way through central North Carolina for 190 miles, from Durham to Charlotte, scooping up isolated precincts with nothing in common save a large number of minority voters." The newly created 12th District was dubbed "the I-85 District" because it followed the interstate highway, at some points no wider that the highway itself. In June of 1993, the Supreme Court considered the 12th District in the case of *Shaw v. Reno;* the 5 to 4 decision found that majority and minority districts drawn with little regard for any factor other than race may be unconstitutional, remanding the case to the district court for further consideration.[1]

Though the new map helped Democrats across the state by adding two new majority black districts, it helped McMillan by removing areas of the district, particularly in inner-city Charlotte, that previously had voted for Democratic House candidates. Daisley commented that it would not have surprised him if no Democrat had run in 1992; Hair said the district had become "more Republican by a mile." Only Blake, the pharmacist who filed for the Democratic House nomination, contested the conclusion that the newly drawn 9th District gave incumbent McMillan a virtual lock on the seat.

The new 12th District opened up attractive opportunities for a host of black candidates from Mecklenburg. Indeed, one of the most well known and highly regarded Mecklenburg County Democratic activists, Mel Watt (who managed the Senate campaign of Harvey Gantt in 1990) won the 12th District party nomination and easily defeated Republican Barbara Gore Washington, 72 percent to 28 percent. In the plan of the 9th District that was thrown out by the Justice Department, Watt—and several other prominent black politicians—would have been potentially attractive candidates. As the district is drawn now, the pool of prospective candidates in the current 9th District includes only three black activists.

The Democratic Pool of Candidates

Despite the Republican dominated electoral history of the 9th District, the names of forty Democrats were mentioned as potential candidates by those we interviewed. Twenty-two names were mentioned only once; it seems clear that some of the respondents were developing "wish lists" as much as identifying individuals who have indicated an interest in candidacy. For example, John Murphy—appointed several years ago to the high-profile post of superintendent of schools for Charlotte-Mecklenburg—was named by one respondent as an attractive future possibility despite being a newcomer with no stated political ambitions. Others on the list include the president of a local college, a prominent local banker, and an import/export businessperson. This is an "amateur" group to be sure (Canon 1990a); indeed, when asked about the individual involved in the import/export business, one of the most knowledgeable informants responded, "Who is he? Is he a Democrat?"

The biggest fish in the Democratic pool, it seems, are six individuals who received five or more mentions from the respondents. Five of the six have previously run for or held office; the sixth, a local attorney, has never run for public office but has been involved in district politics for almost ten years.

The most frequently mentioned potential candidate is Fountain Odom, a senator in the North Carolina legislature. Ten interviewees suggested Odom in response to one or more of the questions about potential candidates in the district. Six respondents suggested that Odom would run if McMillan decided not to seek reelection. Five respondents said they would like to see him run for the seat.[2] Republican informants referred to Odom as "the best of the Democratic candidates," adding the caveat that it would be "an uphill battle" with the newly redrawn 9th District. Another Republican informant stated succinctly of Odom: "viable candidate but couldn't win."

D. G. Martin, Parks Helms, and Mike Daisley were mentioned by six respondents. Martin has run for the House seat twice against McMillan, losing narrowly in 1984 and by several thousand votes in 1986. Martin is currently a legislative liaison for the North Carolina state university system and no longer lives in the district, though he retains close ties to it. Martin's name surfaced several times as an ideal candidate for the 9th District, but only one respondent indicated that Martin might return to run if Representative McMillan left his seat.

Parks Helms is an attorney in the district with an extensive history of local political involvement. He served ten years in the North Carolina House of Representatives and recently was elected with the highest vote total for one of the three at-large seats on the Mecklenburg County Commission—a high-profile position viewed by many district political watchers as a natural rung on the ladder to higher office. One Republican informant suggested that Helms had "run for county commission as a stepping stone for the congressional nomination." Five of those who mentioned Helms said they would like to see him run for Congress.

Mike Daisley is also an attorney (in the same Charlotte firm as Odom) who has been involved both as a candidate recruiter and as a candidate recruited by others in 1990 to challenge McMillan. He demurred at that time, and as one respondent said, Daisley is "attractive, photogenic, has paid his dues, and has congressional ambitions, but he is a cautious guy." Daisley's name was mentioned in response to seven of the eight pool questions; perhaps it is significant that only one respondent suggested they would like to see Daisley run, though three interviewees mentioned him as someone apparently grooming himself for a congressional race. No other individual in either party received as many "grooming" references.

Two potential candidates, both women, were mentioned by five of the interviewees. Martha Alexander, who until recently had never held elective office, is a member of the state legislature and the executive director of the Charlotte Council on Alcohol and Chemical Dependency. Winning the Democratic primary against well known Charlotte attorney Sydnor Thompson, Alexander faced no Republican challenger in her bid for state representative. Four of the five people naming Alexander encouraged her candidacy. Also receiving five mentions was Cyndee Patterson, a Mecklenburg county commissioner and one-time leading vote-getter for the commission, an honor that resulted in her selection as the commission's mayor pro tem. Patterson was described by one respondent as an ideal candidate with a strong likelihood to run should McMillan vacate the seat. According to one Republican informant, "the only way a Democrat could win would be with a woman with a strong community focus and she [Patterson] has this."

Six other individuals received three or four mentions, including Harvey Gantt, former Charlotte mayor and unsuccessful U.S. Senate candidate (against Jesse Helms) in 1990; Liz Hair, a former county commissioner now in her seventies; Ray Farris, Charlotte attorney; and Leslie Winner, a liberal local attorney who served as legislative counsel for the state redistricting committee. Winner recently was elected to her first term in the North Carolina Senate, garnering 60 percent of the vote.

Perhaps the most distinctive feature of the pool of potential Democratic candidates is its extensive level of political experience. Using Canon's distinction between amateurs and experienced candidates (Canon 1990a, 165-166)—"experienced" is defined as having held prior elective office— the 9th District Democratic pool includes sixteen experienced candidates and twenty-three amateurs. Many of the amateurs, however, have run for public office before. Five amateurs ran for area offices in November 1992 (three have had earlier unsuccessful races), with two pairs of amateurs contesting one another for Democratic nominations for two local posts; both winning amateurs went on to win the general election. Another three candidates in the amateur category have run and lost in previous years. Only fifteen of the forty individuals in the pool, in sum, could be classified as pure amateurs, highlighting the wealth of Democratic talent in a historically Republican dominated congressional seat.

The Republican Pool of Candidates

Democrats and Republicans alike readily acknowledge the lock that both the incumbent McMillan and the Republican party has had on the 9th District. We asked each informant and potential candidate to identify Republicans who might seek the House seat if the incumbent retires. No interviewee suggested that Representative McMillan would face a serious challenge for the Republican nomination. Only if he were to retire or run for higher office—a possibility which became a reality in 1994—did it appear likely that other Republicans would reveal congressional ambitions. One informant did mention, however, that the only way to beat McMillan would be to run a strong, pro-choice Republican woman against him.

Twenty-four Republicans were mentioned as potential House candidates, an impressive figure given the presence of a secure incumbent. The list includes three former members of the Mecklenburg County Commission, Charlotte's incumbent mayor and the major who preceded him, three local well known state legislators, a district court judge, a U.S. attorney, and several Charlotte attorneys. It is a virtual list of "Who's Who" of area Republicans, perhaps not surprising given the four-decade-long party control of the seat.

Most frequently mentioned as a potential candidate was former Mecklenburg County Commissioner Carla DuPuy. Fifteen interviewees identified her as a potential House candidate; in fact, four people (more mentions than for any other Republican) suggested that she is grooming herself for congressional candidacy. Richard Vinroot, Charlotte's current mayor and a former basketball player at the University of North Carolina, was mentioned ten times—with several interviewees contending that he would make "an ideal candidate." Vinroot was viewed as an especially formidable candidate, with several of the potential Republican candidates reluctant to challenge Vinroot in any potential primary for the House seat.

Rod Autrey, an at-large county commissioner until his defeat in 1992, was mentioned by nine respondents, with several suggesting that he was grooming himself for candidacy. Five of the respondents simply said they thought it was likely that Autrey would run if the incumbent retired, with some expressing uncertainty over what Autrey's recent electoral loss would do to his future political viability. Another at-large county commissioner who lost in the 1992 election, Peter Keber, was mentioned four times. Jerry Blackman, a state legislator with name recognition, also was mentioned four times.

Like the pool of potential Democratic candidates, the Republican pool is rich with experienced and high-visibility prospects. Of the twenty-four Republicans mentioned, only nine of the potential candidates could be classified as amateurs. It can be argued that as the occasion to seek the Republican nomination for the House of Representatives never presented itself (until 1994), politically ambitious Republicans found other ways to channel their zeal for public service.

Context, Ambition, and the Decision to Run

Potential Democratic as well as Republican House challengers in the 9th District were affected most profoundly (and understandably) by the presence of a strong incumbent and a new district map that entrenched him even more securely than ever. Indeed, a year before the campaign the district might have appeared winnable for the Democrats. McMillan's name was mentioned as a candidate for statewide office; the governorship was opening up and a Senate seat held by a relatively weak Democratic incumbent was to be defended in 1992. The Republicans had won the two most recent gubernatorial elections and Senator Helms had shown repeatedly that a Republican Senate candidate could win in North Carolina. If the state legislature had left the 9th District untouched during the redistricting process or had redrawn the map to weaken the Republicans, a number of quality Democrats would have seriously considered entering the race. If the

1984 Democratic primary is an indication, a spirited fight among several Democrats might have resulted. That such a contest did not materialize, especially given the wealth of the candidate pool, is a measure of the critical importance of incumbency and districting. The interviews suggest that other factors—such as the large amount of money necessary to run— would not have kept some of the prominent Democrats out of the race.

The Competitive Context: Incumbency

For potential Republican candidates, there was unanimity of opinion that the seat belonged to McMillan "as long as he wants it." With the redistricting and the move of the heaviest concentration of black voters to the 12th District has come a confidence on the part of Republicans that the 9th District will continue to be represented by their party even if McMillan decides to retire or seek other office.

The ability of the incumbent to discourage potentially strong opposition is certainly not surprising (Kazee 1983), even though many of the Democrats interviewed argued that McMillan lacks charisma and a "common touch" with the district. Louise Brennan, a prominent local Democratic activist, described him as "relatively stand-offish in his personal relations ... he needs to be more in touch." Despite the fact that several respondents viewed McMillan as relatively shy for a politician, there was a widespread consensus that he has done an effective job of avoiding controversy and cultivating a generally positive image in the district. Brennan said that "his strength is that he looks like a congressman." Alexander told us that McMillan was "too well respected ... people like him. . . . He hasn't done enough wrong." Hair, while also using the term "stand-offish" to describe McMillan, nevertheless said that he would not attract serious opposition as long as he stayed in office:

> Alex is a remarkably good congressman for a Republican. His manner is too patrician, and his voting record is bad on some issues, but he doesn't have that many liabilities. He wife is attractive and takes to politics. He is from an old Charlotte family. . . . He has learned to be more helpful to constituents. His issues are more thought out. . . .

One potential challenger assessed his own assets and liabilities and those of the incumbent and declared:

> I'd give Alex a hell of a race—he wouldn't know what hit him. He'd have trouble with me, but he'd beat me—53-47, perhaps, but that would be a waste of time. Why run if you can't win?

Only Blake, the one individual who decided to run against McMillan, came to a different conclusion:

> On the surface he looks like someone who would be very hard to beat, but he hasn't done anything ... he's so out of touch. . . . Redistricting

affected my decision to run. We've taken in areas that I'm better known in, though I hate that they've taken away the black vote. . . . The logical outcome is for us to win.

Thompson, the most active recruiter of Democratic House candidates, reiterated the common sentiment: "Alex is not very vulnerable, if we're realistic."

Resource Obstacles

After incumbency and redistricting the contextual factor most important was campaign financing, with noticeable differences in the responses from Democrats and Republicans. While all respondents were cognizant of the resource challenge a congressional race presents, Republicans viewed fund-raising for an inevitable primary as the chief obstacle; otherwise the potential Republican candidates were confident of sufficient funds for the general election. Three of the potential candidates estimated a general election cost of $1 million or more. Only two interviewees projected a general election cost of less than $500,000. Two respondents were reluctant to give a precise figure, suggesting a range with a lower limit of as little as $100,000. This is an unrealistic figure in light of the district's spending history (approximately $1.5 million was spent in 1984) and McMillan's apparent ability to raise spending levels to meet any serious challenge. One interviewee, recognizing the difficulty of raising such sums, said that he would challenge McMillan on campaign spending:

> He can keep his perks, but he must limit his spending to $250,000. I'll agree to limit my own to $150,000. He will say no, of course, but you have to make the issue campaign spending.

Notwithstanding the daunting task of campaign fund-raising, few of the candidates suggested that this obstacle would be a sufficient deterrent. Optimism that adequate funds could be raised is perhaps an explicit recognition of the interrelationship of incumbency, district political context, and campaign finance. In the minds of the Democrats, if the seat was more winnable—in other words, if the incumbent left office and the former 9th was still a reality—a great deal of money could be raised (as it was for D. G. Martin in 1984). In the minds of the Republicans, fund-raising efforts would "depend on the opposition" in the primary as well as the fact that the Democrats "would make a stronger run without Alex."

The Personal Context

Personal factors were cited by all of those interviewed, both Democrat and Republican, as having an important influence on candidacy decisions, but these factors generally worked to *encourage* rather than to *discourage* running for office. Most of the interviewees described supportive families and occupational situations that would not be affected adversely by a run for Congress—even if the effort proved to be unsuccessful.

Of the sixteen interviewees who acknowledged having thought about running for Congress, twelve characterized family reaction as supportive, two as unsupportive, one as mixed, and one as unsure. When asked if she had ever discussed the possibility of running for the House seat with her family, Hair said, "My husband said 'do it!'" Blake said that his family's reaction was "initially negative, but I've been able to explain to them that we can win . . . it's not a dream anymore." Not all families are thrilled at the prospect of candidacy, of course. Helms described the conversion of his wife from a positive to negative orientation:

> I like politics—I enjoy it. . . . My wife has always been my strongest supporter. When I ran for lieutenant governor in 1988 she helped me day in and day out. We lost, and she was very bitter. She remembered all of those people who had, at various times, promised their support . . . and then didn't provide it. "The next time you run for office," she told me, "why don't you do it with your next wife."

While speculating on a potential House race, Republican Autrey cited his family as supportive but added that he himself "would not want to raise a family in D.C." DuPuy was emphatic that the leading personal sacrifice she would have to make would be loss of privacy, stating that "you're reading all of your remarks in the paper, even some quip . . . you give up that part of yourself . . . often to the point that you can't be yourself." Others cited the personal sacrifice of time and the strain of dislocation as factors to consider but not sufficient to rule out candidacy.

Despite such anecdotes, the pattern of responses makes clear that most of those committed to politics as a vocation or even an avocation are surrounded by families who have made peace with their loved ones' participation in the political arena. Helms's wife apparently has not made good on her threat: he ran a successful campaign for the Mecklenburg County Commission in the fall of 1992—and he is still married to her.

Access: The Role of Parties in Candidate Emergence

Little formal recruitment activity takes place in the 9th District, and then only on the Democratic side. It is unfortunate for the Democrats that organized recruitment activity is a clear signal that a noncompetitive House election is upcoming. The Republicans have been concerned with identifying a candidate only in the two instances in the past forty years when the seat was open, and only in McMillan's case was there significant primary opposition. It is not surprising that the GOP sees little need to recruit for a seat they have held for two generations. The Democrats, however, have had to look hard to find a candidate willing to challenge popular Republican incumbents. While the Democratic party has a mechanism for candidate recruitment in the form of the Mecklenburg County Democratic party and the 9th District Democratic Committee, evaluations of their effectiveness were not complimentary.[3] One informant echoed a common perception when asked about party recruitment activities: "The Democratic party organization is pretty much a joke in this district."

Most prominent in the recruitment of Democratic House candidates has been Thompson, current Mecklenburg County Democratic party chair and past chair of the 9th District Democratic Committee. In recent years several local party activists, including David Erdman (a local attorney and Democratic party activist) and Michael Daisley, have taken a more pronounced recruitment role. In 1992, for example, Thompson and Daisley "drew up a list of about ten people who we thought might make good candidates." Their efforts to attract politically experienced, well known challengers have borne little fruit. Thompson apparently was instrumental in recruiting the candidates who ran in 1978, 1980, and 1982; each recruit ran against James Martin, the popular Republican incumbent, who won with 68 percent, 59 percent, and 57 percent during those years. When Martin left the seat to seek the governorship, several candidates—all self-starters—sought the Democratic nomination. On the heels of D. G. Martin's losses to McMillan in 1984 and 1986, Thompson encouraged Mark Sholander, then a 34-year-old labor arbitrator, to run. Sholander was opposed for the nomination by David McKnight, a little known local musician. Sholander won the nomination but was defeated handily by McMillan in the general election. McKnight ran as the Democratic candidate in 1990, winning the nomination, as one Democratic activist told us, "by default," and lost to McMillan in the general election 66 percent to 34 percent.

Blake, then a 41-year-old pharmacist with no history of party involvement or previous elective office experience, was the 1992 Democratic candidate. He was a self-starter and an amateur; indeed, Erdman was not aware at the time of our interview that anyone had declared for the House seat, although Blake had announced his candidacy several weeks previously. Other interviewees had never heard of Blake, and even those who knew he was running knew little about him. As one Democratic informant stated, "he's just off the street . . . he has no money, no party support whatsoever . . . he'll get 10 percent of the vote."

The Democratic party thus has played a role in the recruitment of 9th District candidates, though party activity appears primarily to be the result of one official's efforts and is most consequential when the nomination is least attractive. Thompson said, "My theory is that you run someone even if it isn't winnable." When the nomination is attractive, as it was when the seat opened up in 1984, the party need not recruit; candidates—three strong candidates in 1984—emerge.

While the Republicans resemble the Democrats in having a formal mechanism for candidate recruitment, it has not been active at the House level. All of the Republican informants and potential candidates stated that no one in the district is active in encouraging candidates to run for Congress. This appears obvious in the face of a strong and successful incumbent, but an interview with McMillan, as well as a small item in the *Charlotte Observer* during the fall campaign, revealed that McMillan was contemplating what so many members considered during 1992—the frustrations of a gridlocked Congress and the decision to retire.[4] When asked if anyone in the district was waiting to hear if he was going to run in 1994 before deciding whether or not to enter the race, McMillan replied "well, yes . . . I've put out some signals that I might not run." All of the Republicans interviewed said that they would expect a vigorous primary should McMillan vacate the seat, a prediction that turned out to be correct when the incumbent announced late in 1993 that he would not seek reelection. Demonstrating the depth and breadth of the Republican pool, five Republicans, ranging from the state legislator David Balmer to former Charlotte mayor Sue Myrick, jumped into the race for the 1994 GOP nomination.

Other Contextual Factors

Expectations of limited party support, low name recognition, and the national political context apparently have little impact on the political calculations of those we interviewed. As to the likelihood of help from the Democratic party, longtime party activist Doris Cromartie said "the party has no money either at the state or local level. Our [local] chairman keeps us afloat . . . we wouldn't have an office if he didn't pay the rent." The national Democratic party was seen as the source of some services and advice, but not a single interviewee expected the Democratic Congressional Campaign Committee (DCCC) or other party entities to provide significant financial support. An interview with Martin Hamburger of the DCCC in the summer of 1991 revealed that the national party was only vaguely familiar with the redistricting efforts concerning the 9th District and even less aware of potential candidates except for those who had made a bid before (such as D. G. Martin) or who were well known (such as Harvey Gantt). The lack of national party support was not a significant disincentive, however, because potential candidates understood candidacy and fund-raising to be a highly personal venture.

All of the potential Republican candidates, however, had expectations of support from both the local and national parties. One potential candidate "would expect lots of support." Autrey said any Republican candidate should "expect significant help from the party locally and nationally because this is a traditional Republican seat." The potential Republican candidates did share the view that the party could not offer support in a contested primary.

Only one of the interviewees, a Democrat, saw low name recognition as a potentially fatal problem if he were to run for Congress, and he suggested that the problem might be more serious in the primary than in the general election. The lack of concern about name recognition, especially on the part of the Democrats, is perhaps a result of D. G. Martin's 1984 campaign experience. He was not well known before the Democratic primary, but the free publicity resulting from his two campaigns for the nomination was sufficient to make him a relatively well known figure before the general election campaign commenced.

While Democrats and Republicans alike do not view low name recognition as a significant impediment, the potential Republican candidates, most of whom currently hold public office or have done so in the quite recent past, are relatively confident of the public's familiarity with their names. One potential candidate stated:

> Generally, people don't know where you are on specific issues but they have a general sense of you as a liberal or conservative and your style. People probably couldn't tell you specifically where Alex [McMillan] stands but they see him as hardworking and conservative."

Potential Republican candidates expressed similar opinions with regard to character and stands on issues. DuPuy felt that voters thought of her "as a fair person and one whose judgment you could trust."

National political factors were mentioned by several of those interviewed as important for running an effective campaign, although only four individuals identified such factors as highly important for district success. One respondent cited the importance of an issue critical to 9th District voters, and "a firebrand opponent to give voters a reason to take him down—a Harris Wofford type." Most important, however, was "a Democratic landslide at the top of the ticket." Bob Walton, a Mecklenburg county commissioner, also identified the need for a strong Democrat at the top of the ticket because district politics are affected "more by national candidates than by national issues." The only specific reference to the importance of national issues came from Blake, the 1992 Democratic challenger. Blake asserted that "this one [the 1992 election] better be affected by those issues . . . after all, Alex McMillan is the state campaign manager for George Bush." [5] Mayor Vinroot argued, as did most others, that Charlotte is "not a national trend city and despite the fact that the House seat has been held for the last forty years by Republicans, there is lots of Democratic representation in the city council, the county commission, and the state legislature."

Ambition and Candidacy

How ambitious is this pool of potential candidates? One measure is simply the number of those interviewed who have thought about running for the 9th District seat. Discounting the informants, eleven of thirteen Democrats said that they have thought about running—a proportion particularly notable in a district that has not seen a successful Democratic House candidacy since 1950! While the Republicans sensed that McMillan might retire or seek other office soon, all of the Republicans interviewed—all of whom had given some thought to running—were circumspect in their willingness to display ambition for the seat. As former Republican County Commissioner Keber stated, "I have thought about the *idea* of running but not really of going down and filing because the opportunity was never there."

Ambition for a House seat manifests itself in different ways. When asked whether she had thought about running for the 9th District seat, Cromartie said "Yes . . . and then I took two aspirins and tried to forget it!" Discussing her love of politics, Cromartie described her state legislative candidacy of two years ago: "I went down to the Elections Commission and waited to see who would file against David Balmer. When *no one* did, I filed at 11:55 A.M. Right after I filed, I got the fever . . . I got 45 percent of the vote . . . we had tons of volunteers." Another respondent, otherwise ambivalent about the personal costs of candidacy, said that his conversations with others who have run for office all lead to the same conclusion: "Everybody I've ever talked to has said, 'great experience,'—there is real dignity in running for office; it is a thrill." Autrey described his ambition more in terms of "being part of the process . . . the ability to create, to build and to help people . . . there are other ways to do that than the House seat."

Two of the three interviewees who were least positive about running for Congress were attorneys who had not run for public office before. One attorney said that it was "unlikely" that he would run for Congress in the future: "I have a very active life. To make an impact would require an *enormous* commitment. I'm not sure you can make a difference in the House, and if I cannot, why would I want to take a substantial cut in compensation and incur new debt?" The other attorney said that he was " . . . 100 percent committed to my family. I have two daughters, and I want to be their daddy. If there is any glory in running for office, it is lost on me."

Mayor Vinroot, frequently mentioned as an ideal Republican candidate, is not shy about his political ambition or his desire for a future in politics but has no apparent interest in the 9th District House seat: "I cannot envision myself there, and nothing would change the situation that I can see . . . it's not that I have no interest in other offices . . . someday I might want to consider the Senate seat, but serving as mayor of Charlotte strikes me as better than being 1 of 435."

Such sentiments were the exception rather than the rule. Politics is appealing, particularly for those who have some prior exposure to elective office, either through serving or running. One interviewee commented that running for office requires sacrifices of "time and energy—but I love it."

A Summary of Factors Affecting Candidate Emergence

For both Democrats and Republicans, variables affecting the competitive balance in the district had the greatest impact on decisions about candidacy. Other potentially important contextual variables appear to play very limited roles in the emergence process. Structural variables such as media markets and geography simply were not considered by most of those we interviewed. While all recognized the importance of fund-raising, the majority of the prospective candidates did not view this as an insurmountable obstacle. Most potential candidates viewed voter perceptions of their characters as more important than any litmus test on certain issues; local or national issues did not appear to enter into the candidates' calculus for running, and only one potential candidate explicitly cited the national political context as important in influencing his decision to run.

Prospective candidates do, however, pay close attention to the district's competitive balance and to factors that might upset that balance. Of significant concern, for example, is the partisan and racial balance of the district. Discussing his decision to run for the open seat in 1984, McMillan said that previous Republican domination of the House seat did not change the fact that the district he faced "was registered 2 to 1 Democrats . . . you had to get some of the Democratic vote." The partisan and racial balance of the district was changed notably with the redistricting of 1992. The loss of black voters both has removed the potential for a black Democratic candidate from the 9th District as well as reduced the number of reliable votes for 9th District Democrats. Despite the redistricting, the foremost fact for the Democrats remains the presence of a strong incumbent. With a relatively popular incumbent with no real vulnerabilities, the Democrats have had to face the continuation of Republican domination and the removal of the House from the opportunity structure of quality challengers. On the Republican side, the long electoral histories of incumbents, with the exception of the few instances of an open seat, has removed the House seat from the immediate opportunity structure for politically ambitious Republicans. Both talented and ambitious Democrats and Republicans alike have focused their energies on highly visible and respectable positions such as members of the Board of County Commissioners and the City Council, as well as opportunities in the state house and senate. Holding office in one of these capacities, coupled with an active record of community service, produces a number of attractive potential candidates from both parties.

With few exceptions, potential candidates were convinced that the benefits of public service outweigh perceptions of personal sacrifice. While some candidates have reservations about raising a family in Washington, D.C., most of those interviewed indicated substantial family support. The potential candidates—with the anomaly of the Democratic nominee in 1992, Blake (who believed redistricting *helped* Democrats)—are sophisticated and realistic in their understanding of the time and energy demands of both campaigning and serving in the House of Representatives. Again, most of the potential candidates, Democrats or Republicans, are ambitious—an ambition demonstrated by a willingness to entertain some scenario by which, given an open seat, they could win the nomination and perhaps even the general election.

Conclusions: Competition in the 9th District

On the surface, North Carolina's 9th District appears to be an area in which real electoral competition does not exist. The seat has been held by the Republican party for forty years. However, the pool of potential Democratic challengers in the 9th District is deep and of relatively high quality. Indeed, the first redistricting plan passed by the North Carolina legislature must have caused ambitions to stir among those who might have been able to mount credible challenges. Odom, Alexander, and Helms, perhaps Daisley and Erdman, likely began weighing the possibility of a successful challenge to McMillan. The question any candidate must ask—can I win this district?—surely must have tipped closer to an affirmative answer. For Odom, the risk of giving up his seat in the North Carolina Senate perhaps seemed less intimidating when measured against an increased chance of winning. Daisley, reluctant in 1990 even with the promise of seed money, might have justified the great effort required to mount a competitive campaign if a real possibility of winning existed.

It was this same district, after all, that produced three credible and attractive challengers to run for the open seat in 1984. D. G. Martin was a formidable contender, described as "nearly an ideal candidate, a former Green Beret, an athletic hero. . . ." Acceptable to the area business elite and possessing an impressive record of community service, Martin was, as one respondent said, "soaked in Charlotte."

The pool of potential Republican challengers is also of high quality. It is clear that numerous Republicans have the reputation, the resources, and the redistricting edge to attempt to continue their party's domination of the House seat in the 9th District. As one Republican informant put it, "there would be lots of competition in the GOP if the seat were open; lots would see themselves as heirs to the throne." Indeed, when McMillan decided in 1993 to retire at the end of the term, five Republicans stepped in to seek the Republican nomination. Three of the candidates, state legislator David Balmer, city councilperson Don Reid, and Sue Myrick, the former mayor of Charlotte who sought unsuccessfully a Republican nomination for the U.S. Senate in 1992, are well known, experienced politicians. As might have been expected in a district that is perceived by most local observers as safe for the Republicans (after the 1992 redistricting fight), a less impressive set of Democratic contenders emerged. Rory Blake, defeated by McMillan in 1992, and law student Dale Dixon filed for the Democratic nomination.

In the 9th District, then, the latent competition apparent during the tenure of incumbent McMillan became real competition in 1994—at least for the Republican nomination. As our interviews revealed, the district harbored the ambitions of numerous potential candidates with rich political experience. If many districts are like the 9th, we may begin to understand more fully the dynamics of incumbent behavior and electoral change. The high rates of incumbent success may mask an electoral insecurity well grounded in perceptions of the latent competition present in the district. Attentiveness to the district is one way to discourage latent candidacies from becoming real. In the same vein, "retirement slump" (Brady 1990)— that is, the drop-off in the share of the vote won by the candidate of the previous incumbent's party—becomes understandable largely in terms of candidate emergence. The incumbent may have constructed a nearly impregnable personal vote (Alford and Brady 1989), but this appeal is not transferable to his or her successor when the out-party has attractive, often experienced activists waiting for an opportunity to run for the open seat.

Notes

1. Writing for the majority, Justice Sandra Day O'Connor argued that a redistricting plan based on "individuals who belong to the same race but who are otherwise widely separated by geographical and political boundaries and who may have little in common with one another but the color of their skins, bears an uncomfortable resemblance to political apartheid" (*Shaw v. Reno,* 113 S. Ct. 2816 (1993)).
2. The total number of mentions adds up to more than nine because of multiple mentions by respondents. Odom, for example, was cited twice by five respondents (in their answers to different questions) for a total of fourteen mentions.
3. The "9th District Democratic Committee" is our designation for an informal committee with no apparent formal name. It is perhaps revealing to note that none of our respondents were aware of an official name for the district party group.
4. Timothy Wirth, Democratic senator from Colorado, received widespread attention when he wrote "Diary of a Dropout," a cover article for the *New York Times Magazine,* in which he detailed his decision not to seek reelection and in which he noted his frustration "with the posturing and paralysis of Congress" (1992, 16).
5. While McMillan was active in Bush's reelection effort, Gov. James Martin (former 9th District representative) was North Carolina chair for the Bush campaign.

7

Old Style Politics and Invisible Challengers: Iowa's 1st and 4th Districts

John Haskell, Kerry Sutten, and Peverill Squire

A cursory examination of Iowa's 1st and 4th Districts in early 1992 would have suggested that conditions were ripe for a sighting of that rarest of birds: a high-quality candidate challenging a House incumbent. Redistricting created an electoral map that appeared to weaken incumbents in both districts, and the growing national anger with politics-as-usual seemed to be building to an anti-incumbent pitch. Moreover, in the 1st District the incumbent was a Republican, apparently suffering affiliation with the Republican White House at a time of substantial economic distress, both nationally and in important areas of the district. In the 4th District the Democratic incumbent was the powerful chair of an appropriations subcommittee, a Washington insider who steadfastly refused to criticize the way things worked in Washington. Yet no strong challenger came forth in either district. The incumbent in the 1st District faced a little known candidate scorned by activists in his own party. The incumbent in the 4th District was challenged by a candidate he had defeated soundly four years earlier.

Despite the similar outcomes, the absence of competition is a result of different forces operating in the two districts. In the 1st District, a rich candidate pool failed to produce a quality challenger willing to battle an incumbent who was widely viewed as doing a good job. In the 4th District, the pool of potential challengers was very shallow. The Democratic incumbent, who worked hard to "re-secure" his district after new lines were drawn, was the beneficiary of a district and state context that appears to produce few viable House contenders in the Republican party.

The Rise of an Invisible Challenger: The 1st District

Iowa's 1st District is represented by Republican Jim Leach, first elected in 1976 after an unsuccessful House bid two years earlier. Leach has gained a reputation as a thoughtful, intelligent, issue-oriented representative who is more interested in making good public policy than in fighting political battles. He won high praise even from many of the more partisan Democratic members of his constituency.

Leach has had little competition after his initial win, securing reelection by comfortable margins. The sweep of Michael Dukakis in Iowa in

1988 coincided with Leach's vote percentage decreasing a bit to 61 percent from 66 percent two years earlier, but in 1990 he ran unopposed. Leach campaigns have been heavy on policy-oriented speeches and media advertising and light on backslapping, handshaking, and personal appeals. In 1990 and 1992, his campaign relied on billboards around the district that simply read "HONEST, Congressman Jim Leach."

Leach is considered one of the most (and one of the few) liberal Republicans in the House. Leach often finds himself voting with the Democrats on social and foreign policy issues, but he takes more moderate stands on economic issues. In recent years, Leach enhanced his positive image with voters by being one of the first members of Congress to warn about problems in the savings and loan industry. Leach won support from Democrats for being one of the first Republicans to support cutting off U.S. trade with South Africa, and for opposing restrictions on grants by the National Endowment for the Arts. Leach has never accepted political action committee money, and was praised for sponsoring campaign finance reform legislation that sought to ban or limit the influence of PACs.

Leach's reputation as a moderate and the strong public perception of his integrity made it appear to many observers that it would be difficult for any Democratic challenger to unseat him. But there were political forces at work that kept those contemplating a challenge interested in the race. Aside from the changes brought on by redistricting, many observers thought Leach might retire from the House out of frustration with his lack of influence within the increasingly conservative Republican party. Others thought he would move into the Bush administration because of his close relationship with George Bush—in 1980, 1988, and 1992, Leach served as chair of Bush's presidential campaigns in Iowa. Other rumors had Leach retiring for health reasons.

A Winnable District for the Democrats?

Redistricting substantially altered the political environment in Iowa's 1st District in 1992. The plan produced by the nonpartisan Legislative Service Bureau and adopted by the state legislature created a political map of Iowa that changed a primarily rural district spread over sixteen counties to a surprisingly urban district containing six of Iowa's larger cities: Bettendorf, Cedar Rapids, Clinton, Davenport, Iowa City, and Muscatine. Only three of the counties from the old 1st District remained in the new redrawn district; Leach retained only 35 percent of his former constituents. Almost two-thirds of the constituents were new to the 1st District and to Jim Leach, although some of them had been represented by Leach in the 1970s.

The partisan makeup of the district also changed with redistricting. Johnson County, home of Iowa City and the University of Iowa, and Linn County, home of Cedar Rapids, were both new to the 1st District and represented half of the eligible voters. Both counties were considerably more Democratic than any county in the old district. The new 1st District

Figure 7-1   Iowa, 1st and 4th Districts

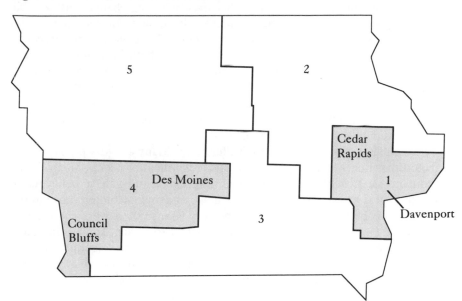

contained more than 30,000 additional voters who cast ballots for Dukakis in 1988 and 17,700 fewer voters who supported Bush than the old 1st District. Republicans made up 31 percent of the old district but only 28 percent of the new 1st District; registered Democrats represented 37 percent of the old district and 36 percent of the new one, figures that probably underestimate the district's Democratic leanings.

In addition, the news media in the old district were based primarily in the Quad-Cities (Davenport and Bettendorf, Iowa; and Moline and Rock Island, Illinois), a market shared with eastern Illinois. Many of the residents in the new district lived in Linn and Johnson counties, where local news comes from television stations and newspapers based in Cedar Rapids, Waterloo (which is still outside of the 1st District), and Iowa City. The media in these communities had been focused on the activities of the representatives from the 2nd and 3rd Districts, not on Jim Leach. Thus many of the incumbent's new constituents were not well informed about his activities or opinions. Democrats all over the 1st District began to ask themselves, "Is this the right time?"

Democratic County Chairs and Their Assessments of the Race

County chairs and local activists split in their evaluations of a challenge to Leach. Many saw this election as an opportunity to win the House seat;

others viewed the race as a tough, uphill battle undertaken only to build name recognition for a future run. Activists believing change was possible cited many of the factors discussed previously. In addition they noted with particular excitement that the pool of possible challengers in the new district was large and of exceptional quality. They believed that if one of these potentially strong challengers ran a vigorous, grassroots campaign, he or she could unseat Leach. Moreover, these activists were confident about the abilities of their local party to win elections. Party activists in Johnson County, for example, took credit for getting Dave Nagle elected in the former Republican-leaning 2nd District.

Confidence was not unanimous, however. Many activists privately predicted that Leach would win in the end, regardless of his opponent. They thought that Leach's reputation as an intelligent and honest policymaker would appeal to many of the district's new residents, including those in the university community of Iowa City, the very voters others were counting on to carry a Democratic candidate. The real risk to Leach, some informants thought, was a challenge from within his own party, which seemed possible because some area Republicans were unhappy with Leach's moderate views. They hoped that a tough primary fight would weaken the incumbent enough to entice a strong Democratic challenger to enter the race. But, while Leach had had primary opponents in the past, no one saw any on the horizon in 1992.

Democratic leaders and party activists agreed on the characteristics of the ideal challenger. The strongest candidate would be a woman who was already known to the voters of Linn and Johnson counties. Many activists argued that a woman would attract a substantial share of the female vote and could secure specific sources of campaign funds intended for women. Most informants acknowledged that a campaign against Leach would not be based on issues—given the small differences between Leach and most Democrats—and they concluded that having a woman candidate might be one way to offer voters a meaningful choice. A candidate known in Linn or Johnson County would allow the Democratic campaign to concentrate on areas of the district in which Leach was already known and strong. It would also force Leach to spend time away from his base in the old parts of the district and campaign in a more Democratic region.

Thirty-nine individuals were identified by informants as potential Democratic candidates. The list of potential challengers included state officeholders, well known attorneys, county officials, former candidates for Congress, the Riverboat Gambling Commission chair, and a former football player for the Miami Dolphins. Seven names were mentioned most frequently by informants. All had considerable political or electoral experience. Most frequently mentioned was Rep. Minette Doderer of Iowa City. A former state senator and candidate for lieutenant governor, Doderer currently was serving in the Iowa House of Representatives. State Sen. Rich Varn represented Johnson County and was known to have an intense interest in the job. Mary Neuhauser, another state house member from Iowa City, was mentioned frequently. State Rep. David Osterberg was known throughout the state for his work on environmental issues and was considered a likely candidate. Jean Lloyd-Jones, the president pro tem of the Iowa Senate, was actively recruited by the 1st District Democratic Central Committee. Finally, former House challengers Steve Sovern and Bill Gluba were mentioned as possible candidates. Most others cited were local figures with little or no name recognition outside their home areas.

Potential Challengers and Their Assessments of Candidacy

Although all seven of the individuals mentioned frequently by informants declined to challenge Leach, their rationales varied, often intertwining personal and political concerns. The stories of the seven potential challengers and the one surprise candidate who did enter the race show clearly how ambition and context interact to influence candidate emergence.

State Representative Doderer was the most often mentioned individual in the study, and to many observers she seemed the ideal candidate. She had run twice for lieutenant governor and was known throughout Linn and Johnson counties from having represented the area in the Iowa legislature for more than twenty-six years. Her efforts on behalf of women were well known by many voters throughout the state. Doderer believed that Leach could be beaten and she admitted that she would like to challenge him. She was one of the few candidates to question Leach's credibility, calling him "intellectually dishonest." But she decided not to run against him because she did not think she could raise enough money to run a competitive campaign. She was the only strong potential candidate in the 1st District to raise that concern. Other women candidates in Iowa thought differently. Indeed, Iowa Secretary of State Elaine Baxter had entered the congressional race in the 3rd District in southern Iowa, a contest that in many ways mirrored the 1st District race. Running against a four-term Republican incumbent, Baxter intended to raise $600,000 and she believed that figure was attainable. Doderer, however, commented that she did not enjoy soliciting campaign funds. She said "when a little old lady gives me a few dollars out of her purse for the campaign, I just know the money is all that is left from her last Social Security check. My reaction is to simply give it back to her but I can't without offending her." Moreover, Doderer did not like to campaign and found it extremely difficult to take on a race requiring her to canvas every cafe and county fair in the district. About campaigning she said, "It hurts me when I can't remember the name of someone I run into at an event who thinks that I should remember." Finally, Doderer believed that she had a problem with name recognition, both inside and outside her district. As she put it, "I represent a college town. Every four years my constituency completely changes. I spend all of my time just reintroducing myself to my own constituency."

Varn had expressed an active interest in running for higher office and he seemed particularly interested in a seat in Congress. An ambitious state senator from the Johnson County area, Varn is young, energetic, articulate, and sharp. Midway through his second four-year state senate term, he had the opportunity to run against Leach without giving up his seat. Varn thought he could beat Leach because of his vigorous campaigning style. "With about $250,000 and a well run, grassroots campaign like the kind Nagle ran the first time around I could beat Leach." Without question, Varn possessed all the traits needed to run a congressional campaign and the intense interest to propel him quickly into the race. But he declined too. He and his wife were expecting their third child. He wanted to be home for the first few months of the baby's life. As a law student in 1986, Varn had run for the state senate and he regretted the time he spent away from home during that first year of his oldest child's life. In addition, his responsibilities in the state legislature and on national commissions left him little time to raise money and organize an effective campaign. Finally, as a practicing attorney, he had an active law business to which he had to tend.

Like Doderer, State Representative Neuhauser was suggested as an ideal challenger by activists in and around Iowa City. But when told she had been mentioned by a number of individuals as a potential challenger against Leach, she began to laugh and said emphatically, "No! I'm not interested." Indeed, Neuhauser said that she had never considered running for higher office. She was happy with her position in the Iowa House. She and her husband recently had built a new home in another state house district to avoid running against another Democratic incumbent when their old districts were combined through redistricting. She said, "It would be silly to build the new house and then not run for the state legislature." Furthermore, Neuhauser said she had no interest in running against Leach. "Why run against someone you like? He is bright and full of integrity. He was one of the few that stood up early on and expressed a concern about the savings and loan industry." She believed Leach had a strong chance of being reelected, but noted that: "Everyone is beatable, no matter how much of a 'sure thing' the race seems."

Another widely mentioned potential candidates was Osterberg, a state representative from Linn County who has a solid reputation as an effective legislator, particularly on environmental issues. He also repeatedly had expressed an interest in running for Congress. But Osterberg did not believe he could beat Leach because, he said, "I have no policy disagreement with Leach on which to base a campaign." Osterberg echoed Varn's estimate that $250,000 would be needed to run a good campaign against Leach and that the money could be found. He pointed out that if he were to run in 1992, it would be to develop name recognition in the district for a future run; he preferred to develop district support behind the scenes. Osterberg planned to spend more time in Johnson County and other counties in the new district to prepare for a future campaign. Several activists thought that

Varn would be a good candidate but would only be interested in a race in which his chances of winning were high.

One of the more revealing stories of potential candidates was that of State Senator Lloyd-Jones. Having expressed an interest in running for higher office, Lloyd-Jones was actively recruited to run by members of the 1st District Democratic Central Committee, as well as Representative Doderer. A state central committee member commented that Lloyd-Jones would make an excellent candidate because, "She's articulate, Episcopalian, and tall. She could give Leach a run for his money." Moreover, Lloyd-Jones, like Varn, was at the mid-point in her four-year state senate term and would not have had to give up her seat to run for higher office. Although not widely known throughout the new district, she chaired a much publicized state senate ethics committee that had the potential to increase her name recognition. Lloyd-Jones eventually passed up the House race to run instead against the state's most popular politician, Republican Sen. Chuck Grassley. Lloyd-Jones said she chose to run an uphill Senate race rather than a more winnable congressional race because:

> You have to want to beat someone to run against them and I have always found myself agreeing with everything Jim Leach stands for. It would be very difficult for me to define a difference between us. Now Grassley, there's a difference. The environment, women's issues, the family; there are vast differences in our beliefs in these and other issues. I decided to run against Grassley while I was attending a women's conference meeting in the Senate Caucus Room, the same room in which the Hill-Thomas hearings were held. The hearing was still fresh in the minds of all of us when Pennsylvania Senator Specter walked into the room to speak to the group. Everyone at my table was outraged and we started to talk that something had to be done. I decided then and there to take on Mr. Grassley.

Lloyd-Jones's decision reflected a calculation of costs versus benefits primarily based on policy considerations. She had the opportunity to run for Congress with the possibility of winning—but only by defeating a candidate whose policy position she respected. However, she also had the chance to run in the Senate race with little chance for success but far greater personal benefits if she won. After weighing the costs and benefits, she chose the Senate race.

Two other individuals mentioned frequently by informants as possible challengers were Sovern and Gluba. Sovern had run for the House twice before, getting 42 percent of the vote in a losing bid against Tom Tauke in 1980, and then losing again in the Democratic primary in 1990, when Tauke stepped down. Sovern had built a loyal following in Linn County during his earlier campaigns in part because of his refusal to accept PAC money. The 1st District Democratic Central Committee members approached him about running but he repeatedly rebuffed their efforts, citing personal reasons. He recently had sold his business and returned to law school. He planned to devote his energies to finishing his degree.

Gluba had run against Leach in 1982 and 1988, getting 41 percent and 38 percent of the vote. Many informants thought he might be interested in the 1992 race but most hoped he would not try again. Having lost twice already, they thought another try would be futile. Gluba made no moves to be involved in the race.

In addition to the frequently mentioned prospects, a number of other individuals were suggested as possible House candidates. Many of the informants from the Clinton area, for example, said they would actively support Jack Wolfe, an attorney and political activist, if he chose to run. Although he had never run for political office, he and his family had been outspoken about a number of issues, including Desert Storm (which he opposed), aid to the contras in central America, abortion, and the Grenada invasion. Wolfe was reluctant to run, however, concluding that he could not raise enough money for a credible race.

In summary, the reasons for eschewing a challenge to Leach were varied. Personal reasons such as family and school prevented Varn and Sovern from running. Osterberg assessed the chances of winning and decided against it. Neuhauser asked herself the question "Do I want it?" and answered no. Doderer was not willing to pay the cost of raising the funds and running a campaign to challenge Leach. Only Lloyd-Jones had the ambition, the opportunity, and the will to take on a race for higher office. She chose the Senate race because the possible benefits of winning against an incumbent who she believed represented the wrong ideals were great enough to overcome the financial and personal cost of that race.

The Invisible Challenger

The candidate who did surface to run against Leach, Jan Zonneveld, was not welcomed by local Democrats. They thought he was responsible for the loss of the House seat two years earlier, which was vacated by Republican Tauke who ran for the Senate. Zonneveld, running as an independent, received 2,200 votes; the Democratic nominee lost by 1,500 votes.

A retired actuary from Cedar Rapids, Zonneveld decided to run again in 1992 because of his frustration with the political system. "I'm mad as hell. Mad at everything in Washington. I'm against the crookedness, the robbery, and the outrageous spending." But he characterized his race as "a gamble at best" (Yepsen 1992). Zonneveld had been prompted to run for Congress in 1990 by the passage of the Catastrophic Health Care Act. As he saw it, that law taxed senior citizens at a much higher rate than it did everyone else. The legislation generated enough protest from seniors that Congress eventually repealed it. But Zonneveld continued to rail against the federal government's policies toward the elderly, even claiming in a January 1992 guest editorial in the *Cedar Rapids Gazette* that the government was trying to economically eliminate the elderly.

Zonneveld cited Ross Perot as evidence that 1992 was a different sort of political year, one in which incumbents were more likely to lose. He noted that he, like Perot, was a political outsider and hoped that the Perot campaign would boost his own. Acknowledging that his chances of beating Leach were slim, Zonneveld argued that he did not care about winning. Said Zonneveld,

> Leach is a very nice fellow and I wouldn't hesitate to vote for him if the times were different. I see three problems with Leach. He has no enemies. He makes friends of everyone. How can anything ever be done without making some enemies? Also, Leach is now a ranking member of the House Banking Committee. Where was he before the Savings and Loan Crisis happened? Finally, Leach is also on the House Foreign Relations Committee and look at our relations overseas. At the Rio Conference we were outcasts. Japan and other countries are making better products and conducting better research. I could just as easily go to Congress and do nothing but make friends. As the wind blows, so blows my jacket.

Zonneveld's issues in 1992 were the problems of the elderly, a single-payer national health care program, and a balanced budget. Activists expressed concern about his lack of political experience and the sense that he did not realize what was required to run a political campaign. During the campaign Zonneveld expressed disappointment that no invitations had been offered for him to speak to political and civic groups. He attended some county conventions at which he addressed those in attendance. But, according to Zonneveld, one convention would not allow him to speak at all.

The media and the Democratic establishment ignored him. At one 1st District Democratic Central Committee meeting, the candidate was asked about his position on a federal bill to prohibit companies from hiring replacements during a strike. When he waffled on his answer, one member of the committee slammed her fist on the table and yelled at Zonneveld, "You're no Democrat. I've been an active Democrat for a long time in Johnson County and you do not represent me or the Democratic party!" Discussions at other meetings of the committee sought ways to avoid turning over the campaign war chest raised to help the Democratic nominee. In the end, the committee chose to use its funds to support Democratic registration programs in the district rather than give it to Zonneveld.

Zonneveld's reason for running had nothing to do with victory but came out of a sense of frustration with the current system. He calculated the probability of winning, factored in the costs of running, and still found the personal benefits of running a campaign were enough to convince him to announce. On November 6, after spending about $350 on his campaign, Zonneveld received 81,225 votes—31 percent of the vote.

The 4th District: Old Style Politics in a New District

Democratic incumbent Neal Smith in the 4th District has carved for himself an electoral niche that gives potential challengers pause. The major difference between Smith's district and Leach's district is that Leach faces a pool of House aspirants that is rich in depth and quality; Smith has so dominated congressional politics in the district that few are willing to admit that they have even considered challenging him.

Smith was first elected to the House in 1958, beating a Republican veteran with more than a decade of service at a time when Iowa was not at all hospitable to Democrats. It was in large measure a result of the efforts of politicians such as Smith and party leader Lex Hawkins that the most heavily populated areas of the state in and around Des Moines became organized as effective Democratic strongholds. Polk County—which includes Des Moines—was poorly organized on the Democratic side until Hawkins began working precinct by precinct in the early 1960s. At the same time other Democratic leaders, future Sen. John Culver, for example, were organizing in the eastern part of the state. Smith's party ties in the district have remained strong during his entire tenure in the House. Smith is now the second-ranking majority member of the Appropriations Committee, and recently lost in his bid to be elected chair of the committee. He will become chair of the Subcommittee on Labor, Health and Human Services, and Education, a panel with control of about $260 billion of the federal budget.

Redistricting

On April 16, 1991, the day after the Iowa redistricting plan was announced (Iowa lost a seat), the headline in the *Des Moines Register* read: "Grandy Is a Clear Winner, but Smith's Future Cloudy." Though Smith's district was to remain the most Democratic in the state (44 percent of the registered voters were Democrats, 33 percent were Republicans in 1992), he would lose strongly Democratic Story County, home of Iowa State University, for whom Smith had been a major benefactor. Moreover, the new 4th District picked up several predominantly Republican counties that had supported Republican House member Jim Ross Lightfoot when they were part of Lightfoot's 5th District. Indeed, Lightfoot had protested vociferously when the redistricting plan was proposed, although the alternative probably would have pitted him against fellow Republican Fred Grandy (representative for the new 5th District).

The new part of Smith's district seemed to be fertile ground for a Republican opponent. Much of the new area is in an entirely different media market; this is a change from the 1980s when all of his district was in the Des Moines vicinity, receiving the moderately liberal *Register*. Voters in many of the western counties in the district are likely to receive the *Omaha*

World-Herald, which has a decidedly conservative editorial policy.

The structural context of the district has changed, then, in ways that appear to threaten Smith's dominion in the district. Smith had faced weak opposition in the old 4th and had spent, on the average, only $87,202 in his past four elections. The last time he was held under 60 percent was in 1980. His opponent that year, Donald C. Young, got a critical infusion of money orchestrated by the National Conservative Political Action Committee (NCPAC) late in the campaign. Smith's 1992 opponent, Paul Lunde, raised virtually no money, just as in his previous run in 1988. Neither Lunde nor Robert Lockard, the Republican challenger in 1984 and 1986, ran with the advantage of close ties with the GOP establishment in the district.

The Absence of a Candidate Pool

Redistricting, though making the district more winnable for a Republican House challenger, has had little apparent impact on the pool of prospective candidates. Politicians, party leaders, and journalists familiar with the politics of Des Moines, Council Bluffs, and the surrounding rural counties were hard-pressed to come up with a single name of a person thinking of running for the Republican nomination. Smith's administrative assistant of twenty-two years, Tom Dawson, said that a running joke is that many aspiring Democrats have died waiting for Smith's seat to open.

The state media's "great mentioner," David Yepsen of the *Des Moines Register,* said that "no one even talks about challenging Smith." Yepsen did mention in his column two Republicans early in 1992 who were considering contesting the primary. Neither was regarded as a strong candidate. One did run, but lost in a low-key primary to Lunde. The dearth of potential candidates is exemplified well by the response of one Republican activist whose favorite prospective candidate lives in Dubuque—about two hundred miles east of the 4th District.

State Rep. Brent Siegrist was mentioned by one informed observer as a possible attractive candidate. When interviewed, Siegrist stated unequivocally: "I have not even thought about running." Siegrist was preoccupied with a hotly contested (and ultimately successful) race to keep a seat in the legislature. Other legislators and former elected officials also denied any interest in running for the Congress. A prominent Republican closely connected with the legislature (who preferred to remain anonymous) corroborated the denial of interest on the part of these Republicans. He claimed that "replacing Smith is not a topic of conversation among Republicans." Former state Republican party co-chair David Oman stated bluntly: "We do not consider the 4th District a priority in terms of recruitment and financing for the party." He indicated that scarce resources were better channeled by the party to legislative races and to the House races in the 2nd and 3rd Districts, both of which were hotly contested in 1992.

Most remarkable about this district is the absence of a talent pool on the Republican side. An aide to Representative Lightfoot, referring to potential talent in the new western part of the district (formerly a part of Lightfoot's district), noted that most of the people active in Republican politics in that part of the state are relatively old. Both Joe Brennan of the *Omaha World-Herald* and Smith aide Dawson had nearly identical reactions. "Many of the prominent Republicans in the Council Bluffs area are part-timers and too old to consider a run for the House," according to Brennan. The most they seem to seek is power in the state legislature. Lightfoot's aide said that the new part of the district is "largely irrelevant." He went on to claim that "Smith could easily win while ignoring the new counties . . . he has an unbeatable stronghold in Polk and Dallas counties."

Were Smith to retire unexpectedly, the field would be wide open in both parties. On the Republican side, the only person with enough name recognition and fund-raising ability potential to prevent a competitive and divisive primary would be Oman. Oman appears not to be interested in the House seat at this time, however. He has expressed interest in running for governor, but chose not to in 1994.

Mike Glover of the Associated Press believes that "a Republican challenger [to Smith] would have to come from Polk County or the Des Moines area," corroborating to some degree the contention of Lightfoot's aide that Smith could ignore the western counties and still win. Oman suggests that optimally a challenger would have grown up in the southwestern part of the state, but would now live and work in Des Moines. Glover suggested two future possibilities: Steven Churchill of Johnston, a first-time candidate for a state house seat in 1992, and O. Gene Maddox, longtime mayor of Clive who ran for a state Senate seat in 1992. Neither has expressed interest in the House seat.

In short, Smith's opponents in the past fifteen years have been little known, underfunded challengers, with no apparent ties to politically well connected groups. This again appears to be the case in the 1994 race. Lunde will be competing for the GOP nomination, to be joined by Des Moines plastic surgeon Greg Ganske, a political novice without strong organizational ties.

Ambition and the Political Career

Why is the pool of ambitious House aspirants in the 4th District so limited? One factor dampening the enthusiasm of potential candidates is Iowa's opportunity structure, which, though sufficiently fluid to permit movement from a variety of elected positions, generally seems to preclude amateurs as viable candidates for the U.S. House (Representative Grandy—a former television actor— is a conspicuous exception).

Another factor may be more partisan in nature. In his book, *The United States of Ambition* (1991), Alan Ehrenhalt postulates that nationally there are fewer skilled, ambitious, up-and-coming politicians to choose from on the Republican side. Electoral politics now requires a full-time commitment in many parts of the country, and more of those with a commitment to using government to address social conditions are likely to put in the time and effort needed to win office. A conservative who philosophically does not see an expansive role for government is less likely to be attracted to politics as a career, therefore. In short, Democrats derive more satisfaction from a career in politics and government. Gary Jacobson offers empirical support for Ehrenhalt's argument, noting that fewer Republican challengers have prior elective office experience than Democratic challengers (1990, 50-54, 72-73).

The central assumption in Ehrenhalt's theory holds true in Iowa. Politics is starting to become a full-time job, making necessary a higher level of ambition and a willingness to be a self-starter. Oman said, "The people we *have* to recruit to run for the state legislature usually make poor candidates." The self-starters are the ones who are willing to put in the necessary time and effort to be truly effective candidates. If it is true that making politics one's full-time occupation is important in order to compete successfully in the 1990s, then Democrats may have an advantage in the candidate pool in Iowa. In the Iowa state legislature, far more Democrats than Republicans list their occupation as "politician," "party official," or "consultant." Fourteen Democratic and seven Republican members of the state legislature list an occupation related to politics. Only two of the self-described politicians are Republicans in the 4th District—and of these two, neither is at the career stage in which a run for the House is realistic. No informed observer considered them potential candidates, either.

The Resourceful Incumbent and Challenger Emergence

In the end, however, the best explanation for the absence of ambition in the 4th District is to be found in a combination of the competitive and resource contexts. Smith has suppressed competition by developing an effective home style, adapting effectively to a changed political environment (that is, a newly drawn district), and building bridges to the business community—the most likely source of funds for an emerging Republican challenger.

In 1992, Smith's only television advertisements were short name identification spots, not very widely distributed, broadcast in the last weekend of the campaign. The only campaign advertising that the typical constituent would be exposed to is a billboard. Smith's version of campaigning "doesn't look like campaigning," says administrative aide Dawson. Such an appearance should not conceal the seriousness of Smith's reelection efforts; having beaten an entrenched incumbent in 1958 himself, he is fully prepared for a significant challenge.

Each Smith reelection campaign starts out with a budget of approximately $200,000, though he has not been forced to spend the full amount in the past ten years. Even faced with a weak challenger in 1992, Smith did not ignore his opponent. He spent $15,000 on polling during the summer, and his billboard expenditures reached $20,000, according to campaign finance reports.

Smith is his own campaign manager and has a very small campaign staff. Most of his appearances are made alone, and the media are not notified. Glover describes seeing Smith show up alone at a bankers' association meeting in Des Moines. The representative did not draw attention to himself and went unrecognized by some. Smith typically returns to the district three weekends a month. Often a county party chair will arrange a coffee meeting with business leaders to "Meet Neal Smith." Starting in 1992, in the new parts of the district, Smith stepped up the regularity of these sorts of meetings. They are informal, with no agenda, and almost always include Republicans and independents.

Redistricting has caused Smith to concentrate on an important question to which congressional scholars have paid little attention: how does an an incumbent solidify his electoral base after redistricting produces major changes in his district? In Iowa's 4th District, Smith redoubled his efforts to meet with community and business leaders with whom he previously had had little contact. He met with educators, labor leaders, local bankers, realtors, and others, in Council Bluffs, sometimes in meetings arranged by the local party chair. In this era of candidate-centered campaigns, Smith does not have a personal campaign apparatus independent or exclusive of the party. Some independent candidate organizations do exist in Iowa, but Smith remains committed to working through the existing county officers.

Smith also appears, often alone, at auctions, farm sales, or other similar events. By all accounts, he connects well with people at a personal level. In a rural state such as Iowa, his ability to empathize with farmers (and even to fix their equipment—a story heard more than once attesting to the Smith legend) holds him in good stead. Iowans "instinctively dislike flash," says Glover. "Smith and [Senator Charles] Grassley are a lot alike—both highly successful down-to-earth politicians," he said.

But an effective home style (Fenno 1978) might not be enough to foreclose opposition in a sprawling district with a substantial Republican base. What has made Smith safe is his delivery of services to his district to an extent that few in Congress rival. And he has delivered in ways that have served the interests of the people likely to fund potential challengers in his district. The grooming process for congressional hopefuls has been short-circuited by Smith's cordial relations with the business community in Des Moines, the main source of in-state GOP money for the district.

Smith's approach is nonconfrontational, nonideological, and nondivisive. Although his voting record across a range of issues leans in the liberal direction, he never broaches, and seems to have no interest in, the ideological social issues that animate so many election campaigns at all levels across the country. Smith is pro-choice and supported the Equal

Rights Amendment to the Iowa State Constitution that appeared on the ballot in 1992, but he downplays these positions. While he is a strong supporter of labor and generally receives high marks from civil libertarians, he has never received high marks from environmental groups. But Smith has found a middle ground entirely acceptable to the business elites in Des Moines.

Of particular importance to the business community has been Smith's role in the revitalization of downtown Des Moines in the past decade or so. The tightly knit Des Moines business community, including the major fund-raisers for Republican candidates in the state, has worked successfully with Smith in securing funds for numerous improvements for the city. He was instrumental in providing a downtown convention center, a skywalk system, and other improvements. These projects and many more, including the creation of a resort lake built by the Army Corps of Engineers near the city, might not have happened without him.

Party officials and journalists in the district told us that the business community, far more Republican and independent than Democratic, does not want to see him lose his seat. Business leaders have paid tribute to him in the traditional ceremonial ways, as well as by refusing to instigate a grooming process for a challenge. The politically active, GOP-oriented firms traditionally have been at the core of Republican politics in the district and statewide. These leaders would have played an active and indispensable role in supporting and perhaps even recruiting a challenger, were they not favorably disposed to Smith. Some Republican leaders, such as Polk County Chair John Schaffner, talk of various tactical campaign scenarios by which Smith might be challenged effectively. But this appears to be just talk; the reality is that Smith, after having secured his Democratic base early in his career, has always worked well with the business community, and they have helped protect him in recent years by not opposing him.

A Challenge from the Christian Right?

In the late 1980s and early 1990s a new force has emerged in the politics of the 4th District. Gaining steam with the presidential campaign of Reverend Pat Robertson in 1988, Christian conservatives have tried to take control of the Republican party apparatus across the state. Iowa is an important target for the group because of the prominence of the state's presidential precinct caucuses. Christian activists controlled the state party's platform convention in 1992, producing a document that was a virtual manifesto of the Christian right. In part as a result of an aggressive media campaign by the Christian Coalition against it, in 1992 the state's voters defeated the Equal Rights Amendment to the state constitution.

The Iowa GOP traditionally has been controlled by moderates who favor some forms of government intervention in the economy (especially farm programs), are relatively dovish on foreign policy (Senator Grassley voted against President Bush on the crucial Gulf War authorization vote), and maintain moderate positions on social issues such as abortion. The consensus has been shattered by the insurgency from the Christian Coalition. In 1992, many Republican legislative candidates distanced themselves from the party platform by openly supporting abortion rights and the Equal Rights Amendment referendum. In effect, the Christian Coalition has introduced serious divisions within the Republican party, encouraging an intra-party contentiousness that did not exist before.

The split within the Republican party has important ramifications for candidate emergence. As we have seen, for the past ten years a candidate for the 4th District House seat has been forced to look away from the traditional business-dominated party sources for campaign funds. The business community has made its peace with the moderately liberal Democratic representative whose accumulation of seniority often serves their interests in Washington. The resource breach left by business leaders may soon be filled by christian conservatives and the candidates they support.

Candidate Emergence in Two Iowa Districts

An assessment of the causes of candidate emergence in the 1st District must focus on individual decision making. Personal reasons were powerful factors in making the decision of whether to run. Varn, ambitious and confident of success, was held back by family commitments. Sovern, too, would like to hold public office, but law school forced him to skip this race.

Assessments of the competitive context also played an important role in the 1st District. Osterberg, Lloyd-Jones, and Zonneveld all were eager to run. Each analyzed their chances of winning and made different choices. Osterberg decided he could not win and decided not to run. Zonneveld also recognized that his campaign would not succeed but he still undertook it. Lloyd-Jones believed she had a chance to beat Leach, but entered another race because of the higher personal payoff.

The key to understanding 1st District politics, then, is that a substantial number of activists have considered running for the House seat and have been reluctant to do so largely because of the presence of a popular incumbent—an incumbent with whom many potential candidates are in substantial agreement on policy issues. If Leach retires from the House, competition for the congressional nominations in both parties is likely to be intense and the winner drawn from a rich pool of activists.

In the 4th District, however, the incumbent has not only avoided significant challenge, but appears to have so locked up the House seat that few district politicals will admit to even having considered a run for Congress. In short, we see the stifling effect on candidate emergence of a strong incumbent and the unwillingness of a cohesive and influential wing of a party to use that influence in House politics. The absence of active support for a challenger to Smith by the 4th District business community has made it difficult for a prospective candidate to raise sufficient money in the state—and outsider money is not always welcomed. Such conditions produce challengers such as Lunde, who has twice won the Republican House nomination and twice lost convincingly to Smith. Lunde, with a more advantageous district and an apparent anti-incumbent sentiment growing across the nation, still managed only 37 percent of the vote in 1992.

Moreover, incumbent Smith has had success in working with leaders in both parties. Smith has steadfastly avoided the divisive social issues that have made consensus politics so difficult in this country in the past twenty-five to thirty years. E. J. Dionne (1991) suggests that Americans hate politics because the politicians are battling over social issues that are falsely polarized in the national discourse by groups taking extreme positions. These battles poison the atmosphere in Washington, D.C., and around the country and make it difficult—if not impossible—for politicians to get anything done. Smith's style of nonconfrontation and consensus, by contrast, reflects the political culture of his state. He meets informally with business leaders and other influential people and by and large delivers the improvements requested.

Iowa is one of the most ethnically homogeneous of all the states, a quality that may produce a type of politics more focused on common goals than in states with more diverse populations and interests. But, as with a number of other states, some fraying at the edges is evident. The Christian Coalition has divided the Republican party and has introduced a level of political discord heretofore uncommon in the state. Their efforts are well organized, and they appear to be in Iowa to stay. The strains they have placed on the GOP in the 4th District are similar to those increasingly evident in the party at every level, including presidential politics. Consensus politics of the Smith variety will thus be, if not impossible, at least more difficult in years to come.

8

The Closing of Political Minds: Noncandidates in the 4th District of Oklahoma

Gary W. Copeland

The 4th Congressional District of Oklahoma is an extreme example of what many have concluded is wrong with congressional elections today: it is a typical district in which the incumbent has made himself seemingly impervious to electoral challenge. This situation is not a new one in the 4th District—it has had only two House representatives since 1948. Tom Steed (D) served from then until his retirement in 1980. Dave McCurdy, one of several candidates in 1980, won a Democratic party runoff with 51 percent of the vote and then went on to win the general election by an identical margin. The next two elections saw Republicans mount serious challenges, but they captured barely more than one-third of the votes. Since 1986, McCurdy has faced either no opposition or faced self-starters who have failed to wage vigorous campaigns and have managed to capture only about one-fourth of the votes. We will discuss the electoral security of the district's incumbents in sections that follow, but of greater importance is the conclusion that the presence of a seemingly impregnable incumbent transforms the political ambition of others in the district and the incumbent's presumed victory becomes a given in the calculations of political activists: it closes the political minds in the district.

The story of the 4th District is uncomplicated. Though the district is full of potential candidates who would be quality challengers, not a single person with impressive political credentials gave serious consideration to running for Congress in 1992. Moreover, throughout the district McCurdy is seen as secure and, largely, as a very good representative who deserves to be secure. Indeed, political activists have difficulty imagining the district being represented by anyone who does not share McCurdy's characteristics.

An Overview of the 4th District

Oklahoma's 4th District encompasses part of southern Oklahoma City (including the large Tinker Air Force Base), Norman, several small towns and a substantial number of agricultural communities southward to the Red River, and westward to include Lawton (the state's fourth largest city and home to the large Fort Sill Army Base) and Altus (the site of a modest air force base).

Figure 8-1   Oklahoma, 4th District

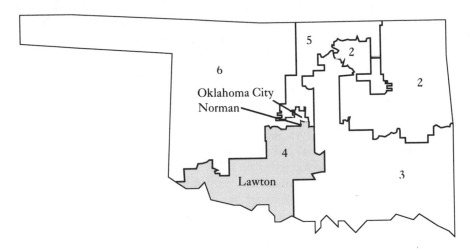

The district, then, has an obvious and strong military component, is home to the University of Oklahoma and two other substantial state universities, and has an urban component—encompassing all or part of three out of four of the state's largest cities. It includes suburban areas of Oklahoma City and Norman as well, but the political and cultural character of the district remains substantially rural.

It is relatively diversified economically, but the district has not fared well recently. Agriculture, oil and gas, and the public sector (military, state government, and higher education) dominate. The agricultural and oil and gas components of the private sector economy have suffered in an extended downturn. The public sector also has suffered, indirectly through the loss of state revenues, and directly through military cutbacks. Generally speaking, the economic hardship felt by much of the nation in the early 1990s hit Oklahoma and the 4th District earlier than it hit most of the rest of the nation and the district actually was experiencing a relative (and modest) rebound by the 1992 election.

The district is like much of the nation demographically: overwhelmingly white with only a small number of African Americans (6 percent), Hispanics, and Native Americans. Politically, it is heavily Democratic by registration (68.9 percent) and by state legislative representation, but it is Republican in national politics, voting overwhelmingly for Presidents Reagan and Bush. The office of House representative is transitional—races for offices above it are competitive and frequently are won by Republicans and races below it are overwhelming won by Democrats (with the exception of some Republican state legislators representing suburbs). In theory, the congressional seat is winnable by a Republican, but most observers of politics in the area have forgotten that fact; the only election the GOP won in the district was in 1920. Only two people have represented the district for nearly forty-five years. The first, Steed, was elected initially in 1948 and often was reelected easily or was unopposed. But he also was vulnerable to a serious challenge; in 1966 (a bad year for Democrats nationally) he escaped with a 364-vote margin. During his last campaign in 1980, he won a contested primary with 65 percent of the vote and the general election with 60 percent. At that point, Steed opted to retire, opening the way for a hard fought campaign to succeed him.

In 1980 McCurdy was only 30 years old, with limited political experience, but with substantial political ambition. McCurdy, some believe, may have sought election to Congress in 1980 even had Steed not retired. McCurdy faced three other Democrats—most notably James Townsend, a seasoned political veteran with substantial ties to traditional Democratic constituencies. In the primary, McCurdy received barely more than one-third of the votes cast, but the weaker candidates kept Townsend's number down also (40 percent), forcing a runoff. In the runoff, McCurdy triumphed by about 1,600 votes.

The general election proved to be equally hard fought. McCurdy was challenged by Howard Rutledge, one of several former Vietnam-era POWs seeking election as a Republican in 1980. Except for the fact that Rutledge also was politically inexperienced, the two candidates were quite different. Rutledge was in his fifties, a war hero, and a Reagan conservative; McCurdy was young, had served in the Air Force Reserve, and followed two unpopular Democrats on the ballot. Local political watchers (who prefer to remain nameless) like to joke about McCurdy "back then." They tell (undoubtedly exaggerated) stories about how little McCurdy knew about issues ("He didn't know the difference between Davis-Bacon and a side of bacon") and discuss his "Safeway strategy" for victory. (The "Safeway strategy") had the handsome, young McCurdy standing outside of grocery stores for hours on end introducing himself to shoppers—mostly female. Obviously, subsequent events have shown McCurdy to be much more politically astute than those detractors give him credit for, but McCurdy did lack experience, had not received the candidate training his opponent had, and did not run a strong issue-based campaign. But, except for crediting his political savvy and hard work, there is no way to account for his electoral victory in a district that provided 60 percent support for Ronald Reagan that year.

Immediately after the 1980 votes were counted, McCurdy started two new campaigns. One was to make himself a real "player" in Washington—which he did, gaining appointment to the Armed Services Committee and playing pivotal roles on key votes during his first term. The other was to ensure that he could gain reelection. His Washington successes, especially the Armed Services appointment, eased the latter task. In 1982, he again confronted a challenge from Rutledge, but this time the results were dramatically different. National political forces worked in McCurdy's favor in

1982, but he also had overcome all of the apparent advantages that Rutledge seemed to hold in 1980. By 1982 McCurdy, not Rutledge, was the military expert. In public campaign forums McCurdy would correct Rutledge's errors and claim credit for strengthening the nation's defense. The outcome was a predictable landslide, with McCurdy winning 66 percent of the vote.

Republicans, though, still felt that the seat was winnable, especially in a year when Reagan would be on the top of the ticket. In 1984 they recruited what they thought was a viable challenger in Jerry Smith. Smith did run a respectable campaign; McCurdy only outspent Smith by $263,000 to $206,000. The result, however, was the same: McCurdy received 65 percent of the votes cast—nearly doubling Walter Mondale's portion in the district. Since then, McCurdy has not faced a serious challenge; when he has been opposed, he has received about three-fourths of the votes.

McCurdy's electoral hold on the district corresponds with the development of his national reputation as a power-broker among moderate Democrats. His Armed Services appointment helped him gain a reputation as a hard worker, as knowledgeable, and as supportive of a strong military. His national reputation has been enhanced further by his leadership roles in the Democratic Leadership Council and the Mainstream Forum, both aimed at moving the party toward the center of the political spectrum. His personal presidential ambitions came into public play for a few days in 1992 when, during a period when the Clinton campaign appeared to be faltering, McCurdy let it be known that he was considering a run for the White House. Instead, McCurdy offered strong backing and support for Bill Clinton.

Potential Candidates in the 4th District

The strength exhibited by McCurdy is all the more impressive when one considers the long list of high quality potential candidates in the district. Among those are about a dozen Democrats, many in the state legislature, who have strong personal and political appeal, secure political bases, and the experience and background to run a campaign against Representative McCurdy. None of them, though, are likely to give the possibility serious thought; if anyone made the run it would have the potential to tear the party apart, after which McCurdy would probably win and the challenger would face devastating personal and political consequences.

The list of potential Republican challengers is possibly even stronger, with several Republicans who would attract the attention of the national party, interest groups, and the media. Three prominent Republicans said they could raise plenty of money to carry out their campaign as desired and all three are probably correct in that conclusion. The collective mind-set of the district, however, is that the incumbent could not—*and should not*—be defeated in 1992. In the end, no credible candidate gave serious consideration to running against McCurdy in 1992.

The long list of potential Democratic candidates is simply a result of the political character of the district—there are lots of Democrats. Moreover, the state legislators from that part of Oklahoma are unusually capable and would be taken seriously if they sought election to the Congress. Within that group, the first name mentioned is routinely that of Senator Cal Hobson from Lexington, who represents a primarily rural district that also includes part of Norman. Hobson, first elected to the state house in 1978, toyed with the idea of running for Congress in 1980. Instead, he filed for reelection to his state legislative seat, and devoted his efforts to leading the McCurdy campaign. In 1990, he gave up his seat in the Oklahoma House to challenge the incumbent Republican state senator. By any standard Hobson is a quality candidate—his politics are reasonable for the district (although a little liberal-leaning), he is experienced in the legislature, has proven himself to be a tough campaigner, and has been a respected and influential legislator. In the words of a potential rival, Hobson is "politically adept, experienced, a proven winner, and a proven leader." While Hobson is well located for a run for Congress *without* the presence of McCurdy, *with* him Hobson's location would make a challenge to the incumbent virtually impossible because of their shared constituency.

Other Democratic legislators have some of the same advantages, but also would draw from different geographic bases than is McCurdy's natural constituency. Among those are Oklahoma Representative Loyd Benson (from rural Frederick), retired Oklahoma Representative Sid Hudson (from Lawton), Oklahoma State Senator Butch Hooper (from Lawton), and Oklahoma State Senator Dave Herbert (former mayor of Midwest City). Benson would have appeal in distant rural areas; the base for Hudson and Hooper would be the second largest city in the district, which is also geographically separated from Norman; Herbert could possibly draw votes in the suburban Oklahoma City area. McCurdy is also strong in all of those areas, but it would seem that a successful Democratic challenger would have to draw votes from outside of McCurdy's Norman base.

Other Democrats were mentioned periodically as potential candidates, but only after substantial probing, usually in the form of "Suppose, for some reason, McCurdy did not seek reelection. . . ." Under those circumstances, some additional names were offered, generally centering on Norman-based candidates. The present and former mayors of Norman, the county sheriff, and McCurdy's administrative assistant for district affairs, Vaughn Clark, all were considered possible candidates by at least one politically knowledgeable person in the district. In fact, with the possible exception of the sheriff (who was defeated for reelection), all of those mentioned, especially Clark, would be strong candidates. The most telling comment, however, was that a strong candidate would "be some Norman attorney they would get together and put up." That conclusion may well be accurate, for McCurdy himself was a relatively unknown Norman attorney prior to campaigning for Congress.

Five or six quality Republicans are on the list of potential congressional candidates. The candidate who would attract the greatest national attention is J. C. Watts, a former quarterback from the football glory days of the University of Oklahoma. Needless to say, Watts has very high name recognition. He is also the only African American Republican in the nation currently holding a statewide elective office. Watts is an articulate speaker who conveys a sense of confidence, social concern, and practicality in his talks; his message carries a populist tone that fares well in Oklahoma. One admirer said, "his speech to the state party convention was one of the finest I've ever heard. He even outspoke Guy Vander Jagt [R-Mich.]." His skills in oratory (and perhaps his race) led him to be selected to provide one of the seconding speeches for George Bush in 1992. Watts currently is a state corporation commissioner (providing regulatory oversight and utility rate setting). Watts may eventually seek election from the 4th District, but he never gave it serious consideration in 1992, opting instead to remain in his current position despite its well deserved reputation as being fraught with political dangers.

A second Republican who could raise interest in the 4th District election is Marc Nuttle. Nuttle is currently an international trade and investment banking attorney in Norman. Nuttle, however, has a substantial political reputation, having served as executive director of the National Republican Congressional Committee, advising hundreds of congressional candidates, and serving as campaign manager for Pat Robertson's 1988 presidential campaign. Nuttle is undoubtedly better known in Washington, D.C., than in Noble, Oklahoma ("he's been in D.C. more than he's been here," is the way one state-based politician put it), but his contacts and expertise would enable him to run a credible, well financed campaign. However, Nuttle may be seen as too ideological in a district that values moderates and independence. "He's too one-dimensional and too tied to Pat Robertson," said a Democrat who would be happy to see Nuttle run.

The third strong Republican is Tom Cole, executive director of the Republican National Congressional Committee during the 1991-1992 election cycle. Cole has been around politics for a long time, has served in the state senate, was the state party chair, and would be positioned to attract talent and money to his campaign. Cole's electoral strength would be his ability to draw votes in the suburban Oklahoma City areas and, perhaps, in Norman, but there are not many Republican votes outside of those areas. Democrats throughout the district are not unaccustomed to voting for Republicans, but Cole has been identified so strongly with the Republican party that he might have problems drawing the votes of Democrats.

There are at least two other candidates who could be very attractive given sufficient resources. One is Gary Gardenhire, a former state senator (defeated for reelection by Hobson) who established solid conservative credentials without appearing too strident when serving in the state legislature. A second is State Rep. Ed Apple, who is a rare elected Republican in the southwest portion of the state. Apple could draw votes in areas that Republicans normally have to forego. Both have military ties (Gardenhire is currently in the reserves and Apple is a retired Marine pilot) and both are articulate and think well on their feet. Gardenhire also falls into the category of "Norman attorney," while Apple can claim a business background.

The district is replete with talent and people who could run respectable campaigns against McCurdy, but have no interest in doing so. As a result, McCurdy again encountered no opposition in his party's primary and only token opposition in the general election. Howard Bell, then a 69-year-old insurance unit manager, ran for the fourth time against McCurdy in 1992. Bell however, did not have the field entirely to himself. Within the Republican party, he had opposition from Robert Best, who identified himself only as a disabled veteran, and mounted little or no campaign. My efforts to locate him failed—as did those of the state Republican party. One final individual merits note as a potential challenger. William Tiffee, a student, attorney, and engineer, is quite dissatisfied with McCurdy's representation and is equally disturbed by McCurdy's aura of invincibility. In both 1990 and 1992 Tiffee considered a campaign as an independent and even took several steps toward launching a campaign, but ultimately shied away from the race. As it turned out, Bell was McCurdy's only threat, but the result for Bell was even worse than his previous attempt—he only captured 29 percent of the vote in 1992.

The Mood of the 4th District

The political ambitions and calculations of these and other political activists and potential candidates in the 4th District cannot be understood without appreciating the dominant political mood in the district. There is a conventional wisdom, even a certitude, about the invulnerability of the incumbent that hangs over any discussion of politics in the district. That impression not only colors evaluations of the incumbent, but also calculations about the political future of the district and how it might be represented.

No one seriously believes that Representative McCurdy might be vulnerable to defeat, and certainly no politically ambitious person is willing to consider testing that proposition. Put simply, I did not talk to *anyone* in the district who felt that McCurdy could be beaten under current conditions—or under just about any conceivable set of circumstances. Routine comments included: "No one can beat McCurdy—Republican or Democrat." When asked if McCurdy was vulnerable several interviewees simply said, "No." As one interviewee concluded, "No one can beat him. The incumbent would have to lose it; have to slip." Or, in the words of another, he'd "have to make a major, major mistake."

Tom Cole, in his position at the Republican Congressional Committee, hinted that Republican party polls suggested that McCurdy was quite secure. Another potential candidate confidentially shared some polling results taken when President Bush's approval rating in the district was two-thirds and when some were thinking about McCurdy as a possible presidential candidate. The poll pitted McCurdy against Bush in a presidential matchup. The outcome was that "McCurdy won overwhelmingly." My source added, "If a popular Republican president can't beat McCurdy, who can we get to beat him here?"

Moreover, virtually everyone—whether Democrat or Republican—concluded that McCurdy deserves to be electorally safe. The quotes that follow may sound as if they were taken from McCurdy press releases, but they were instead made during interviews with friends and foes alike:

> He has so few liabilities; he is so politically skilled. He looks good in Washington, like he is making the courageous decision, but for his district he is really doing the politically correct thing.

> [R]unning against McCurdy is not a doable deal unless he does something incredibly stupid . . . and he won't.

> He is so savvy; smart enough to get in on a hot issue and turn it around to his advantage. No one in the state could beat Dave in his district. He is well liked, respected, and he stays in touch.

One Republican even asked, "Why would we want to beat him? He's pretty good on the issues and represents the district well."

I pressed my subjects for hints of vulnerability: "If you had to go after McCurdy, how would you do it?" Several Republicans hinted that if someone had lots of money and was willing to go negative, McCurdy might be vulnerable. One person said, "Some people have told me that they are unhappy with McCurdy, but I don't know if that's a very broad picture." A number of political watchers hinted at minor political or personal matters that might be used negatively, but it was clear that they were reaching, trying to come up with something to make their interviewer happy or to allow a slight ray of hope to shine through for their party. The clearest example came from Nuttle, a person with great political savvy. He said that McCurdy is "not very" vulnerable, but when asked if he could be beaten, responded: "Sure. You would have to tell the people something they don't know about Dave McCurdy and that is negative. It would have to be decided on character, but that's not my style. . . . I don't know what that negative would be either." Potential independent candidate Tiffee considers a defeat of McCurdy unlikely, but a possibility "with a well-financed campaign. You'd call in big guns. Run a negative campaign. Run commercials with what others have said negative about him. Talk about how he doesn't stay in touch; does not spend a lot of time in the district. You might get a coalition together to get him out—but you may not keep it together for reelection."

Ambition and Context in the 4th District

Most people in the district think that a challenge to McCurdy would be futile. In rational-actor terms, they clearly had reached the conclusion that the utility function for a rational office seeker is inevitably negative because there are costs to a campaign and because the probability of success is zero.

In the interviews, however, potential candidates were encouraged to consider what might happen if McCurdy would disappear from the scene or if McCurdy had run for president. They asked what contextual factors would have the greatest impact on the decision to run.

The state of the economy and presidential coattails are factors which might encourage some prospective candidates to seek the House seat. But the general consensus was that the effect would be minimal. One state legislator said:

> National issues can have a great impact, but the issues ebb and flow. We could get caught up in something—abortion, the Gulf War—depending on the timing it might matter. But, the constituency who wants a say is going to be local and on-going and will exist regardless of national issues.

Democrats interviewed tended to discount national forces—several, in fact, quoted Tip O'Neill's apothegm that "all politics is local," while some Republicans explained that issues such as abortion and family values could be used to their advantage. Still, one of the most ideological of the potential Republican candidates offered the more realistic appraisal:

> A member of Congress is like being the complaint officer at the window of Macy's. *U.S. News and World Report* said that and it's true. Issues aren't very important and national issues, especially, aren't important.

As for structural factors, potential candidates do not seem to think that Oklahoma's relatively late primary and runoff are relevant to any strategic decisions because none of them felt an early start would be necessary or wise for a campaign. The opportunity structure in the district for potential candidates is virtually irrelevant because of the unusual electoral history of the district (and, for that matter, because Oklahoma is a state in which longevity of congressional service has been the norm). There is no predictable path to the office so no one is automatically included or excluded as a viable candidate.

Most of those interviewed believed that the district is Democratic, but that it is winnable by either party absent an incumbent. Most also see the district as having a political focus centering around Norman and south Oklahoma City. But, as McCurdy pointed out, he does not see it that way and has worked hard to establish a strong political base throughout the district. Candidates of both parties will have to consider geographic appeal, but the issue might be more important for Republicans who feel that they have to draw votes from traditionally Democratic parts of the district. Several commented that one of Watts's potential strengths would be pulling some black votes in Lawton away from the Democrat.

The competitive context, though, is dominated by short-term district forces and how they mix with the subjective assessment of the chances of winning—in other words, the presence of a seemingly invulnerable incumbent. The only option for those determined to run for a House seat seems to be to seek office elsewhere. One Republican potential candidate has moved to a different district; another told me that he seriously considered running for Congress in a different district in 1992; and a third told me that if he opts to build a personal electoral base, it will be in a different district.

Personal considerations appear to have varying effects. One potential candidate said: "The costs would be very high. Politics are brutal on families and tough financially." But when asked how his family would receive a candidacy he gave an answer that reflected more resignation than acceptance on both his and his family's part; "Oh, they'd be adamantly opposed [to my running] . . . but, they'd trust me to make the right decision. They have always supported me."

But the one person who nearly ran for Congress (in a different district) was dissuaded, at least in part, by family considerations. The move for his family would have been a double move—to the new district and then to Washington, D.C., in the case of success. He concluded, "Town X is the only place [my children] know. They would not want to move and it wouldn't be fair to them to move them now." He added, "I don't know where in my life I will be in four years; where my kids will be."

Little detailed thought was given to the question of the financial consequences of seeking office because no one expected to do so in 1992. The one potential candidate had decided to resign his current position had he run for Congress, but felt that win or lose he would not suffer financially in the long term. Most simply felt that the question lacked any concrete referent and that they would confront it when—and if—it became relevant.

Emergence in this district, then, is dominated by the short-term evaluation of the probability of success. Other contextual factors can be seen as theoretically important, but have been given little consideration by potential candidates in light of McCurdy's lock on the district.

The Closing of Political Minds in the 4th District

It is very hard to spend much time with the political elite in the district and not begin to feel that McCurdy is held in political awe. These overwhelmingly positive evaluations have serious negative consequences for the district in three ways. First is the obvious fact that political competition has disappeared. Second, the political elite, as reflected in the previous comments, have lost their ability to provide reasonably balanced evaluations of McCurdy's performance. Third, the district has lost even its ability to think creatively about what type of person would be a good representative for the district. The district is hamstrung by an image of a near perfect representative who should be replaced—if necessary—by someone just like him. These consequences for the district, of course, are largely negative. On the positive side, however, the politically ambitious in the 4th District have gone on with their lives and are making their contributions to society according to their interests and talents and not being held up by a passion to serve in

Congress that might otherwise overwhelm all other ambitions.

McCurdy's dominance has not caused political ambitions to disappear. The individuals to whom I spoke would happily serve in the U.S. Congress. They very much act like most politically ambitious individuals found throughout the nation and described in much of the recruitment literature. They follow the pattern discussed by John Hibbing (1991, 11-12) by not awaiting invitations to power, but by actively working to shape their own futures. They have ambition; they have progressive ambition, but they do not define "progressive" the way many political observers do. Rightly or wrongly, these individuals have concluded that the path for the exercise of their ambitions does not run through Congress.

The district has lacked a serious challenger for a decade. In 1992 the home district of the executive director of the Republican Congressional Committee, Cole, was left without a serious Republican contender while he otherwise was proclaiming the large number of quality Republican challengers around the country. This set of circumstances has closed the minds of the political elite in the district in a variety of ways. For example, my interviews suggest that most people have grown to believe that the district's representative should "be like Dave." Only one person actually used those words, but they all seemed to be describing him. In fact, many did not even seem to be aware that they *were* describing McCurdy when talking about what a good candidate or representative should be like. One said, [an ideal candidate] would probably need to be a male who could appeal to both rural and urban voters. He would need to have a military background and be able to talk about the details of economic development." Another sounded similar tones, saying, "he'd have a military background, some ties to the University, be religious, and energy conversant. He'd have to be knowledgeable about agriculture." Or, "he'd have to have credibility in both the military and business communities." Other words commonly used were "independent," "looks good," "good on T.V.," and "good family support system." A good representative, then, has come to be defined as someone sharing the characteristics of the current incumbent.

Another approach used to explore what underlying factors may encourage or discourage challengers was to ask directly what would make 1992 a particularly good or bad time to run for Congress. The answer was always the same. What made it bad? "Dave McCurdy's running for reelection." What would make it good? "If McCurdy did not run for reelection." Nothing else was relevant.

Minds were even closed about potential opportunities for challenge. No one felt that any national issue could influence the race. "McCurdy was right on the Gulf War," or "the pay raise [in Congress] won't be an issue," were the kinds of comments made. It was concluded that the state of the economy would be irrelevant. The much-ballyhooed anti-incumbency feeling evidently never reached the 4th District. When specifically asked if a campaign could be made using that appeal, no one thought so. Even bounced checks

did not raise the interest of potential challengers as one Republican informant said, "His checks are not bad enough to hurt him. Not with Mickey
[Edwards] next door." (Mickey Edwards (R), listed as an "abuser" of the
House bank, was defeated in his party's primary.) In short, potential opposition declared all possible issues to be non-issues.

The consequences of that degree of closed mindedness are not appealing. The incumbent cannot be held accountable for his or her activities,
performance, or positions when potential challengers declare all differences
to be unimportant. Regardless of the specific merits surrounding McCurdy's
job performance, the tone of the district is such that anything but the most
egregious lapse in his performance will go unchallenged.

The closing of the minds of the politically ambitious in the district does
have a positive consequence. The 4th District does have its share of politically ambitious people, but none of them make plans around someday being
elected to Congress. Many would love to, but have decided not to wait for
the opportunity to arise, but instead, to pursue other facets of their ambitions. Rather than wait to run for Congress they have "got a life." Frankly,
the politics of the district and nation have benefited from the fact that many
of these individuals have found alternative ways to achieve their goals. Those
with blind ambition have moved on completely, while those with a balanced
notion of ambition have pursued other avenues of public service. As a result,
it seems that those who remain in serious contention to run for Congress
someday are those who have balanced personal ambition with some broader
conception of public service.

Payne has identified a number of sources of political ambition, an ambition he labels a "quasi-compulsive drive" (1984, 6-7). He identifies the
following motivations: (1) the need for prestige and public recognition, (2)
the need to work on specific, concrete policy issues, (3) the need to please
others and gain their approval, (4) the need to follow one's conscience and
engage in "morally correct behavior," and (5) the need to compete with
others in a structure that is rife with intellectually challenging interactions
(1984, 10). Congressional service is one way to achieve those goals, but
there are many. In fact, it seems that those with blind progressive ambition
fueled by the more negative of these motivations are likely to be driven to
other endeavors when their paths are blocked. But those with the more
positive motivations are more likely to accept alternative venues to exercise
their ambitions and reach for other aspects of public service.

The politically ambitious in the 4th District have become particularly
adept at seeking positive alternatives. One state representative vowed to
retire soon and to work to improve the system "to upgrade our methodology
of government, to train candidates, to train them after they get elected, and
to encourage grassroots participation and preparation." Another said, "I don't
feel a need to be in elective politics, but public service is the only thing I
have really wanted to do." A third said, "I expect to stay in the public service
sector my entire life, but not necessarily in politics at all."

One who typifies this positive outlook is Watts. He indicated that he was engaged in public service before being encouraged to pursue politics and, regardless of politics, will continue in public service. "I don't want to sound like a humble former quarterback, who had the world come to my door," but that is close to what did happen. He added, though, that "most of us in politics have an ego. I have seen what decision makers can do and have enjoyed that." He said, however, that "my life does not revolve around that," adding that he is also a full-time youth pastor and might be happy coaching high school football. Watts is ambitious, but serving in Congress is not a "quasi-compulsive drive." In short, the service of the people in the 4th District who might be quality candidates for Congress, but who have sought other outlets for their ambitions has enriched the quality of life in the district, the state, and the nation. The closing of the political mind as it relates specifically to the 4th Congressional District has opened minds when it comes to public service.

Conclusion

The 4th District in Oklahoma in many ways typifies districts across the country. The incumbent first sought office under adverse circumstances, prevailed, and made himself secure in that seat. Like many districts, there are numerous quality candidates who could run strong campaigns and provide good service to the district if elected. In this case, though, the incumbent has been so successful that no one considers a campaign to be a viable option. Over time, that conclusion has grown to dominate overwhelmingly the thinking of the politically active in the district.

Such a lack of competition is not worrisome because McCurdy is inadequate or deficient as a member of Congress. In fact, this situation could develop only when the incumbent is a good representative and serves his or her district well. The key is that politics in the district has become personalized. Only when campaigns are centered on the candidate—controlled by the candidate and focused solely on the candidate—can this emotional link to the incumbent as an individual be found. Only then can we see the incumbent become a filter for the interpretation of other political events. A key to incumbents' success is that they are seen as likeable individuals in an otherwise highly impersonal government. When that image consistently goes unchallenged, it eventually becomes hardened. Competition is the key to exposure to alternative viewpoints; without it, political minds become closed.

Without competition, the right person—as McCurdy is—has the opportunity to define the politics of the district. Given that McCurdy has successfully done so, what will happen when he moves on? I suspect the next incumbent will define a new image in his or her own terms. Once the *person* of McCurdy is gone, so is the *image*. The only electoral advantage that a candidate "like Dave" will have is in the initial stages being better able to convince others, including contributors, that he or she is electable. After that first post-McCurdy election, the new incumbent will have the opportunity to build the same type of following. Should that person prove to be as politically astute as McCurdy, he or she can look to define the politics of the district for the next era.

For now, the political elite (and perhaps the constituents) in the district can hardly envision the district without McCurdy and have come to believe that he is the embodiment of quality representation. If a good representative must be "someone like Dave," then the district loses its ability to choose quality representation from among competing models. If this district offers a lesson it is that unless candidates offer themselves as alternatives, the district has no choices and even begins to fail to see what alternatives might be attractive.

9

Biding Their Time in the Illinois 9th

Anne C. Layzell and L. Marvin Overby

In an era of safe incumbents, candidate-centered campaigns, and negative public evaluations of Congress, the 9th District of Illinois is an excellent laboratory in which to study the phenomenon of challenger emergence—or to put it more pointedly, challenger nonemergence. It is a place where the prospect of enduring a tough campaign against an incumbent most observers consider unbeatable is enough to deter most serious potential candidates. But it is also a place where, every two years, some candidates do put themselves forward to run the good—if ultimately unsuccessful—race and where many more potential candidates are waiting patiently, strategically holding their ambitions in check for a more propitious opportunity to run for Congress. Investigating the emergence dynamics in such a district illuminates how an entrenched, popular incumbent is able to prevent all but quixotic challenges, even following redistricting in an anti-incumbent election cycle.

The 9th District

Beginning in Chicago's Lake View neighborhood on the Near North side, the 9th District travels north along the lakeshore to the city's uppermost limits where it fans out westward to include the suburbs of Evanston, Skokie, Lincolnwood, Morton Grove, and parts of Niles and Glenview, as well as some of Chicago's northwest wards. It combines the wealth of the lakefront and the suburbs with what the authors of *The Almanac of American Politics* called a "grimier, more diverse Chicago" (Barone and Ujifusa 1989, 376).

The southern, urban portion of the district includes some of what have been termed Chicago's "mixed" neighborhoods. Within the confines of these communities are a combination of African Americans, whites, and Hispanics; wealthy and poor; yuppies and homeless; a large concentration of the city's gay and lesbian population; and the campuses of two major universities. Many of Chicago's young professionals and a large percentage of the city's Jewish population live in the high-rise condominiums along Lake Shore Drive and Sheridan Road. Traveling westward, however, both the high-rises and the wealth begin to disappear and the district picks up some of the city's working- and middle-class neighborhoods. There are

Figure 9-1   Illinois, 9th District

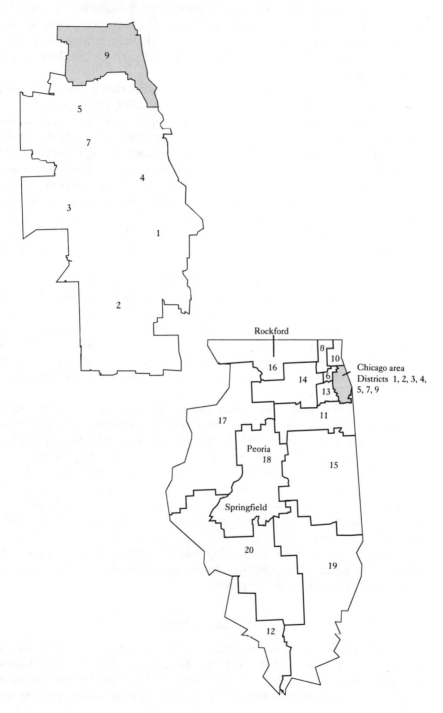

large concentrations of Hispanics in these areas—9 percent—and pockets of African Americans throughout—12 percent of the district's population. Whites make up the majority of the population in these city wards, as they do in the district as a whole (68 percent), and there is a growing Asian American community (roughly 10 percent) centered in the New China Town neighborhood.

Over the years, the district has moved steadily north. Once contained within the city limits, the 9th District now includes all or part of seven suburbs, most of which fall into middle- or upper-class ranks. The demographic makeup of this suburban portion of the district parallels that of the city wards. The opulence of the lakefront continues through Evanston, the home of Northwestern University and the Women's Christian Temperance Union, where the lakefront neighborhoods are anything but poor. With a black population of more than 20 percent, Evanston also contains the largest concentration of African Americans in the district. Skokie, Lincolnwood, and Morton Grove constitute most of the rest of the suburban part of the district, and are distinguished by their large Jewish populations.

The 9th District historically has been a liberal district and the last two remappings have done little to change that. The authors of the 1984 edition of *The Almanac of American Politics* claim that the district "[i]s the one large part of the city where the dominant political tone is intellectual and where voters' gut preference is for reform over the machine." While the district is traditionally heavily Democratic, these voters are by no means traditional Chicago Democrats (in other words, blue-collar, white, ethnic, ward-oriented partisans).

Through the years, the urban part of the district has been largely Democratic but has retained its commitment to reformism by voting faithfully against the party machine of former mayor Richard J. Daley, providing critical support in both 1983 and 1987 for Harold Washington, the city's only black mayor. The suburbs, which were once bulwarks of Republican strength, have become strongly Democratic as the city's young professionals have moved northward. In presidential politics, the 9th District has gone Democratic in each of the past six elections, giving the Democratic candidate an average of 58 percent of the vote. This is in stark contrast to Illinois as a whole, which voted Republican in these same elections. In 1988, for instance, while the 9th District gave Dukakis 58 percent of its vote, Illinois gave him only 49 percent.

The Incumbent

The 9th District has been represented by Chicago-born, Jewish Democrat Sidney Yates since 1948—with the exception of the two years following Yates's unsuccessful Senate bid in 1962. In that time, he has become so ensconced in area politics that during the recent redistricting process one member of the Illinois General Assembly admitted that for all practical purposes Yates "could draw his own map." He has been able to maintain cordial relations with the official Democratic "machine" in Chicago, while at the same time expanding his appeal to more independently minded, reform voters. As a result, Yates invariably is endorsed by both the official Democratic party organization and such groups as the Independent Voters of Illinois-Independent Political Organization (IVI-IPO).

Yates began his term in the House and on its Appropriations Committee in 1949, well before any other current member of the House, with the exception of Jamie Whitten (D-Miss.). Had Yates served consecutively since 1949 he would be second in seniority after Whitten. In 1962, however, Yates made a serious political miscalculation—one of the few in his long career—when he decided to challenge popular Republican senator and minority leader Everett Dirksen. With little support from President John Kennedy (whom, it is alleged, believed any other likely Republican leader would be more difficult to work with than Dirksen), Yates lost, although narrowly. After serving two years as Kennedy's appointee to the United Nations Trusteeship Council, he was reelected to the House in 1964 and began again the climb up the seniority ladder. Currently, Yates is the fourth most senior member of the Appropriations Committee and since 1975 has chaired the panel's interior subcommittee. With his low profile on the floor, he generally is regarded as courteous and mild-tempered. His overall voting record is consistently liberal, and he typically earns ratings from the Americans for Democratic Action above 90 and scores from the American Conservative Union of below 10.

Although he uses his position on the "college of cardinals" to benefit his constituents, Yates's home style is low-key—so low-key, in fact, that he spends little time in the district. As one state representative noted, "He's always in Washington; he never misses a vote." This does not seem to hurt Yates much, however. While it is often said that "if Sid Yates has a weakness, it is that he doesn't spend enough time at home," the emphasis is invariably on the first part of the sentence rather than the latter.

Yates has made the 9th District as safe as any House member could want. He has won every election since 1958 with more than 60 percent of the vote and has averaged 70 percent. As state representative Louis Lang put it: "[h]e can't lose a primary or a general election as long as he's alive . . . and he's in good health." The question, then, that haunts potential candidates in the district is whether or not Sidney Yates will ever retire. There has been speculation in every election since the mid-1980s that "this will be the year Sid steps down." But at age 84 in 1993, Representative Yates has yet to make such a decision and continues to have a firm grip on his seat.

One of the reasons that Yates has entrenched himself so firmly in the 9th District is that he has responded aggressively to the few serious challengers who have emerged over the course of his career, including two during the past decade. In 1982, when the district moved into the suburbs for the first time, the Republican party pitted then 32-year-old Catherine Bertini against him. Bertini waged an aggressive, well financed campaign, attacking Yates's age and alleging that he had lost touch with his constituents. Worried that the new, suburban portion of the district might prefer the Republican Bertini, Yates campaigned more strenuously than he had in years, making special efforts to meet his new suburban constituents. This work paid off and he won easily with 67 percent of the vote—underscoring the conventional wisdom that even in a redrawn urban-suburban district Yates was virtually invincible to Republican challenges in a general election.

Eight years later, in 1990, Yates encountered what he and others saw as a greater threat to his security: a serious, aggressive, well funded challenger in the Democratic primary. Edwin Eisendrath, then a 31-year-old, liberal, well financed, Jewish alderman from Chicago—who, as one local political observer noted, could distinguish himself from Yates only on the basis of age—mounted a major effort to unseat the incumbent. Using the same approach that Bertini had employed, Eisendrath campaigned on the theme that it was time for a change. It was a bitter and expensive fight.[1] Eisendrath charged that Yates ignored the needs of younger generations, had grown out of touch with the 9th District, and was "more interested in self-preservation and pet projects than in our needs" (Hardy and Dold 1989). Yates responded more vigorously than many had anticipated. He raised more than $800,000 for the primary, called in many old favors, and brought in a number of Democratic heavyweights to campaign on his behalf. These included not only both of Illinois's senators (Democrats Paul Simon and Alan Dixon) and Chicago Mayor Richard M. Daley, but also House Speaker Tom Foley (D-Wash.) and Rep. Beryl Anthony (D-Ark.), then the chair of the Democratic Congressional Campaign Committee, who rarely interceded in Democratic primaries (Dold 1989). In the end, Yates glided through the primary, capturing 70 percent of the vote. Yet, to be on the safe side, when the region was redistricted the following year, Eisendrath's ward was drawn carefully out of the new 9th.

What happened in the 9th District in 1990 tells us a great deal about candidate emergence. Even though Eisendrath eventually lost the race, the fact that he decided to run in the face of such inhospitable objective conditions indicates the powerful role of personal ambition in the emergence process; the fact that he was able to raise more than half a million dollars for the effort provides further evidence that in even the most "secure" congressional district high levels of latent competition may rest just below a seemingly placid political surface.

In terms of this study, the 1990 primary battle was important because it had repercussions that helped set the tone for the 1992 election cycle, repercussions that are still being felt across the district today. Yates removed any doubts that anyone might have had about his stomach for a tough fight. Moreover, the negative public reaction to Eisendrath's challenge speaks volumes about Yates's status in the 9th District—he is considered more than just a politician, he is a political icon. As such, younger Democratic challengers risk not only losing badly, but seriously damaging their political futures if their challenges are considered hubristic or disrespectful. Strategic considerations, therefore, counsel even the most ambitious potential challengers to bide their time not just because they are unlikely to unseat Yates, but because an unsuccessful challenge—far from building name recognition for an eventual victory—might so damage their reputations as to make their political futures uncertain.

The Decision to Run for Office

None of the eight strong potential candidates identified by our survey of district political elites opted to challenge Yates in 1992.[2] On the other hand, four lesser-known challengers, two Democrats and two Republicans, did emerge. The Democrats who challenged Yates in the March 17 primary were William McTighe, a ward superintendent in the Chicago's Department of Streets and Sanitation, and Glenn Sugiyama, an Asian American who owns a local restaurant chain and sits on the board of directors of the Chicago Bulls basketball franchise. The Republicans who sought the nomination were George Larney, a labor mediator from Evanston, and Herb Sohn, a urologist, lawyer, and perennial candidate who had run against Yates in four previous elections. Yates easily outdistanced his Democratic challengers with 65 percent of the vote (Sugiyama finished second with 23 percent, while McTighe polled 13 percent), and Sohn won the GOP primary, beating Larney 56 percent to 44 percent.

Incumbency and the Competitive Context

In a district such as Illinois's 9th, assessments of the incumbent's electoral strengths are far and away the most important in determining which latent candidates decide to become actual challengers. The potential candidates have to determine if the incumbent's margin of victory has declined in recent years; if his age is a factor; if the incumbent has lost touch with the district; and if his voting record reflects the interests of the district. The answers to such questions are often quite subjective, and we expected and received several elaborate rationalizations to justify the different political decisions made during the 1992 election cycle.

None of the potential or actual challengers we interviewed indicated that they believed Representative Yates to be very vulnerable on any important dimension. Those who opted to get into the race, however, convinced themselves that Yates was vulnerable enough to at least open the door to a challenger. Democrat McTighe, for instance, argued that Yates's "base of support has evolved, and moved," making it less reliable for an incumbent who rarely comes home or provides much help for the district. Republican Larney came to a similar conclusion:

> Yates's strength is incumbency, but it's also his weakness. This year the issue is incumbency. He is one of the old men in Washington's elite club who is very insulated from his district and divorced from the affairs of daily life. He is an incumbent with 42 years of service, yet he does not head a powerful committee. What's more, he's like Mao Tse Tung— never seen here among the people.

As previously suggested, those who decided not to challenge Yates in 1992 were influenced by the events of 1990 and what they said about the strength of the incumbent. Potential Democratic candidates not only unanimously viewed Yates as virtually invulnerable, most volunteered the opinion that good Democrats *should not* challenge him. The following comments were typical of those we heard: "In 1990, Edwin Eisendrath launched a vigorous challenge . . . and people resented it. They felt that he ran an ageist campaign. [Eisendrath] felt that even if he lost he would move to the next position, make himself the next one in line, but that wasn't the case. People really resented him." Another told us that Eisendrath's effort ". . . was outrageous. I thought it was a terrible thing for him to do. He had no chance of winning even if Sidney died." And finally, "There is a bad image associated with trying to topple so good a person as Sid Yates. If it ain't broke, you don't try to fix it." Due consideration of the quality of service Yates has provided, combined with an understanding of how badly Eisendrath jeopardized his political future in 1990, has counseled well positioned, strategic politicians to put any congressional ambitions on hold until the seat becomes an open one.

Our interviews revealed another factor related to incumbency that affected the decisions of the potential candidates—the fact that this is considered by many to be a Jewish district. State Representatives Lee Preston and Louis Lang indicated that retaining a Jewish seat in the House was more important to them than running for office, and both had to factor such a consideration into their personal decisions. Focusing on the future and the inevitable scramble for the nomination once Yates steps down, Lang said that he would prefer sitting down and deciding who the strongest Jewish candidate would be, even if it was not him: "This seat was developed as a Jewish seat. . . . [And] I would not want to be a party to making this a non-Jewish seat." Preston, also acknowledging the importance of retaining a Jewish representative from the 9th, said that "[t]here are very few Jewish leaders in elective office. . . . I would not want to go to my maker knowing that I had [been a party to abolishing a Jewish seat]."

The Resource Context: Campaign Costs

Both the academic literature and our own instincts about the 9th District suggested that potential challengers' evaluations of the financial costs of unseating an incumbent would loom large in their decisions. Yates has shown exceptional fund-raising capabilities, moving his campaign spending levels into six digits early in the 1980s and, as already mentioned, setting the curve in the 1990 primary season by spending more than $800,000. However, even with the high stakes in this district, the ability to raise money did not seem to be a decisive factor in potential candidates' decisions of whether to run for Congress.

When we asked potential candidates how much they expected a campaign would cost in this district, the responses were generally realistic, ranging from $500,000 to $1 million for both primary and general elections. Perhaps less realistic were the potential candidates' evaluations of their abilities to raise such funds. Of our interviewees, only Larney and Preston expressed reservations in this regard. Most of the other potential candidates indicated that they believed money would be available, especially when Yates has retired. One candidate, however, believed he could do well without copious campaign funds. McTighe declined to discuss the cost of his primary challenge, but acknowledged he was running a targeted campaign designed to turn out his supporters without arousing what he hoped was a complacent incumbent. He stressed that by meeting 2,000 voters per day (which was his goal) and not spending enough to trigger Yates "to dump tons of money into the race," he could squeak by the incumbent in the primary.

The principal difference between Republican and Democratic potential candidates in terms of their evaluations of fund-raising concerned *when* they thought they would need the money. Given the Democratic makeup of the district, all of the Democrats we interviewed said they viewed the Democratic primary as the principal race and that when the seat becomes open a serious candidate would probably have to spend hundreds of thousands of dollars to win the nomination. Republicans, on the other hand, indicated that the GOP primary is likely to remain a rather low-cost affair as a result of limited competition, but that to be competitive in the general election—against Yates or any other Democrat—would be an uphill struggle requiring perhaps $1 million.

The Personal Context

Considerations of family and personal costs had only a limited effect on the candidates' decisions to run. While some admitted that the thought of sacrificing family privacy to run for public office gave them pause, all of those who got into the race felt that they had the support of their families in their decisions to run for Congress and most said they would be willing to do so again. While all acknowledged that a campaign puts a strain on family life, none admitted that such concerns were major factors in determining whether to run. McTighe, who has two small children, said that he "had never worked so hard" in his life and that he barely saw his family in the weeks before the primary. He concluded, however, that he enjoyed the campaign and that outweighed his family considerations. Personal financial considerations did limit what some of the candidates were willing to do, however. Despite his estimates of what a competitive campaign would cost, Larney, for instance, "never considered borrowing a lot of money to make this run. I have to pay for my children's education and I'm not prepared to take out a second mortgage to fund my campaign."

Those who decided not to run, all of whom are current elective office holders, also concluded that family considerations were not critical to their decisions. As public officials they already willingly had made certain familial sacrifices. When asked what personal concessions he would have to make to run for Congress, Preston responded "none that I haven't [already] made for a very long time." In a similar vein, Janice Schakowsky said that other than surrendering her seat in the state house, running for Congress would not affect her much except in terms of "personal time and privacy . . . and they can go."

Although minor in comparison to the incumbency factor, professional considerations did play an important role in the individual decisions to run for Congress. For those in the private sector, the impact was basically a wash—helping some, hurting others. Urologist Sohn believes that his biennial challenges to Representative Yates are good for business. "The name recognition I get from running helps me build my practice, since people who know my name will come to me. And [campaigning] is the greatest education I've ever gotten . . . it's a fantastic education in terms of building people skills." For labor negotiator Larney, the stakes were higher and the calculus less clear-cut: "I don't know what this will do to my career. Generally you don't take high power political stances in negotiations nor do you want to be associated with them. I have taken a big risk professionally and I tend to think the professional impact will be negative, but then again most people know me well enough to know I'll be impartial."

For those currently holding elective office, professional considerations strongly counseled against running for Congress, especially against a powerful incumbent. Most indicated they have given serious thought to their positions and feared the worst case scenario—losing both their current position and the election:

> If I ran and lost, [the committeeman would have to find someone else to run in my place]. Two years from now, he or she is not just going to step aside so that I can run again [for my old seat]. It's hard to get back into the game.

> [The prospect of losing my office] is very important. I have been known to take a risk, [but] I am very happy doing what I'm doing—I like the people I'm serving. I don't think I would give that up lightly.

Few of the elected officials among our interviewees totally ruled out the possibility of someday running for Congress, and more than a few volunteered that they would be eager to run if the odds were good. But with more to lose than most, they are particularly averse to rash decisions and more than willing to bide their time until Yates's retirement.

Strategic Considerations

Since this was the first election cycle after a decennial census, political decisions in the 9th District were made against the backdrop of two important and related strategic considerations—redistricting and name recognition. In a real sense, redistricting determines the universe of potential candidates and can have a substantial impact on political outcomes; in the 9th in 1992, however, its importance was more problematic and probably helped more than hurt the incumbent. Since Illinois lost two House seats in this reapportionment, significant remapping occurred in many of the state's congressional districts and there was some speculation early in the process that the 9th might be split up between several other districts, especially if Yates decided to retire. But that did not happen; Yates actually became even more firmly established since Eisendrath's ward in the south was drawn out of the district and several additional, liberal, largely Jewish suburban neighborhoods were added in the northwest.

The only potential challenger significantly affected by redistricting was McTighe, whose home in northwestern Chicago was drawn into the new 9th in 1992. According to McTighe, redistricting "played a big part" in his decision to run, not only because it moved him into the 9th but because he decided that "Yates could be beaten" in the redrawn district with its new voters and the new northwestern Chicago neighborhoods that gave him a base of political operations.

Name recognition was the other strategic consideration potential challengers had to weigh. In an urban area such as "Chicagoland," increasing name recognition via the mass media is complicated both by its large expense and by the difficulty in concentrating advertising on a targeted population. Challengers, therefore, face an added difficulty and often are forced into a more "retail" political style. With the exception of Sohn, none of the people we interviewed felt that his or her name recognition was as high as it needed to be. While many acknowledged that they were well known in the portions of the district in which they lived or worked, all indicated that their district-wide profiles could be much higher. This did not, however, seem to be a major deterrent to running for office. Several of the potential candidates who did not run in 1992 indicated that over the course of a campaign they thought they would be able to enhance their visibility considerably, and three of the actual challengers volunteered that they believed campaign activities such as rush-hour El stop visits and small-scale, local debates helped them raise their electoral statures among voters.

At least one actual candidate also developed a complicated rationale concerning how other factors would offset his relatively low-level name recognition in the Democratic primary. Before the Democratic primary, McTighe admitted that his name recognition was "next to none" along the populous lakefront, but predicted he might win anyway. He noted that his name was the first on that section of the ballot; that Yates's name was the smallest and was "stuck" between his and Sugiyama's; that McTighe was the first Irish name on the entire ballot (and, we were left to conclude, likely to get a disproportionate share of the Irish American vote); and that he had received the same ballot number as well known incumbents Dan Rostenkowski and Bill Lipinski in other parts of the city.

Party Support

It is not surprising, given the diminution in their traditional recruitment roles, that the political parties were not major players in the 1992 election cycle in the Illinois 9th. On the Democratic side, the fact that both party organization and independent Democratic groups have strongly supported Yates for years left his primary challengers largely on their own. As Nicholas Blase, a local Democratic committee member, put it, with Yates as the incumbent, local and state Democratic officials paid little attention to the 9th and were "more worried about getting someone in [Rep. Henry] Hyde's district [the Illinois sixth]." As a result, none of the Democrats we interviewed mentioned active involvement by either local, state, or national party organizations, although each of the actual candidates felt it necessary to inform local party officials of his intentions—a feeling that was echoed by several potential candidates who indicated that they would certainly contact the party to "estimate support" if they decided to run at some future date. The general feeling among Democrats is that even when Yates has passed from the scene there will be little organized party activity in the recruitment of his replacement and little need for it. In the words of one potential candidate, "we have so much quality here . . . you don't need to *recruit* candidates."

As the minority party in the district for more than forty years, the local GOP is unorganized and usually much more interested in the area's competitive General Assembly races than in trying, yet again, to unseat Yates. Even though 1992 looked to be a bad year for congressional incumbents, local Republicans had no luck during 1991 identifying and recruiting a strong challenger to Yates. So, local party leaders turned reluctantly once again to Sohn, who had decided to run with or without their endorsement.

It is symptomatic of the difficulties that modern party leaders face that Republicans in the 9th were unaware of Larney's political ambitions and his willingness to enter the race. Although Larney had been in contact with officials at the Republican National Committee and GOPAC, a political action committee affiliated with Rep. Newt Gingrich (R-Ga.), for months during 1991, the local party neither contacted nor even knew about Larney. The national party contacts were critical for Larney, however, and convinced him to enter the race. "GOPAC was very supportive," he recalled.

> [A]nd the [national] party reenforcement was a stimulus. Had they been less supportive, I might not have run. As it was, there was a snow-balling effect . . . [as they] sent training videos, literature, issue position papers . . . called on a regular basis . . . [and] set up conference calls with other [potential Republican] candidates in the state.

Larney learned, however, that his national party contacts were not appreciated by many local Republicans. "There was a real lack of communication between the local and national levels," he recounted, "and a resentment on the part of local party people regarding national party activity." As a result, when he filed for the Republican primary on December 6, 1991, he received a "cold reception" from his local committeeman. While Larney acknowledges that "there would have been more enthusiasm [among local Republicans] if I'd been identified earlier," his relationship with the local establishment remained distant throughout the campaign. While he received some "under-the-table support" from party leaders dissatisfied with Sohn, they remained officially neutral during the primary and concentrated most of their energies on the reelection of a local state senator.

National Political Conditions

In a congressional campaign in which the focus tends to be on district-specific interests, national political conditions are less likely to influence a candidate's decision to run for office than the more immediate personal and strategic considerations. However, it is generally believed that national economic and political conditions do influence the way people vote and candidates are forced to take this into account. During the 1992 election season the national political mood became particularly turbulent in response to events such as the Clarence Thomas confirmation hearings, the House banking scandal, and the faltering national economy, resulting in strong pro-women and anti-incumbent sentiments.

These national tempests did little to roil the political waters in the 9th District, however. With only four overdrafts, Yates was not seriously tainted by the House banking scandal, and his liberal record on such matters as abortion rights and a national family leave policy has earned him the support of many women's groups. Moreover, the relative wealth of the 9th—in which the 1990 per capita income was $18,691—insulated the district somewhat from the national economic sluggishness. As a result of these factors, the nation's general political mood did not seem to have much effect on the decisions of potential congressional candidates in the Illinois 9th. Only Republican Sohn mentioned the nation's anti-incumbent mood as an important factor in his decision, and his comments were general, not specific. Asserting that 1992 "was a good year" to enter a congressional race, he expressed the opinion that "the anti-incumbent feeling . . . would force people to see that there are good people [besides Yates] around [to run for office]."

The Waiting Game

What is most interesting about the 9th District in 1992 is not that several weak candidates emerged to confront Yates, but that once again most politically savvy potential candidates made the strategic decision not to emerge as challengers—deciding instead to continue playing the waiting game, hoping for a better opportunity in the future. Since Yates remains in good health and is seeking reelection in 1994, their long wait seems destined to continue.

In the meantime, for serious potential candidates, the most politically relevant question is how to structure their careers to be in position to run a competitive race when the opportunity arises. Given the political dynamics of the district, that is not an easy question to answer.[3] Yates has so dominated congressional politics and the district has changed so much since the last time he was seriously threatened (he last garnered less than 55 percent of the vote in 1956) that it is not clear what career platforms would best position potential candidates for a future campaign. An examination of the other twelve House members from the Chicagoland area, however, might provide some clues. Of these, six served in the state legislature before running for Congress, three as Chicago aldermen, and the remaining three came from nonpolitical backgrounds. This predominance of state legislators is also reflected in the pool of potential candidates in the 9th. Of the eight potentially serious candidates identified by district observers, three were state representatives and three state senators.

While it is unclear that these politicians "planned" their state legislative service with an eye toward one day running for a congressional seat, it does seem that they—more than local officeholders—are well poised for such a run. In addition to general advantages of campaign expertise and policy mastery (Berkman 1993), in a split urban-suburban district that is increasingly suburban, state legislators enjoy another pronounced advantage over aldermen: they are less likely to be associated with urban machine politics. This seems to be especially important in the heavily Jewish 9th. As Barone and Ujifusa (1993, 408) put it, "Chicago's North Side Jews, on the lakefront or in neighborhoods like Rogers Park and nearby suburbs like Skokie and Niles, have been a solidly Democratic voting bloc, but skeptical of the old Democratic machine." Since these voters hold the balance of power in the district, those with realistic hopes of representing the 9th one day seem to be following career paths that take them through Springfield rather than through the wards of the city.

Conclusion

Since the principal strategic factor in the district is the incumbent's longevity, it is worth concluding with a brief consideration of what is likely to happen when the seat becomes open: will the rush to succeed Yates look like a busy day at O'Hare Airport, or will one or two strong contenders push their ways to the top and dissuade others from running? Many of the local politicians we interviewed believe that once the obstacle of incumbency is removed from the equation, the race for the House seat, at least in the Democratic camp, will be a battle, with numerous quality candidates climbing into the ring. Such a conclusion, however, may be too facile. Since the 9th is still considered by many to be a "Jewish district," local Jewish politicians and organizations have an interest in avoiding a divisive Democratic primary and maximizing the likelihood of electing another Jewish representative. It is possible that they might dissuade some potential candidates while encouraging the most electable ones to enter the race, resulting in the emergence of only one or two quality, strategic candidates (State Rep. Janice Schakowsky and former State Sen. Bill Marovitz are the names that were mentioned most frequently, although Marovitz's 1992 reelection loss has tarnished his political image).

In the meantime, strategic politicians in the district must plan their careers in the shadow of Yates. While most of the politicians we interviewed stressed that they were content in their current positions and were not currently making plans to run for the 9th District seat, many also indicated that they had at least allowed themselves to speculate about an eventual campaign for Congress.[4] Given the nature of the constituency, with its large liberal Jewish population, university communities, and sizable minority components, it is likely that whoever succeeds Yates will be similar to Yates—Jewish, Democratic, liberal, and activist. Despite their personal ambitions, "politicians-in-waiting" who do not share these qualities are likely to face serious—perhaps insurmountable—difficulties in the post-Yates 9th.

The Illinois 9th provides a textbook example of how strategic politicians make decisions that will determine their political and professional fates. Yates, who has represented the district for more than forty years and shows no signs of diminishing support, presents a formidable "incumbency factor" against which most of the area's politicians have decided not to risk their assets and, more importantly, their careers. Instead they have decided to bide their time until more favorable conditions arise.

Notes

1. According to Federal Election Commission figures, the Yates-Eisendrath race was the most expensive primary in the nation in 1990. Yates spent $784,129 and Eisendrath $632,807, for a total of more than $1.4 million (Hardy 1990).
2. Based on interviews with twelve 12 local political observers, we identified eight potentially serious challengers for the 1992 race: three state representatives (Louis Lang, Lee Preston, and Janice Schakowsky), three state senators (Arthur Berman, Howard Carroll, and William Marovitz), one suburban mayor (Joan Barr of Evanston, the only Republican whose name was mentioned), and a state circuit court judge (Alan Greiman). Four other candidates (two Democrats and two Republicans) actually ran in the primaries.
3. Neither is it an easy question to ask of potential candidates. The very negative response to the naked ambition evident in Eisendrath's challenge has cautioned many of the district's political candidates to be quite soft-spoken about their political aspirations and to downplay any thought that they are "positioning" themselves for a run at the seat.
4. The exception is Sugiyama, who already has announced his plans to challenge Yates again in 1994 (Barone and Ujifusa 1993, 409).

10

Ambition and Candidacy:
Running as a Strategic Calculation

Thomas A. Kazee

An elusive goal for those studying congressional candidate recruitment is to explain why some people run for office and others do not. Few questions are as central to democratic theory as those relating to candidate emergence. As Linda Fowler (1993) has demonstrated, maintaining electoral competition; assuring officeholder accountability; representing constituent interests, perhaps even the dominant partisan alignments in the electorate—all these are traceable to the process of candidate emergence. In addition, the quality of government in any society depends on the process by which leaders emerge to seek office. Ehrenhalt (1991, 3) states the problem directly: "Is it possible that this is the best we can do, that this is the best political leadership the world's oldest democracy can muster?"

We began with a simple assumption: potential candidates decide whether to run by matching their ambitions to the political context of which they are part. To test this assumption we interviewed prospective candidates to assess their ambitions and to weigh the relative importance of factors in the politicians' environments. Our findings suggest a candidate emergence process dominated by individual considerations of career impact. In short, most potential candidates appear to ask, "In light of my goals as a politician, is this the right time for me to run?" Implicit in this question is the interaction between ambition and context, for "goals" are defined by ambition and "the right time" is determined by contextual factors. The question also hints at the impact of a variety of contextual concerns raised in this book. The emphasis of the question is on personal goals and the right timing assessment for the individual; congressional candidacy is a self-starting business, depending more on one's willingness to undertake it than the need for selection by district power-brokers or party recruiters. Moreover, the question implies that factors affecting the probability of a candidate winning will transcend other considerations; one's goals as a politician are most likely (although not always) served by winning and advancing to higher office. Personal or occupational costs, for example, may be given less weight by ambitious politicians who see opportunities for career advancement.

The Context of Eligibility

In a candidate-centered environment the decision to run may be largely a function of individual motivation, but race, gender, and (in one of our studies) religion nevertheless shapes the pool of those eligible to run. We saw in our nine districts an expanding group of eligibles. While most potential candidates are—as they have been before—white male professionals, females were included on informants' lists in most of the districts. Indeed, in several districts the *ideal* candidate was described as a female. Minority candidates less frequently appeared on candidate lists, except in the two districts created with African American and Hispanic majorities.

Not all barriers have come down, of course; a white male attorney in his forties need not demonstrate that he comes from a racial, gender, or occupational category appropriate to running for Congress. Others, such as minority activists or women, may have to overcome traditional expectations that they should remain on the sidelines. However, in the "Year of the Woman," being female apparently had its advantages. Party activists in Colorado's 2nd District worked hard to recruit a woman, and in North Carolina's 9th and Iowa's 1st and 4th districts political watchers argued that their districts would be particularly receptive to a woman running for Congress. The desire to field female candidates was apparent in both parties. Democrats wanted to take advantage of their pro-choice position on abortion (which was generally viewed as more appealing to female voters) and Republicans, still smarting from backlash of the Clarence Thomas confirmation hearings, wanted to help close the gender gap by placing women on the ballot. Since we saw little evidence of effective *recruitment,* however, ultimately the gender balance of a candidate pool depends on the number of women willing to enter the political arena. We saw many prospective female candidates; few actually sought party nominations.

For African American and Hispanic activists, the doors to candidacy swung wide in North Carolina's 1st District and Texas's 29th District, as the states' mapmakers intended. The election of a nonminority candidate in Texas should not obscure the preponderance of Hispanic candidates who emerged. Indeed, in minority districts the collective action problem David Canon describes in Chapter 2 is fundamentally a problem of ambition: how does one encourage ambitious individuals to put their own career goals on hold for the good of the group?

In our other districts few minority candidates emerged. Bill Cleveland ran for the Republican nomination in Virginia's 8th District, and in North Carolina's 9th several African American activists eyed the Democratic nomination until redistricting essentially removed all black areas from the district. Anne Layzell and Marvin Overby note that religion played a role in the 9th District of Illinois, which is seen by some as a "Jewish seat"; this expectation has important implications for the emergence of Sidney Yates's successor.

The Access Context

Though the recruitment of candidates, in theory at least, is an important party function, parties have for many years played a limited role in this area (Seligman, King, Kim, and Smith 1974; Huckshorn and Spencer 1971). The much chronicled weakening of the American party system has rendered the parties even less capable of identifying and selecting candidates for public office.[1] As former U.S. Sen. Thomas Eagleton put it, "Today, you are either a self-starter or a no-starter" (Hansen 1991, 71).

Despite this general pattern, party organizations in several of our districts worked to influence candidate emergence and selection. Indeed, the 2nd District of Colorado was a near-textbook example of party recruitment. As Allen Hertzke explains in Chapter 5, Republican party leaders aggressively pursued attractive candidates and discouraged those who seemed less likely to run a strong campaign. Colorado's unusual nomination rules, unlike the rules that predominate in the rest of the country, promote formal party involvement in the nomination process. District party conventions control access to the congressional primary ballot; to be listed on the ballot requires the support of 30 percent of the convention delegates. An active party leader such as Colorado Republican Chair Bruce Benson is likely to have greater influence over party nominations in a system that uses the party convention to "qualify" candidates for the primary.

In Chapter 9, Layzell and Overby describe a limited and unsuccessful effort by Illinois 9th District Republicans to find a sacrificial lamb (other than Herb Sohn) to run against Yates. Other examples of party activity were seen in Iowa's 4th District, where John Haskell, Kerry Sutten, and Peverill Squire note that a potential Democratic candidate was approached by members of the party central committee. Paul Herrnson and Robert Tennant portray as well an activist effort to support the strongest Democrats in the 8th District of Virginia in Chapter 4, though such involvement stops short of recruitment in the classic sense.

When parties did get involved the activity often was motivated by a desire to find someone to run in an unwinnable district. When the seat appeared to be winnable, as in the two new districts, many individuals emerged as prospective party nominees (particularly in the dominant party in the new districts). Party recruitment, in short, may not be needed to identify and encourage prospective candidates to run for Congress. Our districts contain many potentially attractive candidates who possess high levels of ambition, ambition that is sufficient to draw them to candidacy if a realistic chance of winning is present.

Discouraging potential candidates from running—"derecruitment"— occurred at least as frequently as did attempts to recruit candidates. In Colorado, Republican leader Benson apparently told a prospective candidate that he did not fit the desirable party profile, and in Iowa's 1st District Jan Zonneveld, who ran and lost in 1990, was discouraged from running a second time by party leaders. In the 9th District of Illinois, George Larney, considering a run for the Republican nomination, received a "cold reception" from his local party committeeman.

Access to candidacy also may be limited by district power-brokers, who may use their control of resources to encourage some prospective candidates to run and to discourage others. In several of our districts potential candidates recognized the political advisability of sounding out district "heavy hitters" to see if they had made prior commitments or would be willing to provide resource support, but in no district were these heavy hitters able to control access to candidacy. A typical example was the business clique of John Belk, Ed Crutchfield, Bill Lee, and Hugh McColl in North Carolina's 9th District. Several political activists suggested that it would be wise for a House aspirant (of either party) to find out where this group stood before entering the political arena; no interviewee, however, claimed that these business people dictated who could or could not run for Congress.

The gradual relaxing of obstacles to candidacy, reflected in both the eligibility and access contexts, has produced an environment in which the key ingredient in the candidate recipe is personal ambition. As Alan Ehrenhalt argues:

> Political careers are open to ambition now in a way that has not been true in America in most of this century. Those with the desire for office and the ability to manipulate the instruments of the system—the fundraising, the personal campaigning, the opportunities to express themselves in public—confront very few limits on their capacity to reach the top. The bosses and party leaders who used to pass judgment on political careers have just about all departed the scene. They are no longer a significant barrier to entry (1991, 272-273).

The Competitive Context

Factors affecting the likelihood of winning or losing dominated the calculus of most prospective candidates. The presence of an incumbent, in particular, deterred many potential candidates from running. Absent an incumbent, the field of entrants in primaries (particularly on the side of the dominant party) was large. Eleven candidates ran for the Democratic nomination in North Carolina's new 1st District, and five candidates competed for the Democratic nomination in Texas's 29th District. In the other districts, the discouraging effect of incumbency was substantial. Gary Copeland argues that Dave McCurdy effectively has eliminated opposition in Oklahoma's 4th District; potential challengers have "closed their minds" to the seat. This has occurred despite the fact that the district has a competitive party balance and a willingness to support Republicans for other offices. McCurdy's stature in the district, however, has driven the House seat from the opportunity structure. Prior to redistricting, North Carolina's 9th District arguably was competitive, but incumbent J. Alex McMillan drew only token opposition in 1988 and 1990. Iowa's 1st and 4th Districts are fertile grounds for congressional challengers looking only at nonincumbency factors, but the presence of Jim Leach and Neal Smith so discourages potentially strong challengers that the nomination is left to what Haskell, Sutten, and Squire describe as "invisible" candidates.

One of the more surprising findings of the district case studies was the extent to which incumbents are regarded as doing a good job by observers in both parties. Indeed, our interviews reveal that often incumbents do not attract stronger opposition because potential challengers see little need to replace them. In six of the eight districts represented by incumbents our interviewees—informants as well as prospective candidates—rated incumbent performance from good to excellent. Copeland notes that "virtually everyone—whether Democrat or Republican—concludes that McCurdy deserves to be safe." Iowa state representative Mary Neuhauser justified her noncandidacy by asking "Why run against someone you like?" Leach is, she declares, "bright and full of integrity." Haskell and his co-authors describe the reluctance of Iowa businesspeople to oppose incumbent Smith, who has supported their efforts to revitalize downtown Des Moines. The business community, which presumably would bankroll opposition to the incumbent, has instead protected him "by refusing to instigate a grooming process for a challenge."

The competitive context is affected as well by the status of other House prospects. For many activists, "Should I run?" is contingent on "Who else is running?" Unfortunately for those contemplating whether to throw their hats into the ring, this is an area of uncertainty. District political watchers may take pains to find out who will be running, but playing one's cards close to the vest may be strategically advisable for some candidates. Occasionally the uncertainty about candidate intentions took on soap opera qualities. Hertzke's description of the on-again, off-again candidacies of Jim Martin and Carol Taylor-Little in Colorado's 2nd District illustrates well the interplay of ambitions in a congressional district. In the two new districts, those uncertainties were of fundamental importance in determining who would run and eventually who would win. The large number of declared and undeclared candidates in Texas's 29th and North Carolina's 1st exacerbated the uncertainties created by an ever-evolving series of redistricting decisions.

Since seven of our districts were represented by an incumbent at the time of our study, potential candidates' knowledge of the incumbent's intentions is of crucial importance. In most of our districts no doubts existed about the incumbent's desire to run again, though in the 9th Districts of North Carolina and Illinois questions about the incumbents' status revealed a deep pool of potential candidates interested in replacing them. In Illinois, Yates's advanced age leads to understandable questions about his durability; in North Carolina rumors of McMillan's dissatisfaction with congressional life stirred the emergence pot.

Other competitive factors proved less critical than incumbency. If partisan balance were seen by prospective candidates as a crucial factor in congressional races, several of the districts likely would produce quality opposition for incumbents. However, weakened partisanship—which produces split-ticket voting and promotes the use of incumbency as a voting cue (see, for example, Hinckley 1981)—apparently minimizes the extent to which district partisan balance encourages out-party nominees to challenge incumbents.

Issues in the district and the local economy also had limited impact on candidate emergence. Such issues could be exploited to take advantage of an already weak incumbent, but few prospective candidates appeared to believe that a candidacy could be based on local concerns alone. Few candidates cited national conditions as factors affecting their decision to run either, a finding of particular significance given the alleged anti-incumbency sentiment that pervaded the 1992 elections. Layzell and Overby found that a primary motivation for Republican Sohn to run against Yates was the perception of an "anti-incumbent feeling," and Douglas Abel and Bruce Oppenheimer discovered a prospective Republican candidate who was depending on President Bush's coattails in the 29th District of Texas. Such instances were clearly exceptions to the dominant pattern in these districts, however. Copeland concludes that "the much ballyhooed anti-incumbency feeling never reached the 4th District" of Oklahoma, and most interviewees dismissed conditions outside the district as factors important to their decisions about candidacy.

The Resource Context

One of the more intriguing aspects of our study was the extent to which prospective candidates deemphasized the importance of fund-raising as a disincentive to candidacy. To be sure, several aspiring House candidates acknowledged the daunting prospect of trying to raise the sums required to run a respectable congressional campaign. Minette Doderer of Iowa City, for example, stayed out of a race against incumbent Leach because she did not like raising money—and did not think she could raise enough of it. Doderer was the only prospective candidate of those interviewed in Iowa's 1st District for whom fund-raising was a prohibitive consideration. Confidence in the ability to raise large amounts of money was widespread, even among candidates who had no previous experience in campaigns requiring such large expenditures. This is not to say that those considering candidacy are naive about how much money it would take to run. Some interviewees produced low estimates of the resources needed, but most understood that a serious campaign effort would require hundreds of thousands of dollars or more. Such optimism may not be realistic, of course, but the perception is critical to understanding why fund-raising discouraged relatively few prospective candidates.

The Structural Context

Prospective congressional candidates paid much attention to the nature of the playing field, particularly when redistricting changed its shape. Most of those we interviewed weighed carefully the partisan and personal implications of redrawn district boundaries. Is the new district more Republican or more Democratic? Are the lost neighborhoods or cities or counties areas of strength or weakness? An additional consideration (and complication) for a prospective candidate is the timing and uncertainty of redistricting decisions. Does the potential candidate know what the final map will look like—and *when* will he or she know? Will court challenges to new maps dramatically alter the electoral landscape subsequent to the decision to run?

In the two new districts, the political manuevering associated with the redistricting process left prospective candidates unsure about their chances of winning party nominations. Indeed, in the 1st District of North Carolina potential candidates could not even be certain that the new district would physically include them or their areas of greatest strength—confusion exacerbated by the eleventh-hour U.S. Justice Department rejection of a map approved by the state legislature. Moreover, in both new districts the redistricting process encouraged state legislators, incumbents, and would-be candidates to try to manipulate the outcome to their advantages.

In already existing districts, the impact of redistricting is more variable. In some districts, such as the 1st and 4th Districts in Iowa, redistricting may appear to make the incumbent more vulnerable—though we saw in both cases successful efforts by the two incumbents to solidify their holds on the new districts. Or, as in North Carolina's 9th District, an incumbent may be made more secure by the elimination of unfriendly areas of the district. The impact of redistricting in the latter case was demonstrated by the number of potentially strong Democrats who decided to stay out of the race after the new map was announced. Other structural factors, such as the nature of media markets and geography, are likely to be most important in districts that cover a large amount of territory or that meander through various newspaper, television, and radio markets. These factors seldom were mentioned by our interviewees, due perhaps to the absence of unusually configured districts (with the exception of North Carolina's 1st District) and the more important impact of factors such as incumbency or redistricting. A potential candidate, having decided to stay out of the race because the incumbent appears unbeatable, may give little specific consideration to the more subtle influences of media or district geography.

Racial and ethnic balance, however, were predominant influences on the emergence of candidates in the two new districts. As might be expected, the large number of African American and Hispanic residents in each district drew numerous black and Hispanic candidates into party primaries. What could not have been expected, however, was that the dynamics of candidate emergence and campaign politics would produce an Anglo representative in the new Texas district. It could be argued that a similar outcome could have resulted in North Carolina had not several prospective African American candidates remained on the sidelines. David Canon, Patrick Sellers, and Matthew Schousen's assessment of the "collective action" problem facing ambitious minority candidates (who are no longer in the minority) ought to give pause to those who assume demographics translate easily into representation. The power of ambition is perhaps demonstrated no more clearly than in the Texas case, which saw several Hispanic candidates run in the Democratic primary despite the real possibility (which became the reality) that the resulting divisiveness would help the sole white candidate.

As Joseph Schlesinger (1966) noted, another contextual factor is the opportunity structure of a state or community. Offices with short terms and high turnover are likely to present numerous opportunities for ambitious politicians. If the office is also very visible and provides a jumping-off point for higher posts one would expect it to be entrenched solidly in the opportunity structure of the state. House seats in the districts we studied meet several of these criteria: terms are short, visibility is high, and House incumbents may be well positioned to seek Senate seats (as Yates did unsuccessfully in 1962) or governorships (as 9th District incumbent Martin did successfully in North Carolina in 1984).

Potential candidates in our districts, however, surely have noted the infrequency of turnover for the House seat. Our eight incumbents averaged 15.5 years of House seniority (11.4 years without Yates), and in only four of the districts had the seat turned over in the last decade. It would be an exaggeration to claim that the House seat was no longer part of the opportunity structure in several of these districts, but it would be accurate to conclude that ambitious individuals now look elsewhere as incumbents continue to win reelection, often by increasing margins. Copeland argues that ambitious political entrepreneurs in McCurdy's Oklahoma district "have concluded that the path for the exercise of that ambition does not run through the Congress," a reasonable assessment since only two people have represented the district in the House since 1948. Layzell and Overby note that many House aspirants in Yates's district have died waiting for that seat to open.

Related to the structure of opportunity is the nature of the state legislature. Canon, Sellers, and Schousen find that a state legislative seat is a common first step for U.S. House candidates in North Carolina, despite a rather low level of professionalization in the state legislature. Haskell, Sutten, and Squire claim that Iowans also apparently look to the state legislature for House candidates. In most of our districts, however, the nature of the state legislature appears unrelated to the process of emergence, perhaps because a plethora of elective offices, from the county commission to the upper chamber of the state legislature, are seen as appropriate for nurturing congressional ambitions.

A final structural factor apparent in several districts was the electoral process used to nominate and elect House candidates. In both of the new districts, the use of runoff elections profoundly influenced who won and who lost and, presumably, who decided to run. Indeed, in Texas's 29th District the eventual winner, an Anglo candidate, finished second in the first primary to a Hispanic candidate. In Colorado's 2nd, the use of district party conventions to determine access to the primary ballot was a critical factor in shaping the decisions of a variety of potential candidates.

The Personal Context

Without question, candidacy entails significant personal and occupational trade-offs. Winning a House seat likely means uprooting a family, maintaining a residence in Washington, D.C., and at home, perhaps interrupting a promising and lucrative career in the private sector. Even for those who lose, the campaign may require the investment of personal funds, a leave from work, and a fishbowl lifestyle for the duration of the race. In short, a rational person might conclude that running simply is not worth the cost. Gwenne Hume and Sandy Hume in Colorado were not willing to sacrifice time with their daughter and Parks Helms's wife in Charlotte would have to be convinced that serving in the House was more enjoyable than the North Carolina legislature.

Only in one district—the 2nd of Colorado—does it appear that such factors operate district-wide to diminish significantly the pool of potential candidates. Indeed, a distinguishing feature of most political activists in this study was their acceptance of—and, in most cases, enjoyment of—the life-style politics requires. Ehrenhalt summarizes well the attitude that characterizes many of those included in candidate pools across our nine districts: "A political career in America in the 1990s . . . is not an easy, lucrative, or particularly good route to status in life. This places increased importance on one other motive for entering politics: sheer enjoyment. You pretty much have to like the work" (1991, 17). Many of the professional politicians interviewed (and their families) had long since accepted the demands of political life.

Strategic Ambition and Congressional Candidacy

To assess the role ambition plays in the emergence of congressional candidates, one must look for answers to two questions. First, how ambitious are the activists in these districts? Second, to what extent does their ambition affect perceptions of the political world around them? In other words, does ambition blind them to the reality of most districts—that the odds against winning a House seat are almost invariably long? Or does their desire to advance in politics cause them to become overly cautious—"risk-averse," as Hertzke characterizes it in Chapter 5—and not willing to jeopardize a political career with a loss in a House primary or general election?

As for the first question, almost all of those interviewed would pass the minimal test of ambition, that is, they would accept a House seat if it were offered at no cost.[2] This conclusion is less trivial than it seems, for it runs counter to the claim that the demands of politics are so great and the rewards so few that the pool of office-seekers is drying up. We may be embarking on an anti-Washington and anti-politician era, but Congress still appears attractive to a large number of politically active people in these districts. Only in two districts, and in isolated instances in other districts, was there evidence that political activists did not find serving in Congress appealing. Even among potential candidates who find *running* for Congress distasteful, or who are not willing to make family or occupational sacrifices to win a seat, the appeal of the seat remains. Many of the unseen candidates are apparently like Virginia's Mark Warner, who was described by one informant as "dying to get to Congress!"

Of course, few House seats will ever be won without cost, so at issue is the willingness of prospective candidates to pay the costs associated with winning a House seat and serving in Congress. One way to reduce costs is to underestimate them; ambitious individuals wanting to run for office may distort the electoral environment to minimize costs and justify a candidacy decision that was, in effect, already made. As Sandy Maisel, the Maine college professor who lost in a House Democratic primary, said: "That personal commitment [to run] . . . was probably too strong to be overcome by rational analysis" (1982, 19).

Some distortion of the objective context may be evident in the surprisingly small number of our interviewees who conceded that the need to raise large sums of campaign money was a deterrent to candidacy. Low name recognition seems to have discouraged few congressional aspirants, as well. Many potential candidates apparently have concluded that if the seat was winnable, that is, if the incumbent left office, no other obstacle was insurmountable. Surely such perceptions represent wishful thinking for many individuals. How else can we explain the expenditure of more than $600,000 in a primary to unseat twenty-one term incumbent Yates, a contest in which Yates won fully 70 percent of the vote? Or the quixotic campaigns of Rory Blake in North Carolina's 9th District or Paul Lunde in Iowa's 4th District? What is important is not that these people had little chance to win, however, but that their ambition to run for a House seat seems little diminished by the realities of running an effective congressional campaign.

For most of those interviewed, ambition did not interfere with their abilities to interpret accurately the political context of their districts. Most prospective candidates had taken careful stock of what was going on around them, and in most cases drew reasonable conclusions. What distinguishes the candidates from those who stayed on the sidelines was the ability of those who ran to construct plausible scenarios in which they could win; it is this ability that is perhaps the most direct evidence of ambition's power to distort. Abel and Oppenheimer's candidates in the 29th District of Texas illustrate this phenomenon, for each candidate was able to mold his perception of the objective context to match his desire to win a House seat.

Putting the Pieces Together

Based on this study and work that has come before it, we know (or suspect) a number of things about the people who compose the pool of potential House candidates. We know that most of those identified as prospective candidates are serious politicians. They may not hold elective office, or may work at other ostensibly nonpolitical jobs, but politics is at the center of their lives. As Ehrenhalt argues, these professional politicians are willing to commit themselves to politics and to the pursuit of elective office. We know also that politics has become increasingly centered around candidates; as parties have weakened, candidates have become independent actors, particularly in terms of emergence and campaigning. Ambition is the key in such a system: many of today's activists are driven to succeed in politics and are willing to pay a substantial price to do so.

For the highly ambitious political entrepreneur, risks must be taken only after some calculation. Caution must prevail, for an embarrassing loss in a run for higher office may derail a carefully planned political ascendance. Moreover, the calculations are likely to be based primarily on local political circumstances that affect the likelihood of winning or losing an election. The local political context is the bread and butter of politics for the aspiring House candidate, and is certainly more relevant to reelection than national issues. It is the local voters, after all, who will determine if a politician's ambitions are realized.

In summary, the most common emergence profile is of an ambitious but cautious individual who decides whether to run for Congress based largely on perceptions of the winnability of the seat. Amateurs and professional politicians, particularly those whose background, experience, and access to resources makes them most able to mount effective campaigns, are most likely to be motivated by the desire to succeed. They look to candidacy not primarily to fulfill a civic obligation or to run a respectable, but losing campaign—unless such an outcome increases their chances of winning two years later. Indeed, the most ambitious activists are, in this important respect, perhaps least likely to run absent some reasonable probability of success. They have staked their careers on moving up the political ladder, and a defeat in a House primary or general election may do considerable violence to that goal. Their reluctance to challenge incumbents—

particularly given the advantages incumbents possess—is understandable in light of their motivations for running. Most potential candidates, in short, are self-interested, independent entrepreneurs who must see a reasonable chance to win before they will run. Ambition alone is thus not enough to ensure a supply of candidates who will offer credible challenges to House incumbents.

Given this incentive, the apparent fixation of many of our interviewees on incumbency is not surprising. Several of the scholars in the Candidate Emergence Project lamented the difficulty in getting district activists to think about the political environment of their districts without thinking about the incumbent. For the political scientist, speculating about the future is reasonable and important. For the prospective House candidate, the question perhaps seems fantastic; why guess about an unreal world—a world profoundly altered by the absence of the electoral keystone—when today's congressional aspirations are tied so closely to the status (and stature) of the incumbent? Moreover, the activist is likely to view candidacy in the short term, as a series of steps taken every few years. As long as an incumbent avoids scandal or serious policy missteps, he or she is likely to remain in the seat and ambitious people in the district must look elsewhere for political opportunities. Finally, the incumbent remains the most sizable obstacle to the realization of a prospective candidate's congressional ambitions; any political event that affects the status of the incumbent by necessity affects the status of the activist.

But what if the incumbent were not around? What does the interview evidence suggest about the interaction between ambition and context in that situation? If the premise of high ambition and election incentives is correct, we would expect to see a similar mix of forces operating to influence candidacy decisions. That is, contextual factors that affect the competitive environment in the district would still be uppermost in the minds of prospective candidates. National political forces, party recruitment activities, personal costs—all these would still pale in comparison to contextual factors that influence who wins and who loses. An incumbent would no longer be present, but the partisan complexion of the district, information about other candidates, the impact of redistricting, and so on, would rise to the top of the prospective candidates' calculus.

Does this conception of prospective candidates as cautious entrepreneurs accord with what we know about congressional elections? We know that incumbents win most of the time and that competition in House elections has diminished during the last quarter century. Until 1992, the number of uncontested districts had increased dramatically, and the number of challengers with prior officeholding experience had declined. We know also that open districts are more likely to produce real competition than districts with incumbents. Moreover, Canon (1990a) concludes that a modest but nevertheless surprising number of amateurs are winning nominations and elections. Finally, Ehrenhalt (1991) tells us that activists at all levels of

American politics (particularly in the Democratic party) see politics as a full-time commitment—a profession—and develop career strategies commensurate with that commitment.

These findings are consistent with our characterization of candidate emergence. It is not surprising that competition diminishes if quality candidates pick their spots more carefully: running for Congress in a district represented by an apparently entrenched incumbent is not likely to advance one's career. However, new districts, open districts, or districts represented by discredited or scandal-ridden incumbents are more inviting targets. In their caution, experienced politicians may thus abandon districts that are more vulnerable than they knew; amateurs, having won the nomination by default, are able to reap the benefits of an incumbent's newly discovered vulnerabilities.

This explanation also sheds light on the debate among students of congressional elections, discussed at length by Fowler (1993, 78-79), regarding incumbent versus challenger behavior as the cause of diminished competition. As explained in Chapter 1, several scholars have linked recent declines in the competitiveness of congressional elections to the weakness of challengers. Compared to incumbents, challengers spend less money, are less well known, and have more limited contact with voters. At issue is whether the weakness of challengers is based primarily on incumbent behavior or challenger behavior, that is, do incumbents avoid strong challengers simply by avoiding political problems and delivering satisfactory constituent services? Or are would-be challengers, particularly the most experienced potential candidates, primarily responsible for declining competition as a result of their unwillingness to take electoral risks?

Both processes are at work, of course, but the evidence from the districts makes clear that prospective challenger decision making, contingent largely on an assessment of the probability of winning or losing, leans toward noncandidacy in districts with incumbents running for reelection. Motivated by a commitment to politics as a profession, many prospective candidates are understandably risk-averse in an environment that seems more likely to produce a loss—and its attendant damage to career—than a win. To be sure, incumbents play no small role in this formulation, for it is through careful stewardship of their districts that they avoid raising challengers' hopes, but the absence of competition is a result primarily of prospective candidate decision making.

The Competitive Potential of Congressional Elections

Although many prospective candidates may be unwilling to challenge incumbents, it would be a mistake to conclude that the potential for competition has vanished in most House districts, even in our districts, most of which are represented by apparently well entrenched incumbents. Our districts suggest that the perception of vulnerability apparently shared by most

House members (Fenno 1978) is an understandable consequence of incumbents' own electoral histories and their knowledge of the competitive environment at home.

Four district-based realities discourage incumbent complacency: most incumbents have at one time or another been involved in competitive races for their seats; in most districts the pool of potential challengers—*quality* challengers—is deep; when electoral opportunities arise the number of contenders for party nominations is large; and in most districts ambition for a House seat shows no signs of diminishing even in the face of declining respect for Congress as an institution.

The incumbents in our districts most often won their seats in very close elections, usually winning a bare majority of the vote. Moreover, in subsequent elections a number of our incumbents have had relatively close scrapes, or least faced well funded, aggressive opponents (see Table 10-1). Smith, first elected in 1958, was held to 54 percent of the vote in 1980, and McMillan won reelection in 1986 with only 51 percent of the vote. Yates has never lost a House election and has not received less than 60 percent of the vote since 1956, yet his Democratic primary opponent in 1990 spent $630,000 to unseat him. McCurdy's 1984 opponent spent $206,000 (McCurdy spent $263,000). Even Leach, one of the safest incumbents in our group, was held to 59 percent of the vote in 1982. Thus it is not surprising that most incumbents look over their shoulders: they want to know if someone is gaining on them.

Another indication of the competitive potential of many congressional districts is the size and quality of the candidate pool in both parties. The case studies identify a large number of experienced, ambitious individuals in most districts. The project participants noted apparent gaps in the candidate pool in only two districts, gaps that were limited to one party or one identifiable group. Haskell, Sutten, and Squire comment on the scarcity of well known or politically experienced Republicans in Iowa's 4th District who might challenge Democratic incumbent Leach, and Able and Oppenheimer describe the limited pool of Hispanic candidates in Texas's 29th District. More commonly, the district studies describe a quiescent but crowded contingent of potential contenders for the House seat. This situation, which we term latent competition in our description of the 9th District in North Carolina, is not likely to go unnoticed by incumbents.

Most important, competition for the House seat, perhaps held in check for many years as an incumbent builds on his or her electoral foundation, figuratively explodes when the incumbent leaves office. The battles for party nominations in the 8th District of Virginia in 1980, North Carolina's 9th District in 1984, and Oklahoma's 4th District in 1980 suggest what happens when competition moves from latency to reality. This occurred in several of our districts in *both* parties, which underscores both the personal aspect of incumbency advantage and the latent nature of district competition. The large numbers of candidates seeking nominations in the two new districts is further evidence of the competitive environment that exists absent the inhibiting impact of incumbency.

A Note on Strategic Politicians

Gary Jacobson and Samuel Kernell's theory of strategic politicians is based on the assumption that candidates and contributors are sensitive to the political winds blowing at any particular time. Good times for a party breed good candidates, and those candidates are better able to acquire the resources they need to run effective campaigns. The theory purports to explain why aggregate congressional election outcomes appear to be linked to issues such as national economic performance, despite the absence of evidence that voters are responding to issue cues. Empirical support for the theory could be found in the decisions of potential candidates if they cite national conditions as factors affecting their willingness to run.

Our prospective candidates, however, were nearly unanimous in their neglect of national factors. In only a few instances, such as Bob Walton in North Carolina's 9th District (who said that he would want a strong Democrat in the presidential race), were national factors of any kind mentioned. This omission is particularly significant given the inclusion of specific questions about national considerations on the questionnaire. The districts in our study are not representative of all districts, of course. The relative absence of obviously competitive districts—open districts, in particular—may reduce the number of districts in which the impact of national conditions is most apparent.

But what if prospective candidates in other districts, like those we have examined, generally ignore national political circumstances when they decide to run? How do we then account for the persistent evidence of a connection between national economic conditions and congressional election outcomes? One explanation is that national elites behave strategically—both in their efforts to recruit (or at least to encourage the emergence of) strong candidates in good years, and in their support for candidates once campaigns begin. Candidates may be running primarily in response to local circumstances—as they told us—but, because of the decisions of other elites, are more likely to see an inviting resource environment when they are deciding to run, and to have more abundant resources during campaigns.

Candidate Emergence and Electoral Reform

One proposition undergirds this analysis: a steady flow of citizens willing to enter the electoral arena as candidates is essential for the health of a democracy. As Lawrence Hansen (1991, 1) observes:

The vitality of a representative democracy, and to an extent its legitimacy, is as dependent on the number and quality of those citizens willing to compete actively for public office as it is on the rest of us who are periodically expected to sort out and then choose among the competitors.

In recent decades alarms have been sounded about decreasing competition in congressional elections. Twenty years ago David Mayhew discussed "vanishing marginals" (1974), his term for a dramatic decline in the number of closely contested congressional elections. More recently Fowler and Maisel describe the 1980s as an "era of the 'vanishing candidates'" (1989, 1). They note that "[f]ewer candidates compete in House elections today than in the past, and fewer of those who do run are able to mount a genuinely competitive effort" (1).

Do we need to think seriously about reform? Should we alter the structure of American congressional elections to increase the likelihood that strong candidates will run for House seats, which presumably will increase competition and turnover? Such reforms should be based on an empirical understanding of what is happening in congressional districts, of the factors that affect the decision-making process of potential candidates. Our study of nine districts, though not necessarily representative of all House districts, tells us a good deal about how and why candidates "emerge" to run for Congress.

We saw, for example, little evidence that ambition for a House seat is disappearing. In several districts the distaste for living in Washington, D.C., or the recognition of the limited power of a House member discourages some from running, but more commonly serving in Congress is still desirable. The personal costs of running—family sacrifices, occupational trade-offs, hard-fought and expensive campaigns—seem not to be driving a large number of potential candidates out of the electoral arena. Perhaps this is because most individuals seriously considering running for Congress have long since made their peace with the costs of candidacy.

We also saw that personal ambition is highly strategic; potential candidates are often cautious, unwilling to jeopardize a budding political career with a decisive loss in a House campaign. The important phenomenon of amateur candidacies notwithstanding, many (if not most) of today's political candidates are professional politicians. As Ehrenhalt (1991, 273) convincingly argues, political power "passes to those who want the jobs badly enough to dedicate themselves to winning and holding them." For the professional politician, losing an election is not simply an example of nothing ventured, nothing gained, but a serious setback along a career path.

These strategic professionals run if a seat is perceived to be winnable, a truth readily apparent in our two open districts and in the other districts when today's incumbents first won election. (See Table 10-1.) Once the incumbent has established himself or herself, however, competition—defined here as the number of quality candidates willing to run—

Table 10-1   Incumbent Electoral Performance: Selected Elections

District	Incumbent	Party	Percentage first election (percentage/ year)	Lowest percentage subsequent election (percentage/ year)
Colorado, 2nd	David Skaggs	Democratic	51 (1986)	61 (1990)
Illinois, 9th	Sidney Yates	Democratic	55 (1948)	52 (1952)
Iowa, 1st	Jim Leach	Republican	52 (1976)	59 (1982)
Iowa, 4th	Neal Smith	Democratic	52 (1958)	53 (1960)
North Carolina, 9th	J. Alex McMillan	Republican	50 (1984)	51 (1986)
Oklahoma, 4th	Dave McCurdy	Democratic	51 (1980)	64 (1984)
Virginia, 8th	James Moran	Democratic	52 (1990)	n.a.

drops precipitously. It would be fair to conclude that real electoral competition for the House seat in our seven incumbent districts simply did not exist in 1992. (See Table 10-2 for challenger profiles.) Do we need to make seats more winnable? A more inviting electoral environment would increase the number of strong candidates who emerge to run, which would enhance competition and presumably increase the turnover of House seats.

Assuming that more turnover is desirable, two changes in the structure of congressional elections could raise the probability that more quality candidates would run and that more incumbents would lose. First, the resources available to challengers could be increased. Public financing of congressional elections would eliminate the catch-22 facing today's non-incumbent candidates: money must be sought from individuals and groups that want to support winners, but the contributors' refusal to give to challengers ensures that the challengers will lose. Campaign finance reform is a much needed first step toward nurturing the perception held by prospective candidates that House elections *are* winnable.

If the prospective candidates we interviewed are representative of activists in general, we should recognize that campaign finance reform will not bring a flood of new and talented challengers to battle incumbents. Most of those considering a run for the House said that fund-raising was not a significant disincentive; they knew a great deal of money was needed, but they were confident they could raise it. Nevertheless, to be confident of one's ability to raise money is not the same as knowing that a campaign war chest is available once one meets eligibility criteria. Moreover, we saw some evidence that the daunting prospect of raising a half million dollars or more discourages some from running. In short, it strains credulity to dispute that potential candi-

Table 10-2 Challengers from the Nine Districts Included in the
Candidate Emergence Project

District	Candidate	Age at election	Occupation	Spent	Vote (percentage)
Colorado, 2nd	Brian Day	34	minister	$93,011	35
Illinois, 9th	Herb Sohn	65	physician, lawyer	$12,140	28
Iowa, 1st	Jan Zonneveld	66	retired insurance actuary	$1,044	31
Iowa, 4th	Paul Lunde	56	lawyer, teacher	$11,178	37
North Carolina, 9th	Rory Blake	42	pharmacist	$29,720	33
Oklahoma, 4th	Howard Bell	69	insurance agent	n.a.	29
Virginia, 8th	Kyle McSlarrow	32	lawyer	$416,172	43

Source: Congressional Quarterly Weekly Report, October 24, 1992, 3415-3430.

Note: North Carolina's 1st District and Texas's 29th District were open-seat districts so they are not included in this table.

dates would be more inclined to run if a substantial and guaranteed reservoir of funds were made available to them through public financing.

Another reform proposal, currently enjoying great public approval, is to limit the terms of House and Senate members. From an emergence perspective, the proposal to limit congressional terms is based on the premise that strong candidates are much more likely to run for open seats; we could increase the supply of strong candidates by forcing incumbents to leave office after a specified period.

The arguments for and against term limits are wide-ranging. Proponents claim that term limits would replace careerist, self-interested incumbents—many of whom have become wedded to special interests—with energetic new members motivated by a desire to make good public policy rather than the desire to protect their seats in Congress. Opponents respond that limiting terms forces a loss of expertise and experience, increases the power of legislative staffs and bureaucracy, and diminishes the role played by elections in holding incumbents accountable (see especially Kesler 1992, 247-248). Our discussion will be limited to the arguments that address emergence issues, for the interviews offer some insight into the motivations of potential officeholders.

Periodic forced resignations indeed might increase electoral competition, but, as Gerald Benjamin and Michael Malbin (1992) argue, competition actually might decrease if certain types of rules were adopted. "Simple" limits would place a cap on the length of continuous service in one office, but would not restrict what the officeholder could do later—in other words, after taking a one-term break, the officeholder could return to Congress. "Lifetime" or "combined" limits are designed to discourage legislative careerism by limiting the number of years people could serve in their lifetimes. Benjamin and Malbin conclude that simple limits would probably increase the pool of experienced challengers, increase competition, and allow continued professionalism, while lifetime and combined limits would have the opposite effects (13-15). A number of states recently passed term limits laws that included lifetime or combined stipulations, thus working against the objective of increased competition. Even in those states passing simple limits competition might not increase. Term limits, as Fowler argues, "remove the most fundamental incentive for people to engage in political entrepreneurship": potential candidates will assume all the risks of running for office but will not be able to "capitalize on [their] investments" by staying in office and building a career (Fowler in Benjamin and Malbin 1992, 182).

With respect to the reasons for seeking office, are we to believe that the public-spirited candidates running for a term-limited Congress will be profoundly different in motivation than those now running? Such logic is convincing only if you assume today's House candidates view the seat as a terminal position, seeing themselves in the House far beyond the three to six term tenure allowed by most term limit proposals. We have little empirical evidence of how forward-looking House candidates are, but, as Fowler points out (1993, 171) the mean tenure of a House member today, 5.8 terms (Ornstein, Mann, Malbin 1992, 18-19), is within the range permitted by the term limits initiatives.[3]

Answering the question of whether more frequent congressional turnover is needed depends on the quality of representation delivered by those now serving in the House. With respect to representation, two observations seem appropriate, one empirical, the other speculative. We know empirically that voters have returned to Washington almost nineteen out of twenty incumbents seeking reelection. Given such success rates, one must speculate about the level of dissatisfaction with incumbent performance. Moreover, our interviews show clearly that in many districts elites, even if grudgingly, conclude that incumbents have done a good job representing district interests. Turnover for its own sake is difficult to justify if those in the district are satisfied with the performance of incumbents.

Yet for some, the collective consequence of incumbent invulnerability is gridlock. House members attend only to their district interests, seeing little incentive to take politically risky positions back home even if such action would be in the common interest. Would more competition in congressional elections increase the likelihood that the policy logjam could be broken?

One might ask what campaigns would look like if a larger number of districts were competitive. Would the winners work harder to seek consensus in Washington? Probably not; strong campaigns are often built on the claim that the candidate in question could better represent *district* interests. One consequence of increased competition, in other words, might be that the winners would become even more parochial in outlook. Competition has its virtues, to be sure, but we should be wary of the claim that an obvious consequence of more competitive elections would be higher quality representation of the national interest.

Our skepticism about the specific consequences of enhanced competition aside, James Madison's contention that representative democracy depends on competition—which depends on ambition—is compelling. Attracting citizens to government service requires that a competitive environment exists and is nurtured. Indeed, the most serious consequence of the decline of competition in American elections will be the loss of talented and ambitious individuals who look outside of public service for opportunities to satisfy their ambitions.

Notes

1. This is not to say that parties play no role in the emergence of candidates. As various studies have shown, party officials report considerable recruitment activity (Gibson, Cotter, Bibby, and Huckshorn 1985; Cotter, Gibson, Bibby, and Huckshorn 1984), and the national party organizations have stepped up recruitment efforts in recent years (Herrnson 1988). Based on interviews with thirty-six congressional candidates in competitive districts, Thomas Kazee and Mary Thornberry (1990, 76) conclude that ". . . despite the lack of party-directed recruitment, most candidates had a history of considerable party involvement, a pattern particularly apparent among candidates who won party nominations."
2. We might call this the "Rohde Test," named for David Rohde and his test of progressive ambition among U.S. House members (1979).
3. As Fowler suggests, since many members do not serve past the six- to twelve-year proposed limits, term limits would hit hardest at those in leadership positions—those whose institutional memory, accumulated expertise, and demonstrated attention to constituent concerns at home (attested to by their regular reelection) are greatest (1993, 171).

Appendix

Note: we should be sure to take full advantage of the stimulating effect of the interview. You've invited a district politico to think about candidate emergence. Encourage reflection on this topic. Don't be satisfied to ask only the questions on the questionnaire. Probe; follow-up. This should be a conversation about politics in the district and, as such, should not be inhibited by a rigid question and answer format.

As you read the questions, keep in mind that the specific questions asked in any particular interview (as well as the exact wording of questions) should take note of the time of the interview. Some questions make little sense early in the election cycle; others make little sense later in the cycle. Keep in mind as well that you may revisit the respondent to continue the conversation at a later date. Indeed, we should plan to reinterview all those who, subsequent to an initial interview, announce their candidacy for the congressional seat.

Questions for Informants
(to be asked also of potential candidates)

1. Who would you like to see run for the U.S. House seat in this district?
2. Do you know anyone who is thinking about running for the House seat (or in the Democratic or Republican primary)?
3. Who do you think is most likely to run for the House seat?
4. As someone familiar with politics in this district, would you identify anyone who might run for Congress that others might not identify?
5. Can you name anyone who might make a good candidate but will probably *not* run? (If someone is named:) Why won't he/she run?
6. What would an ideal candidate in this district look like? That is, what personal or political characteristics would an ideal candidate have?
7. Are there any distinctive qualities or characteristics a candidate must have which are particular to this district? For example, does he or she have to have lived here a long time, or have connections to important political families, or a history of party service—anything of that nature?
8. Is anyone in the district active in recruiting candidates to run for

Congress? Is anyone in the district encouraging others to run?

9. I'm going to read the names of a few people in the district. For each name, could you tell me how well known the person is in the district, and if the person is likely to run for Congress. What strengths and weaknesses would each bring to a congressional race?

10. How are things shaping up in the nomination campaigns so far? (This question should be tailored to fit the campaign context at the time of the interview. Relevant considerations: Have any candidates actually entered the nomination campaign? Has advertising begun? Is it possible that more candidates might enter the race?)

11. (For races with an incumbent:) If [name of the incumbent] decided not to run—to retire or run for higher office, for example—who might run for the House seat? In general, how would this change the political scene in the district?

12. Is anyone in the district "grooming" himself or herself for a run for Congress this time around? How about in the future—who seems to have ambitions for the House seat in this district?

13. I'd like to talk for a moment about the incumbent. What are his or her liabilities? Are those liabilities serious enough to encourage people to run against him/her in his/her own party? How about in the other party?

14. Is the incumbent doing anything to minimize those liabilities? (For example, is the incumbent perceived to be out of touch with the district, is he or she making more of an effort to get in touch?)

15. How about policies or issues? Any particular issues which might affect who runs? (Ask specific questions about any locally salient issues of which you are aware.)

16. Are there any people in the district who are influential in determining who runs for Congress? Could you name them?

17. Is any person or group in the district so important that prospective congressional candidates always try to gauge where they stand before deciding whether or not to run?

18. Are there any groups in the district (special interest groups, for example) which encourage people to run for office?

19. How about party organizations? As far as you can tell, do the party organizations in the district help to recruit candidates? Does the party have an official committee which helps to recruit candidates? Generally, what role do parties play in the recruitment process in this district?

20. What is the likely effect of redistricting on candidate recruitment in this district?

Questions for Potential Candidates
(not to be asked of informants)

Personal

21. How old are you?
22. What is your occupation?
23. Have you ever held an elective office (or offices) before? (If yes:) Which office(s)?
24. How long have you lived in this district?
25. Have you ever given any thought to running for the U.S. House seat in this district?
26. What would your family think about you running for Congress? Have you ever discussed the possibility of running for Congress with your family?
27. Outside of your family and friends, is there anyone you feel you would have to talk to before you decide whether to run or not?
28. Have you ever talked about running for Congress with anyone who ran themselves? (If yes:) What did they tell you about candidacy? Was their experience positive or negative?
29. Considering the situation in the district as of today, how likely is it that you will run for Congress this year? (If no chance of running this time:) How about in future years—how likely is it that you will run for Congress sometime in the future?
30. (If the respondent is not certain that he or she will run:) What would it take to change your mind? What conditions would have to be present before you would seriously consider running for Congress in this district?
31. Have you ever thought about running for Congress in some other district?
32. Have you ever thought about moving into another district to run for Congress? (If yes:) Why? Did a new district open up, or an incumbent become vulnerable?
33. Are you well known in this district? For example, would a large number of people in the district recognize your name if they heard it?
34. How much do you think the people of this district know about your stands on issues?
35. Generally, how important is it to you to build a future in politics?

Costs

36. Roughly, how much do you think a primary campaign would cost in this district? If you ran, would you be able to raise that much money?

37. How about a general election campaign? How much do you think that would cost? If you won the party nomination, do you think you would be able to raise that much money?

38. If you run for Congress, what personal sacrifices do you expect to have to make?

39. If you ever decide to run for Congress, what impact do you think candidacy will have on your career? If you ran and lost, would this hurt your career?

40. (For those holding an elective office:) Would you have to give up this office if you ran for Congress? (If yes:) How important a factor is giving up this office in deciding whether or not you'll run for Congress?

Parties

41. Have you ever talked to anyone from the local party about running for Congress? (If yes:) Could you tell me a little about those contacts? For example, did you contact that person or did he or she contact you? How about the national party—have you ever talked with anyone at the national level about running for Congress? (If yes:) Could you describe those conversations? Did you contact them or did they contact you?

42. What were the nature of those contacts? That is, did the party say it could or could not provide any assistance? Did they set any conditions for their help, such as raising a certain amount of money or hiring certain consultants?

43. What effect did your contact with the party have on your decision to run? For example, were you more optimistic or more pessimistic about candidacy after that contact?

44. How much contact have you had with the party organization in the district? Have you ever served with the party organization in any official or unofficial capacity?

45. If you decide to run, how much support do you expect from the party in this district? How about at the national level—would you get support from the Democratic/Republican party in Washington?

46. In general, is there much competition in the party primary for the congressional nomination in this district?

Strategic

47. If you decide to run for Congress, how much opposition do you think you would have in the primary?

48. If you ran for Congress, could you win the Democratic/Republican nomination? How about the general election? If you

won the nomination, could you win the House seat? As a candidate, what would your most important strengths or assets be? How about any weaknesses or liabilities?

District Context

49. Do you think anyone in the district is waiting to hear if you are going to run before they decide whether or not to enter the race?
50. How much are congressional campaigns in this district affected by national issues? Can you think of any specific issues which have affected past congressional races in this district?

Miscellaneous (Incumbency, Timing, Redistricting)

51. (In districts with an incumbent:) How vulnerable does the incumbent seem to be? Can he/she be beaten? What would it take to beat him/her? Does the incumbent stay in touch with the district?
52. What is it about 1992 that makes it a particularly good time or bad time for you to consider running for Congress?
53. If someone were interested in winning the congressional nomination in the Democratic/Republican party, what would be the best time to start putting together a campaign organization?
54. What would be the best time to declare his or her candidacy?
55. Do you expect the state legislature to redraw the congressional district boundaries in this district? Will redistricting have any impact on your decision to run for the House? Do you keep in touch with anyone in the state capitol who is aware of the status of redistricting decisions?
56. Finally, what factor will have (or had) the most important impact on your decision to run (or not run) for Congress?

References

ABC News. 1989. *The '88 Vote*. New York: Capital Cities/ABC.

Abramowitz, Alan. 1980. "A Comparison of Voting for U.S. Senator and Representative in 1978." *American Political Science Review* 74: 633-640.

Alford, John, and David Brady. 1989. "Personal and Partisan Advantage in U.S. Congressional Elections, 1846-1986." In *Congress Reconsidered*, 4th ed., eds. Lawrence C. Dodd and Bruce I. Oppenheimer. Washington, D.C.: CQ Press.

Arnold, Douglas R. 1990. *The Logic of Congressional Action*. New Haven, Conn.: Yale University Press.

Baker, Peter. 1992. "30-Second Politics." *Washington Post*, October 20, D6.

Baker, Peter, and Evelyn Hsu. 1992. "McSlarrow, Butler Win N. Va. Races." *Washington Post*, June 10, D1.

Banks, Jeffrey S., and D. Roderick Kiewiet. 1989. "Explaining Patterns of Competition in Congressional Elections." *American Journal of Political Science* 33: 997-1015.

Barber, James David. 1965. *The Lawmakers: Recruitment and Adaptation to Legislative Life*. New Haven, Conn.: Yale University Press.

Barone, Michael, and Grant Ujifusa. 1983. *The Almanac of American Politics: 1984*. Washington, D.C.: National Journal.

Barone, Michael, and Grant Ujifusa. 1989. *The Almanac of American Politics: 1990*. Washington, D.C.: National Journal.

Barone, Michael, and Grant Ujifusa. 1991. *The Almanac of American Politics: 1992*. Washington, D.C.: National Journal.

Barone, Michael, and Grant Ujifusa. 1993. *The Almanac of American Politics: 1994*. Washington, D.C.: National Journal.

Benjamin, Gerald, and Michael J. Malbin., eds. 1992. *Limiting Legislative Terms*. Washington, D.C.: CQ Press.

Berkman, Michael B. 1993. "Former State Legislators in the U.S. House of Representatives: Institutional and Policy Mastery." *Legislative Studies Quarterly* 18: 77-104.

Bernstein, Alan. 1991. "Judge First Declared Candidate for New Hispanic District Seat." *Houston Chronicle*, August 28, 22A.

Bernstein, Alan, and Jim Simmon. 1991. "Hispanics' Eyes on the Prize." *Houston Chronicle*, December 22, 1C.

Bianco, William T. 1984. "Strategic Decisions on Candidacy in U.S. Congressional Districts." *Legislative Studies Quarterly* 9: 351-364.

Black, Gordon S. 1972. "A Theory of Political Ambition: Career Choices and the Role of Structural Incentives." *American Political Science Review* 66: 144-159.

Bond, Jon R., Cary Covington, and Richard Fleisher. 1985. "Explaining Challenger Quality in Congressional Elections." *Journal of Politics* 47: 510-529.

Boyette, J. Alan. 1992. "Migration of Washington Incumbents Makes 1992 Unlikely Year for Congressional Term Limits." *Comparative State Politics* 13: 15-22.

Brace, Kimball, Bernard Grofman, and Lisa Handley. 1987. "Does Redistricting Aimed to Help Blacks Necessarily Help Republicans?" *Journal of Politics* 49: 169-185.

Brady, David. 1988. *Critical Elections and Congressional Policy Making.* Stanford: Stanford University Press.

Brady, David. 1990. "Coalitions in the U.S. Congress." In *The Parties Respond,* ed. L. Sandy Maisel. Boulder: Westview Press.

Broadcasting Yearbook, The, 1990. 1990. Ed. Sol Taishoff. Washington, D.C.: Broadcasting Publications.

Browning, Rufus P. 1968. "The Interaction of Personality and Political System in Decisions to Run for Office: Some Data and a Simulation Technique." *Journal of Social Issues* 24: 93-109.

Browning, Rufus P., and Herbert Jacob. 1964. "Power Motivation and the Political Personality." *Public Opinion Quarterly* 28: 75-90.

Bullock, Charles S., III, and Susan MacManus. 1987. "Staggered Terms and Black Representation." *Journal of Politics* 49: 543-552.

Bullock, Charles S., III, and A. Brock Smith. 1990. "Black Success in Local Runoff Elections." *Journal of Politics* 52: 1205-1220.

Burka, Paul. 1992. "Battle Lines." *Texas Monthly,* March, 50-56.

Butler, David, and Bruce Cain. 1992. *Congressional Redistricting: Comparative and Theoretical Perspectives.* New York: Macmillan.

Campaigns and Elections. 1993. 13(5): 13.

Campbell, James E. 1986. "Predicting Seat Gains from Presidential Coattails." *American Journal of Political Science* 30: 165-183.

Campbell, James E. 1992. "The Presidential Pulse of Congressional Elections: 1868-1988." In *The Atomistic Congress: An Interpretation of Congressional Change,* eds. Allen Hertzke and Ronald Peters. Armonk, N.Y.: M. E. Sharpe.

Canon, David T. 1989. "Contesting Primaries in Congressional Elections, 1972-1988." Paper delivered at the Annual Meeting of the American Political Science Association. Atlanta, August 31.

Canon, David T. 1990. *Actors, Athletes and Astronauts: Political Amateurs in the United States Congress.* Chicago: University of Chicago Press.

Canon, David T. 1992. "The Emergence of the Republican Party in the South, 1964-1988." In *The Atomistic Congress: An Interpretation of Congressional Change,* eds. Allen Hertzke and Ronald Peters. Armonk, N.Y.:

M. E. Sharpe.

Canon, David T. 1993. "Sacrificial Lambs or Strategic Politicians? Political Amateurs in U.S. House Elections." *American Journal of Political Science* 37: 1119-1141.

Canon, David T., Matthew Schousen, and Patrick Sellers. 1993. "The Supply-Side of Congressional Redistricting: Race and Strategic Politicians, 1972-1992." Paper delivered at the Annual Meeting of the Midwest Political Science Association. Chicago, April 15-17.

Canon, David T., Matthew Schousen, and Patrick Sellers. 1992. "A Formula for Uncertainty: Creating a Black Majority District in North Carolina." Paper delivered at the Annual Meeting of the Midwestern Political Science Association. Chicago, April 9-11.

Canon, David T., and David J. Sousa, 1992. "Party System Change and Political Career Structures in the U.S. Congress." *Legislative Studies Quarterly* 17: 347-363.

Capute, Todd. 1992a. "GOP Has 3-Way Choice for Congress." *Alexandria Gazette-Packet*, May 21, 1, 10-12.

Capute, Todd. 1992b. "Stadium EIS Dies in Senate." *Alexandria Gazette-Packet*, September 24, 4.

Charlotte Observer. 1992. "Three for Congress," October 25.

Clem, Alan L. 1976. *The Making of Congressmen: Seven Campaigns of 1974.* North Scituate, Mass.: Duxbury Press.

Clymer, Adam. 1992. "Colorado's Test for the Religious Right." *New York Times,* October 23, A14.

"Congressional Redistricting: No Grey Areas." 1992. *The Economist* 8 (February).

Cook, Rhodes. 1991. "Incumbents' National Status Breeds Local Distrust." *Congressional Quarterly Weekly Report,* February 23, 483-487.

Cotter, Cornelius P., James L. Gibson, John F. Bibby, and Robert J. Huckshorn. 1984. *Party Organization in American Politics.* New York: Praeger.

Cover, Albert. 1977. "One Good Term Deserves Another: The Advantage of Incumbency in Congressional Elections." *American Journal of Political Science* 21: 523-541.

Crotty, William, and John S. Jackson, III. 1984. *Presidential Primaries and Nominations.* Washington, D.C.: CQ Press.

Cunningham, Kitty. 1993. "Black Caucus Flexes Muscles on Budget— And More." *Congressional Quarterly Weekly Report,* July 3, 1711-1715.

Czudnowski, Moshe M. 1975. "Political Recruitment." In *Handbook of Political Science,* Vol. 2, eds. Fred I. Greenstein and Nelson Polsby. Reading, Mass.: Addison-Wesley.

Darcy, Robert, Susan Welch, and Janet Clark. 1987. *Women, Elections, and Representation.* New York: Longman.

Davidson, Chandler. 1984. *Minority Vote Dilution.* Washington, D.C.: Howard University Press.

Denton, Van. 1992. "House Democrats Offer District Plan." *News and Observer,* January 19, 1A, 10A.

Dionne, E. J. 1991. *Why Americans Hate Politics.* New York: Simon & Schuster.

Dold, R. Bruce. 1989. "Yates' Campaign Gets Some Capital Assistance." *Chicago Tribune,* December 13.

Dold, R. Bruce. 1990. "Yates Asked Art Institute for Money, Opponent Says." *Chicago Tribune,* January 11.

Duncan, Phil, ed. 1991. *Politics in America 1992.* Washington, D.C.: CQ Press.

Ehrenhalt, Alan. 1991. *The United States of Ambition.* New York: Times Books.

Elbert, David. 1989. "Poll: Smith Least Known with Iowans." *Des Moines Register,* July 2.

Ewegen, Bob. 1992. "A Good Woman Hits the Glass Ceiling on Her Way to Congress." *Denver Post,* June 1.

Fenno, Richard. 1978. *Home Style: House Members in Their Districts.* Boston: Little Brown.

Ferejohn, John A. 1977. "On the Decline of Competition in Congressional Elections." *American Political Science Review* 71: 166-176.

Fiorina, Morris P. 1974. *Representatives, Roll Calls, and Constituencies.* Lexington, Mass.: D.C. Heath.

Fiorina, Morris P. 1977. *Congress: Keystone of the Washington Establishment.* New Haven, Conn.: Yale University Press.

Fishel, Jeff. 1973. *Party and Opposition: Congressional Challengers in American Politics.* New York: David McKay.

Fleck, Tim. 1992. "Who Can Tame the Geraldomander?" *Houston Press,* March 5, 35.

Fowler, Linda L. 1992. "A Comment on Competition and Careers." In *Limiting Legislative Terms,* eds. Gerald Benjamin and Michael J. Malbin. Washington, D.C.: CQ Press.

Fowler, Linda L. 1993. *Candidates, Congress, and the American Democracy.* Ann Arbor: University of Michigan Press.

Fowler, Linda L., and L. Sandy Maisel. 1991. "The Changing Supply of Competitive Candidates in U.S. House Elections, 1982-1988." Revised version of a paper delivered at the Annual Meeting of the American Political Science Association. Atlanta, August 31.

Fowler, Linda L., and Robert D. McClure. 1989. *Political Ambition: Who Decides to Run for Congress.* New Haven, Conn.: Yale University Press.

Francis, Wayne L., and John R. Baker. 1986. "Why Do U.S. State Legislators Vacate Their Seats?" *Legislative Studies Quarterly* 11: 119-126.

Frantzich, Stephen. 1978. "Opting Out: Retirement from the House of Representatives, 1966-1974." *American Politics Quarterly* 6: 251-273.

Funk, Tim, and Ricki Morell. 1992. "Wishing for a Better Campaign, Voters Weigh Picks." *Charlotte Observer,* November, 1.

Gibson, James L., Cornelius P. Cotter, John F. Bibby, and Robert J. Huckshorn. 1983. "Assessing Party Organizational Strength." *American Journal of Political Science* 27(2): 193-222.

Gibson, James L., Cornelius P. Cotter, John F. Bibby, and Robert J. Huckshorn. 1985. "Whither the Local Parties?: A Cross-Sectional and Longitudinal Analysis of the Strength of Party Organizations." *American Journal of Political Science* 29(1): 139-160.

Ginsberg, Benjamin, and Alan Stone, eds. 1986. *Do Elections Matter?* Armonk, N.Y.: M. E. Sharpe.

Green, John C., James L. Guth, and Kevin Hill. 1993. "Faith and Election: The Christian Right in Congressional Campaigns, 1978-1988." *Journal of Politics* 55: 80-96.

Greenhouse, Linda. 1993. "Court Questions Districts Drawn to Aid Minorities." *New York Times,* June 29, A1, A9.

Grenzke, Janet. 1988. "Comparing Contributions to U.S. House Members from outside Their Districts." *Legislative Studies Quarterly* 13: 83-103.

Grofman, Bernard, and Lisa Handley. "Minority Population Proportion and Black and Hispanic Congressional Success in the 1970s and 1980s." *American Politics Quarterly* 17: 436-445.

Hansen, Lawrence N. 1991. "The Vanishing American Candidate." Unpublished manuscript. The Joyce Foundation.

Hardy, Thomas. 1990. "Yates-Eisendrath Race Costliest in Nation." *Chicago Tribune,* August 9.

Hardy, Thomas, and R. Bruce Dold. 1989. "Eisendrath Challenges Yates for Congress." *Chicago Tribune,* November 15.

Herrnson, Paul S. 1988. *Party Campaigning in the 1980s.* Cambridge, Mass.: Harvard University Press.

Hershey, Marjorie Randon. 1993. "The Congressional Elections." In *The Election of 1992,* ed. Gerald M. Pomper. Chatham, N.J.: Chatham House.

Hertzke, Allen D. 1993. *Echoes of Discontent: Jesse Jackson, Pat Robertson, and the Resurgence of Populism.* Washington, D.C.: CQ Press.

Hibbing, John R. 1982. "Voluntary Retirements from the House in the Twentieth Century." *Journal of Politics* 44: 1020-1034.

Hibbing, John R. 1991. *Congressional Careers: Contours of Life in the U.S. House of Representatives.* Chapel Hill: University of North Carolina Press.

Hinckley, Barbara. 1980. "House Reelections and Senate Defeats: The Role of the Challenger." *British Journal of Political Science* 10: 441-460.

Hinckley, Barbara. 1981. *Congressional Elections.* Washington, D.C.: CQ Press.

Houston Chronicle. 1992. March 4, 18A.

Houston Post. 1992. February 23, C2.

Huckshorn, Robert J., and Robert C. Spencer, 1971. *The Politics of Defeat: Campaigning for Congress.* Amherst: University of Massachusetts Press.

Jacobson, Gary C. 1987. "The Marginals Never Vanished: Incumbency and Competition in Elections to the U.S. House of Representatives." *American Journal of Political Science* 31: 126-141.

Jacobson, Gary C. 1990. *The Electoral Origins of Divided Government.* Boulder: Westview Press.

Jacobson, Gary C. 1992. *The Politics of Congressional Elections,* 3d ed. New York: Harper Collins.

Jacobson, Gary C. 1993. "Congress: Unusual Year, Unusual Election." In *The Elections of 1992,* ed. Michael Nelson. Washington, D.C.: CQ Press.

Jacobson, Gary C., and Samuel Kernell. 1983. *Strategy and Choice in Congressional Elections.* New Haven, Conn.: Yale University Press.

Jenkins, Kent, Jr. 1992. "Stan Parris Backs Candidate in 8th." *Washington Post,* April 24, B3.

Kazee, Thomas A. 1980. "The Decision to Run for the U.S. Congress: Challenger Attitudes in the 1970s." *Legislative Studies Quarterly* 5: 79-100.

Kazee, Thomas A. 1983. "The Deterrent Effect of Incumbency on Recruiting Challengers in U.S. House Elections." *Legislative Studies Quarterly* 8: 469-480.

Kazee, Thomas A., and Mary C. Thornberry. 1990. "Where's the Party? Congressional Candidate Recruitment and American Party Organizations." *Western Political Quarterly* 43: 61-80.

Kazee, Thomas A., and Susan Roberts. 1992. "Challenging a 'Safe' Incumbent: Latent Competition in North Carolina's 9th District." Paper delivered at the 1992 Annual Meeting of the American Political Science Association. Chicago, April 9.

Keefe, William J. 1991. *Parties, Politics, and Public Policy in America.* Washington, D.C.: CQ Press.

Kesler, Charles R. 1992. "Bad Housekeeping: The Case against Congressional Term Limits." In *Limiting Legislative Terms,* eds. Gerald Benjamin and Michael J. Malbin. Washington, D.C.: CQ Press.

Kingdon, John. 1968. *Candidates for Office.* New York: Random House.

Krasno, Jonathan S., and Donald P. Green. 1988. "Preempting Quality Challengers in House Elections." *Journal of Politics* 50: 920-936.

Lasswell, Harold D. 1930. *Psychopathology and Politics.* Chicago: University of Chicago Press.

Lasswell, Harold D. 1948. *Power and Personality.* New York: Norton.

Leuthold, David A. 1968. *Electioneering in a Democracy.* New York: John Wiley and Sons.

Loomis, Burdett A. 1988. *The New American Politician.* New York: Basic Books.

Maisel, L. Sandy. 1982. *From Obscurity to Oblivion.* Knoxville: University of Tennessee Press.

Maisel, L. Sandy, Linda L. Fowler, Ruth S. Jones, and Walter J. Stone. 1990. "The Naming of Candidates: Recruitment or Emergence?" In *The Parties Respond: Changes in the American Party System,* ed. L. Sandy

Maisel. Boulder: Westview Press.

Mann, Thomas, and Raymond Wolfinger. 1980. "Candidates and Parties in Congressional Elections." *American Political Science Review* 74: 617-632.

Matthews, Donald R. 1954. *The Social Backgrounds of Political Decision Makers*. New York: Doubleday.

Matthews, Donald R. 1984. "Legislative Recruitment and Legislative Careers." *Legislative Studies Quarterly* 9: 547-585.

Mayhew, David. 1974. *Congress: The Electoral Connection*. New Haven, Conn.: Yale University Press.

Mayhew, David. 1991. *Divided We Govern: Party Control, Lawmaking, and Investigations 1946-1990*. New Haven, Conn.: Yale University Press.

Michels, Roberto. 1962. *Political Parties: A Sociological Study of the Oligarchical Tendencies of Modern Democracy*. New York: Free Press.

Moore, Michael K., and John R. Hibbing. 1992. "Is Serving in the Congress Fun Again? Voluntary Retirement from the House Since the 1970s." *American Journal of Political Science* 36: 824-828.

Nelson, Candice J. 1993. "Money and Its Role in the Election." In *America's Choice: The Election of 1992*, ed. William Crotty. Guilford, Conn.: Duskin Publishing Group.

"New Districts, Angry Mood Stir Competition for Congress." 1992. *Congressional Quarterly Weekly Report*. February 29.

New York Times. 1992. November 5.

New York Times. 1993. June 29, A9.

News and Observer. 1991a. "Jones Still Unsure on Re-election Bid" ("Under the Dome" column), September 25, 1B, 2B.

News and Observer. 1991b. "PAC Involved in Redistricting Plan" ("Under the Dome" column), August 25, 1C, 6C.

News and Observer. 1992a. "GOP Assails 'Blatant Gerrymandering' in Plans," January 19, 1A, 10A.

News and Observer. 1992b. "Jones Will Cash in Political War Chest," April 24, 2B.

News and Observer. 1992c. "U.S. Supreme Court Upholds Redistricting in N.C.," October 6, 2B.

Niemi, Richard G., Bernard Grofman, Carl Carlucci, and Thomas Hofeller. 1990. "Measuring Compactness and the Role of Compactness Standard in a Test for Partisan and Racial Gerrymandering." *Journal of Politics* 52: 1155-1181.

"Observer Poll in 14 Counties." 1992. *Charlotte Observer*, November 1.

Olson, Mancur. 1965. *The Logic of Collective Action: Public Goods and the Theory of Groups*. Cambridge, Mass.: Harvard University Press.

Ornstein, Norman J., Thomas E. Mann, and Michael J. Malbin. 1992. *Vital Statistics on Congress 1991-1992*. Washington, D.C.: CQ Inc.

Parker, Glenn R. 1980. "The Advantage of Incumbency in House Elections." *American Politics Quarterly* 8: 449-464.

Parker, Glenn R. 1986. *Homeward Bound: Explaining Changes in Congres-*

sional Behavior. Pittsburgh: University of Pittsburgh Press.

Payne, James L. 1984. *The Motivations of Politicians*. Chicago: Nelson-Hall.

Perdue, Louis. 1977. "The Million Dollar Advantage of Incumbency." *Washington Monthly*, Vol. 9.

Pochna, Peter. 1992. "Martin May Run against Rep. Skaggs." *Colorado Daily*, April 14.

Poole, Keith T., and L. Harmon Ziegler. 1985. *Women, Public Opinion, and Politics: Changing Political Attitudes of American Women*. New York: Longman.

Prewitt, Kenneth. 1970. *The Recruitment of Political Leaders: A Study of Citizen-Politicians*. Indianapolis: Bobbs-Merrill.

Prewitt, Kenneth. 1990. Review of *Political Ambition*, Linda Fowler and Robert McClure (New Haven, Conn.: Yale University Press. 1989). *American Political Science Review* 84: 995-996.

Ragsdale, Lynn. 1981. "Incumbent Popularity, Challenger Invisibility, and Congressional Voters." *Legislative Studies Quarterly* 6: 201-218.

Ratcliffe, R. G. 1991. "Area Dems O.K. Pact to Form Hispanic Congressional District." *Houston Chronicle*, August 24, 26A.

"Redistricting 1991: Legislator's Guide to North Carolina Legislative and Congressional Redistricting." 1991. Mimeo. Research Division, North Carolina General Assembly, February.

Robeck, Bruce. 1982. "State Legislator Candidacies for the U.S. House: Prospects for Success." *Legislative Studies Quarterly* 7: 507-514.

Rohde, David W. 1979. "Risk Bearing and Progressive Ambition: The Case of the United States House of Representatives." *American Journal of Political Science* 23: 1-26.

Roll Call. 1992. May 14.

Ruffin, Jane. 1992. "GOP Sues Over Redistricting." *News and Observer*, February 29, 1A, 17A.

Salmore, Barbara G., Stephen A. Salmore. 1985. *Candidates, Parties, and Campaigns*. Washington, D.C.: CQ Press.

Schlesinger, Joseph A. 1966. *Ambition and Politics: Political Careers in the United States*. Chicago: Rand McNally.

Seligman, Lester, Michael R. King, Chong Lim Kim, and Roland E. Smith. 1974. *Patterns of Recruitment: A State Chooses Its Lawmakers*. Chicago: Rand McNally.

Simpson, Glenn. 1992. "Moran Is Criticized for Defending Directors of Failed Bank Who Contributed to His Race." *Roll Call*, September 28, 24.

Snowiss, L. M. 1966. "Congressional Recruitment and Representation." *American Political Science Review* 60: 627-639.

Sorauf, Frank J. 1963. *Party and Representation*. New York: Atherton Press.

Squire, Peverill. 1988. "Career Opportunities and Membership Stability in Legislatures." *Legislative Studies Quarterly* 13: 65-82.

Squire, Peverill. 1992. "Challenger Quality and Voting Behavior in U.S.

Senate Elections." *Legislative Studies Quarterly* 17: 247-263.

Stone, Walter. 1990. *Republic at Risk: Self-Interest in American Politics.* Pacific Grove, Calif.: Brooks/Cole.

Swain, Carol. 1989. *The Politics of Black Representation in U.S. Congressional Districts.* Ph.D. Dissertation, Department of Political Science, University of North Carolina.

Swain, Carol M. 1993. *Black Face, Black Interests: The Representation of African Americans in Congress.* Cambridge, Mass.: Harvard University Press.

Tierney, John T. 1993. "The Election in Context: The Political and Institutional Setting." In *America's Choice: The Election of 1992,* ed. William Crotty. Guilford, Conn.: Dushkin.

Tobin, Richard J. 1975. "The Influence of Nominating Systems on the Political Experiences of State Legislators." *Western Political Quarterly* 28: 553-566.

Tobin, Richard J., and Edward Keynes. 1975. "Institutional Differences in the Recruitment Process: A Four State Study." *American Journal of Political Science* 19: 667-682.

Wall Street Journal. 1992. "Political Pornography II," February 4.

Wattenberg, Martin P. 1990. *The Decline of American Political Parties.* Cambridge, Mass.: Harvard University Press.

Wattenberg, Martin P. 1991. *The Rise of Candidate-Centered Politics.* Cambridge, Mass.: Harvard University Press.

Weber, Max. 1965. "Politics as Vocation." In *The Political Vocation,* ed. Paul Tillet. New York: Basic Books.

Welch, Susan. 1985. "Are Women More Liberal than Men in the U.S. Congress?" *Legislative Studies Quarterly* 10: 125-134.

Wirth, Timothy. 1992. "Diary of a Dropout." *New York Times Magazine,* August 9.

Yepsen, David. 1992. "Democratic Underdog Challenges Veteran Leach." *Des Moines Register,* September 11.

Young, H. P. 1988. "Measuring Compactness of Legislative Districts." *Legislative Studies Quarterly* 13: 105-115.

Zaldivar, R. A. 1992. "Burned-Out Politicians Kiss Congress Goodbye." *Baltimore Herald Sun,* April 4.

Index